THE FAMILY SAGA

The Family Saga:
A Collection of
Texas Family Legends

Edited by
Francis Edward Abernethy
Jerry Bryan Lincecum
Frances B. Vick

Publications of the Texas Folklore Society LX

Francis Edward Abernethy, General Editor
Shannon Thompson, Assistant Editor

University of North Texas Press
Denton, Texas

10 9 8 7 6 5 4 3 2

Permissions:
University of North Texas Press
P.O. Box 311336
Denton, TX 76203-1336

The paper used in this book meets the minimum requirements of the American National Standard for Permanence of Paper for Printed Library Materials, z39.48.1984. Binding materials have been chosen for durability.

Library of Congress Cataloging-in-Publication Data

The family saga : a collection of Texas family legends / edited by Francis Edward Abernethy, Jerry Bryan Lincecum, Frances B. Vick.
    p. cm. — (Publications of the Texas Folklore Society ; no. 60)
Includes index.
  ISBN 1-57441-168-3 (alk. paper)
  1. Texas—Social life and customs—Anecdotes. 2. Texas—History—Anecdotes. 3. Texas—Biography—Anecdotes. 4. Folklore—Texas. I. Abernethy, Francis Edward. II. Lincecum, Jerry Bryan, 1942- III. Vick, Frances Brannen, 1935- IV. Series.
  F386.6 .F36 2003
  920.0764—dc21
                              2003012346

The Family Saga: A Collection of Texas Family Legends is Number LX in the Publications of the Texas Folklore Society

Contents

14 • FAMILY CHARACTERS: HEROES, BLACK SHEEP, AND ECCENTRICS

Preface

I began this book in 1973 when I first announced my intentions for building one of the Publications of the Texas Folklore Society around family legends as discussed by Mody Boatright. I was surprised that I did not get much of a response from members. I tried again in 1992, sure that I would receive a flood of submissions because of the number of family legend papers that had been presented at Texas Folklore Society meetings over the years. But again, the response was minimal. As I neared the end of my editorial tenure, I decided I could not retire before I did this particular collection. Jerry Lincecum of Austin College was working in the same field, so I felt that with my desire and his energy we could build a book of family legends into a Family Saga—So here it is.

The family legends are contributions by Society members, and because the Texas Folklore Society is mainly white, Anglo-Saxon, and Protestant, the legends are white, Anglo-Saxon, Protestant. This is an explanation and not an apology. Hopefully, some day the Society will be racially and ethnically integrated to such an extent that a future editor can do family saga books on or including Mexicans and African-Americans, among others.

I explain also that we have had some beautiful family legend papers presented at meetings—and I am thinking now of Al Lowman's family stories from Staples—but I have frittered them away over previous miscellany publications and do not want to publish them twice.

While I was still teaching folklore I regularly gave assignments to my students, requiring that they bring in some of their own family legends or family legends they obtained by interviews. Thus, a few of these stories will be about families other than the family of the narrator. I put aside some of the most interesting family stories and came across the student file when I was collecting for this book. I used several of these student papers in this publication, even though I was unable to find some of the writers to get releases. I hope my former students read their stories now and know that I did not make any money out of their labors. And I hope that they will take the time to write me and let me know how and what they are doing.

This editor and the Texas Folklore Society thank Assistant Editor Shannon Thompson, who worked diligently and maintained due process in the preparation of this manuscript. I would have faltered without her assistance. And I thank our office secretary Heather Stumbaugh for taking over in the final phase of production.

> And when like her, O Sakí, you shall pass
> Among the guests star-scattered on the grass,
> And in your joyous errand reach the spot
> Where I made one—turn down an empty glass!
> Tamám

Francis Edward Abernethy
Stephen F. Austin State University
Nacogdoches, Texas
Texas Independence Day, 2003

Photo "The Family," courtesy of the Museum of East Texas in Lufkin

THE FAMILY SAGA:
A Collection of Texas Family Legends

an introduction

From the beginning of man's time, from our be-figged first parents Adam and Eve, the family has been the basic social unit. The family clung together, tightly knit, for simple survival.

The old father, the patriarch, called his bickering sons together, and they sat in the light around the fire. He waved his hand about him, indicating all the points of the compass, and said, "Out there in the darkness lies our destruction. Outside of this firelight stand both man and beast, and they can destroy us one by one if we do not travel together as each other's protection." Then he took a stick and gave one to each of his sons. "Break them," he said. They did so, easily. Then he took the same number of sticks as he had sons and bound them in a bundle. "Break this," he said. None could break the bound bundle.

The old father held up the bundle (called a *fasces* in Latin) in the firelight. "We are as these dry and brittle sticks," he said. "Each of us alone can be quickly broken and tossed into the fire. Only bound together as a family can we survive and not be broken." So they stayed together and grew from family to group to tribe to community to society and finally to a nation that still had a drop of the old man's blood running in its veins. And they continually told the tales of their ancestors and their history.

Of all the family sagas, the Bible—particularly the Old Testament's collection of stories of the Children of Abraham—remains the longest, best

1

written, most complete of all the sagas in existence, from the Judeo-Christian point of view, at least.

By the twelfth century B. C. the Jews were no longer nomadic. They had found a fertile land held by a weaker people; so, blessed by the family gods, they took the land and settled down to enjoy their first permanent home.

Writing was not yet a part of their Hebraic culture, but storytelling was, and their stories of the family formed a saga, a group of related family legends, that went back to what they knew as the beginning of time, to their Eden. Their tales went back to the first parents, to the family in the old country, to their migrations and the wars they had fought. The stories they told went back to the fires and floods and catastrophes that they had endured, to the feuds within the tribe, to the miracles they had known, the animals they had hunted, the treasures they had won and lost. And most of all, the tales they told were stories of the great Jewish personalities—the singers and hunters and fighters—the heroes and heroines who had dominated generations, whose tales still excited wonder and admiration. And the most holy of their men, the priests, were responsible for the survival of these legends of times past.

Likewise, a family's most treasured of kin is the one who knows the stories of his family's past and can relate these tales around the diningroom table to the delight of young and old, no matter how many times the tales are told. My grandad's brother, the last of his family, every Thanksgiving told how in the winter of '98 they were snowbound in a dugout in old Greer County. They had run out of food, but were saved when Uncle Sterle, the eldest brother, came riding through the drifts with a pair of gallon jugs of molasses tied to his saddle horn. Uncle Arthur could never tell that story without getting choked up.

If a family is blessed with enough good storytellers down through the generations—scops, bards, or minstrels who can turn an episode into an *Iliad*—the legend will eventually take on the shape of a short story. The best stories have a natural beginning, middle, and end; it is a matter of natural selection.

The title and the idea for this book began in 1958, when Mody Boatright first published his essay, "The Family Saga as a Form of Folklore." What Mody identified was a long established form of folklore that was firmly entrenched among people everywhere. We would not presume to improve on Mody. We have merely further defined and categorized where Mody left off.

Mody went back to early medieval Icelandic and Norse family sagas for his pattern. Those old sagas, passed along in the oral tradition, told stories of the gods on earth, the adventures of heroes, and the lives of kings. They were an accumulation of heroic legends about one family or hero, brought together and eventually written down in a unified saga.

The family saga—as Mody and this collection defines it—is made up of an accumulation of separate family legends. These are the stories of the old folks and the old times that are told among the family when they gather for funerals or Thanksgiving dinner. These are the "remember-when" stories the family tells about the time when the grownups were children. Families with strong identities and strong bonds eventually have a library of legends, treasures passed along in the oral tradition. Because of shared humanity and common family experiences, the legends of these old families follow a recognizable pattern of topics, some of which are contained herein. A large and chronologically extended collection of family legends brought together under one cover, or one roof, is a family saga.

Only some of the many kinds of family legends are contained herein, but not all. I could have had a chapter on hunting and fishing tales from the families I encountered that believed that these sports were at the core of their family's identity. I gave a talk about family legends to a group of genealogists, and the topic of outhouses came up. I could have done a chapter on family tales that involved adventures in outhouses, like the time Dad and I walked in on a bull snake, for instance, or when my aged aunt was greeted by a skunk. I met with a three-generation family of doctors, and one of them told about putting a football bladder in a patient during some emergency. Mercifully, I have forgotten the details.

A family legend is a type of folklore. It is a traditional prose narrative that has a historical setting and real people as characters. The legend is passed down in the family through the oral tradition, by word of mouth, from one generation to another. As with all folklore, the story exists in variations, its author or first teller is anonymous, and it fits a formula in being true to the spirit of the family but not necessarily to the facts of history.

We recognize that family history is more complex than the isolated legends contained in this book. Each story is told in a particular context, sometimes by a particular person. We also realize that family-story traditions frequently begin their journey through time in the form of letters, diaries, memoirs, and journals. For that reason we vary from the absolute and include some first-person narratives, recognizing that they do not fit the formal definition of a traditional family legend. We also know, however, that first-person narratives—stories one tells about one's own experiences—are honed over the decades by that first person to make a better story and to fit his forever-growing and changing attitudes about life. The personal tale is an example of personal folklore and is a personal legend. When it falls into the flow of tales a family tells, it becomes a family legend.

The family saga, therefore, is *not* history. It is *not* an accumulation and an evaluation of factual and documented details, because most families have few facts and very little documentation. But even though the stories are not history, they are shadows of history, which in one sense is more important than the details. A list of ancestors and how long they lived and whom they begot and how long they lived is important factually, but it does not interpret; it does not reveal a family's spirit nor what it believes nor how it thinks. A genealogical list tells *what*, not *why* and *how*; and the *what* is the beginning, the first step, the introduction. The *why* is the reason for being. And the *whys* of a family are revealed in the family's legends.

The literature of a culture is the key to understanding the mind of that culture and its place in time and history. The legends of a family reveal the same things on a smaller scale. The family keeps and tells the stories that reflect the family's culture and beliefs—how the family sees itself—and it binds them together. It keeps the stories that reflect what that family feels are the strengths of its people or the characteristics that the family still honors. When times and attitudes change, the stories change, or they disappear all together. What we have in *The Family Saga* is a collection of stories that, one way or another, have survived the passage of years and migrations, fires, and floods—and most importantly, of changing attitudes. These stories remain to remind their families that they are a part of a history that goes far back in time, and if the pattern holds, will continue far into the future.

Mody Coggin Boatright (1896–1970) was the Secretary-Editor of the Texas Folklore Society from 1943 to 1963. Before that date Mody helped Frank Dobie with the Society publications from *Straight Texas* in 1937 to *Texian Stomping Grounds* in 1941. Mody became the Society's editor in 1943 with his publication of *Backwoods to Border*.

Mody researched and wrote extensively about frontier humor and oilfield folklore, but this year's PTFS is the result of his thinking and writing about family legends and his essay, "The Family Saga as a Form of Folklore."

The Texas Folklore Society's sixtieth volume, *The Family Saga*, is lovingly and respectfully dedicated to the Society's old friend and mentor, Mody Coggin Boatright.

The Family Saga as a Form of Folklore

by Mody C. Boatright (1896–1970)
Secretary-Editor 1943–1963

[This family saga project began in spirit in Mody's preface to *Madstones and Twisters* (PTFS 28–1957). That volume concluded with four articles that were family legends. In the introduction to the four family legends, Mody defined and described the family legend as we now understand that genre, and in his conclusion he sent out a call to members to submit their own family legends. In the following year Mody published "The Family Saga as a Form of Folklore" in *The Family Saga and other Phases of American Folklore* (Urbana: University of Illinois Press, 1958). In 1973 "The Family Saga" was republished in the Texas Folklore Society publication *Mody Boatright, Folklorist* (Austin: University of Texas Press).]

It is with some hesitancy that I apply the term "family saga" to the subject of this paper. I am not here concerned with the heroic poems of Ireland or Iceland or the North European continent, dealing with battles and trials of strength and the complex genealogies of heroes. Nor may the narratives with which I am concerned be accurately called American analogues to these European works. I use the term mainly to denote a lore that tends to cluster around families, or often the patriarchs or matriarchs of families, which is preserved and modified by oral transmission, and which is believed to be true. Lore that is handed down as folklore is excluded. I am, then, not concerned with a type of tale, but with clusters of types, not with a motif, but with many motifs.

These clusters never form a connected history. Such a coherent narrative requires research in libraries and archives.[1] A history or biography written wholly or largely from oral sources has its values, but they are not the values of history or biography. What Homer Croy learned from the neighbors of Jesse James was folklore, a part of the James family saga.[2]

A consideration of these clusters of lore raises a number of questions, for which I have no final answers: What forms and motifs make up the family saga? What is their relation to history? What kinds of historical incidents survive in the oral tradition with little change? How do incidents, some historical and some folk tales of great antiquity, become incorporated into the family saga?

First, the general observation may be made that each episode has, in Martha Beckwith's phrase, "taken on, through . . . repetition and variation, the character of a group composition," and that it "functions in the emotional life of the folk."[3] For a tale to enter the oral tradition and survive, it must afford emotional satisfaction to the hearers, who then repeat the tale and thus widen its circulation. Nothing could be duller and, even when a product of the imagination, further removed from folklore than inventories of property and lists of offices of honor and trust held by one's ancestors.

An event in the family saga has a relation to a social context and reflects a social value. This does not mean, however, that the event is invariably in harmony with the actual social conditions of the region where it is believed to have happened. Two examples will illustrate this lack of harmony.

In one Texas family it is believed that an ancestress, during the Civil War, seeing a group of Union soldiers approaching the farm, began hiding the things of most value. Her most valued possession was a jewel box and its contents of diamonds, rubies, emeralds, and pearls. It developed that her fears were unfounded, for the soldiers were looking only for food, and when they had obtained it they left, and the mother and children began restoring the hidden articles to their proper places. But for some reason the jewel box was left in hiding. A few days later the mother died very suddenly, and the box, in spite of long and repeated searches, has never been found.

Now since Texas, where the family lived, was never invaded by Union soldiers, either the time or place is wrong. It could be that the troops were those of the occupation after the war; it could be that the story was transferred from the deep South, where the accepted thing was for the mistress of the plantation to bury the silver and jewels or have them carried off by the Yankees. If you wish, you may say that here is an etiological tale explaining the absence of family jewels.

In Massachusetts the accepted thing is for your ancestors to have been abolitionists associated with the underground railroad. Nathaniel Benchley, in a biography of Robert Benchley, writes of the first Benchley "to attract attention in Worcester" that after a political career, first as state senator and then as Lieutenant Governor, he, "feeling that the slavery problem needed more attention than he could give it from the Statehouse . . . went to Texas and set up a station on the underground railroad, helping slaves escape to the North. He was caught, convicted, and spent the rest of the time until Appomattox in a Texas jail."[4]

All this seemed rather strange to a certain Texas historian, Andrew Forest Muir. In the first place there was no reason for helping Texas slaves escape to the North, when Mexico, which welcomed Negroes and granted them full equality, was many times nearer than Canada. Muir looked into the records and established that Henry W. Benchley was in Texas as early as April 12, 1859; that he taught singing lessons first in San Antonio and then in Houston; that after the Confederate Congress had passed an act exempting railroad employees from military service, he was a conductor on the Houston and Texas Central Railroad; and that on one occasion he got up a musical entertainment for Confederate troops. He never went to jail in Texas, and the railroad with which he was connected ran upon a flat coastal plain where not even a single tunnel was required.[5]

The tale clearly originated in Massachusetts in conformity with a pattern of conduct people of that state expect of their ancestors. It does not conform to a long tradition about why people came to Texas.

Long before Texas was a subject of concern to the people of the United States, it was assumed by the conservative well-to-do that anybody who left for the frontier did so for a good but hardly laudable reason.[6] Timothy Dwight thought that the people leaving New England must be a sorry lot, and Virginians used to say of one who left that state that he had gone to Hell or Kentucky. When people from the United States began moving into Texas and the political implications of foreseen annexation became apparent, the tradition that the frontiersman was a fugitive became intensified and localized. Thus a sort of archetype was created, which the Texans did little to refute. Samuel Adams Hammett, who was in Texas from 1835 to 1847, after writing a defense of the settlers, remarked that they were partly to blame for "the contumely heaped upon them. [They] indulged in a sly chuckle over their somewhat dubious reputation, and it was a common joke to ask a man what his name at home was and what he came to Texas for."[7] And according to W. B. Dewees, an early Texas settler, the answer would be, "for some crime or other which they had committed . . . if they deny having committed any crime, and say they did not run away, they are generally looked upon rather suspiciously. Those who come into the country at the present time [1831] frequently tell us rough, ragged, old settlers . . . that they have a great deal of wealth in the States, which they are going after as soon as they find a situation to suit them. But we not relishing this would-be aristocracy generally manage to play a good joke on them in return."[8] One day when a number of these would-be aristocrats were boasting of their "lands and Negroes and their ships at sea," they were thus addressed by "Old Man Macfarlane":

> "Well, gentlemen," he said, "I too once commenced telling that I had left a large property in the States, and in fact, gentlemen, I told the story so often that at length I really believed it true, and eventually started to go for it. Well, I travelled on very happily till I reached the Sabine River. . . . On its banks I paused, and now for the first time began to ask myself, What am I doing! Why am I here! I have no property in the States, and if I did, if I cross the river 'tis at the risk of my life, for I was obliged to flee to this country to escape punishment of the laws. I had better return and live in safety as I have done. I did so, gentlemen, and since that time have been contented without telling of the wealth I left in the States."[9]
>
> The boasters were so angry that they would have injured the old man had his friends not intervened, but this "put a stop to their long yarns."

This attitude of the early settlers has persisted among their descendants, and many a Texas family saga begins with a G.T.T.—gone to Texas—story. That of Dandy Jim Smith will serve as an example.

In 1846, when Dandy Jim was a youth in Tennessee, there were in the community in which he lived two factions: the Mountain Boys and the Valley Boys, or the hill boys and the plantation boys. They crashed each other's parties and dances and had numerous fist fights. Then the Valley Boys brought knives into action, and the arms race was on. The Mountain Boys went to a Valley Boys' dance on a riverboat with hickory clubs concealed in their pantlegs. The fight began on signal. A Valley Boy drew a pistol and shot a Mountain Boy in the knee. But the clubs were more effective than the single pistol, and many a Valley Boy was knocked off into the river. Some climbed back in their wet clothes and re-entered the fight, but when it was over, thirteen were missing. A mob formed and began rounding up the Mountain Boys. But not Jim and his brother Watt. They hid in a cave, where an old fisherwoman brought them food. They eventually got to Texas after shooting two of their pursuers.

I do not know that "Old Man Macfarlane" ever committed a crime in his life, nor do I know why Dandy Jim Smith came to Texas. I have told the story as I have had it from his descendants,[10] and I shall not offend them by trying to refute it.

Its significance in this context does not depend upon its accuracy as a biographical event. It is one example of the continuation of a long tradition with many variants. Sometimes it is the over-successful duelist who flees. Sometimes two men fight on a bridge; one is knocked into the river and drowns, the other goes to Texas. But the deed, whatever it is, must not indicate a criminal mind. It must not be robbery, embezzlement, or murder with malice aforethought. If any of these were the real crime, then the family saga would have to make a substitution or remain silent.

The saga of a pioneer family, as would be expected, will include adventures with wild animals. Because the frontiersman was armed with a superior rifle, and because he had been sufficiently touched by the Enlightenment to look upon the animals as natural creatures that could be killed with powder and lead, these adventures rarely exhibit the superstitious fear characteristic of the older Indo–European folklore. The typical hunt had little in it to catch the popular fancy. As Jim Doggett put it, "It is told in two sentences—a bar is started, and he is killed. The thing is somewhat monotonous." Stories that pass into the oral tradition are likely to reveal (1) the uncommon sagacity of the hunter or (2) show human beings in jeopardy.

The first is exemplified by a story of how Adam Lawrence[12] relieved the starving colony. It was a time of prolonged drought and all the game had left the country, though crows occasionally flew over. Lawrence shot one to learn what it had been eating, and found an acorn in its craw. He knew there "was plenty of fat game where that crow drew his rations." He led a party in the direction the crows had come from, and after traveling many miles, they found oak trees and fat buffalo, bear, deer, and elk.[13]

For a story placing a human being in jeopardy, the panther was the favored animal. He, of course, was not a man-hunter, and it was said that a man could take a willow switch and a feist dog and drive him out of the country. But he would fight when cornered, he might be attracted by the smell of fresh meat, and he sometimes attacked men, or apparently more often women, on horseback, perhaps in search of horsemeat, of which he was fond. There are recorded instances of his having killed children, and he was thought to regard a nursing baby as an especial delicacy.

I shall call the two panther themes occurring with greatest frequency "The Panther on the Roof" and "The Panther in Pursuit."[14]

My example of the first is from the Glimp family saga.[15] The Glimp family went on a bear hunt to lay in a supply of meat for winter, Sarah and her three-month-old baby along with the menfolks. Near where they expected to find bear, they built a log hut with a fireplace and clay-daubed chimney. They laid a roof of unspecified material on pole rafters. The men cut and brought in a supply of firewood, and left Sarah with her baby and a hound while they went to look for bear.

During the afternoon the baby began crying from colic. At dusk it was still crying. As Sarah got up to close the door, she heard a panther scream. He screamed three times, each time sounding nearer. Then she heard him near the door, his snarls answered by the growls and barks of the dog. The next sound she heard was the thud of the panther's landing on the roof, which sagged under his weight as he walked. The baby cried and the dog barked. The panther walked toward the chimney. She knew it was large enough for him to come through. She started piling wood on the fire, and kept piling it on until she noticed that the clay was cracking. If it fell and exposed the sticks, the cabin would burn down. Her problem was to keep just the right amount of heat going up the chimney. Eventually the baby went to sleep. She put him on a pallet and seated herself by the fire with a knife in her hand. She was still sitting there awake when the men returned next morning.

With the dog they soon found the panther not more than a hundred yards away, and shot it. Although the hound was well trained and had always been obedient he leaped upon the panther as it fell from the tree and could not be called away until he had completely ruined the hide.[16]

The motif of the panther in pursuit is essentially that of the fairy tale in which the hero, pursued by an ogre, drops objects which become obstacles to slow down the pursuer. The objects, however, are not bottles of water that become great lakes or twigs that become dense forests.

When J. Frank Dobie was a boy he used to hear a neighbor tell of a turkey hunt he once had. Taking his shotgun, for which he discovered he had only two loads, he got on his horse late one afternoon and rode toward a turkey roost. About a half-mile from the roost he came to a fence. There he tied his horse and walked on. He hid and waited for the turkeys to settle down and for the moon to rise. In the moonlight he aimed at several turkeys lined up on a limb and fired both barrels. Six turkeys fell. He was carrying them toward his horse when he heard a panther scream right behind him. He dropped one of the turkeys and ran as fast as he could. He had not gone far when the panther screamed again. He dropped another turkey. He dropped the last one just in time to leap on his plunging horse as the panther screamed again.

Dobie used to wonder what would have happened if the man had killed only five turkeys or if his horse had been a mile away instead of a half-mile. It was not till years later that he learned that the story had been "told for generations in many localities, pieces of venison or other game sometimes substituting for the dropped turkeys."[17]

Sometimes the substitute is articles of clothing, and the person in flight is a woman with or without a baby. She is riding in a vehicle or on horseback, when a panther screams and gives chase. Purposely or accidentally she drops her scarf or the baby's cap. The panther, attracted by the human scent, stops and smells and nuzzles the article of clothing, giving the woman a chance to get ahead. But he is soon coming again faster than the fastest horse can run. She drops another garment. She may strip the baby before she gets home, but no version has come to my attention in which she had to twitch her own last garment off.

Again, as would be expected, the pioneer family saga reflects the conflicts with the Indians, but here again it is selective. An Indian attack on a settlement or a party of hunters, where little happens except that men on both sides get killed, survives as an item of history. It survives in documents and books, but not in the folk memory. The event will pass into the oral tradition only when there is some added interest.

Sometimes this interest is comic, as in the story of the slow mule. The version that follows is from the Adam Lawrence saga. As Wade had the story, the Indians stole nearly all the horses in the settlement, and Lawrence organized a mustang hunt to replace them. Soon after the party had made camp the first night, a man named Jim Jones rode up on a long-legged mule and begged to join them. Lawrence told him that that would be impossible, for they were going into Indian country and might have to run for their lives. "If that happened," he said, "the Indians would sure catch you on that mule and scalp you."

Jones insisted, however, and was finally permitted to go at his own risk. One day when he and Lawrence were scouting for mustangs some distance from the camp, where pens had been built, they topped a hill and saw about forty Comanches in war paint and feathers not more than six hundred yards away, coming toward them. The Indians raised a war whoop and charged. The two white men made a run for camp. They kept well ahead of the Indians for three or four miles. Then the mule began to "throw up his tail." Lawrence begged Jones to leave the mule and get up behind him, but Jones refused, saying the horse could not carry two men and both would be killed. He gave his watch to Lawrence, asking him to send it to his mother and tell her that nobody was to blame but him. This seemed final and there was no time for further parley. Lawrence rode on.

> Two or three minutes afterwards [Wade has him say] I heard an awful screeching and yelling, and my heart came in my mouth, for I thought they was scalping Jim. But they weren't, for just then I heard a pat, pat right behind me, and I whirled back with my rifle gun cocked, for I thought it was an Indian; but I saw it was Jim, and you ought to have seen that mule, as it passed by me almost like I was standing still. Its nose was sticking straight out and smoke was a-coming out of it like steam out of a kettle. Its ears was laid back on its neck like they was pinned back. Its tail was a-sticking out behind him and it looked like he was jumping forty feet at a time. I noticed three arrows sticking up in that mule's rump. As Jim passed me he hollered back and said, "Farewell, Add!" What was them Indians yelling about? Why they was watching that mule fly. They turned back north.
>
> When I got to camp the boys were behind trees with their guns ready, but I told them that them Indians wouldn't follow us in the timber, for they knowed when we shot we got meat. Jim had his saddle off trying to pull the arrows out of his mule. I roped his fore feet and throwed it and cut them out. I was a little careless when I let it up, for it made a bulge and away it went, looking back to where it had been introduced to the Indians. We never saw hide or hair of it again.[18]

The story of the scalping of Josiah Wilbarger, as will be apparent, is a complex one, combining a number of motifs. In August 1833, Wilbarger was with a surveying party near where the city of Austin is now. At that time the only settlers in the region were Reuben Hornsby and his family and retainers. Six miles from Hornsby's house the surveyors were attacked in camp by Indians. Two men were mortally wounded. One after another Wilbarger's legs were pierced by arrows. The two unwounded men ran for their horses, Wilbarger following after them as best he could. They had mounted when they saw him fall, shot in the back of the neck with a gun. They left him for dead and rode full speed to Hornsby's.

Wilbarger did not lose consciousness, but he knew that his chances of staying alive depended upon his playing dead. This he did successfully, even while the Indians stripped him of all his clothing but one sock, and scalped him. When the scalp was torn from his head, he experienced no sharp pain, but heard a loud noise like thunder.

Then he lost consciousness. When he regained it he was alone. He dragged himself to the creek, rolled into the water and drank and rested. Becoming chilled, he crawled out and lay in the sun. Later he went back to the creek, drank, ate some snails, and began crawling in the direction of the Hornsby cabins. Exhausted, he lay down with his head against a tree.

As he lay there, a form, which he recognized as that of his sister, Margaret Clifton, who lived in Missouri, appeared and said, "Brother Josiah, you are too weak to go by yourself. Remain here, and friends will come and take care of you before the setting of the sun." When she had said this she moved away in the direction of the Hornsby place.

The men who had escaped reported Wilbarger dead. They had seen him fall with fifty Indians swarming around him. That night Mrs. Hornsby woke from a dream, called her husband and told him that Wilbarger was still alive. In her dream she had seen him wounded, naked, and scalped, but alive. Reuben Hornsby, thinking that his wife's nerves had been overwrought by the events of the day, calmed her and told her to go back to sleep. She did, only to be awakened by the same dream, the image of Wilbarger by the tree.

This time she got up, made coffee, and would not let the men rest until they promised to go to Wilbarger's relief at daybreak.

At the time of his rescue Wilbarger told of the apparition of his sister. Mails were slow in those days, and it was not until a month later that he got a letter from Missouri bringing the news of his sister's death on the day before he was wounded. He lived eleven years longer and his descendants still tell his story without significant variation.[19] A text has been in print since 1889,[20] which no doubt has militated against change. Yet one wonders how as a folk tale it could be improved.

The first chronicler, puzzled by the event he had recounted, concluded: "We leave to those more learned the task of explaining the visions of Wilbarger and Mrs. Hornsby. It must remain a marvel and a mystery."[21]

There is no marvel or mystery in the incredible. In most segments of our population the ghost story survives only as a quaint relic of the past. It will not be a part of the living folklore unless it is both marvelous and believable. The Wilbarger story passes this test, as do a few others. A college student has recently written:

> When the writer's great-grandmother was a young girl in her early teens, she attended a slumber party given by one of the neighbors, at which about ten girls were present. Even in those days none of the guests slept at a slumber party. As the night wore on, the conversation turned to ghosts, ghost stories, and cemeteries. All but one girl admitted they would be afraid to go to a cemetery at night. The one girl held fast to her boast that she was afraid of nothing, not even ghosts. The other girls called her bluff and double-dared her to go to the Liberty Grove cemetery, which was about a mile and a half away. She took the dare; and to prove that she had fulfilled her mission, she was to take a knife and stick it in the grave of a person they all knew who had recently passed on. She took the knife and slipped out of the house.
>
> Next morning she was found stretched across the grave, her face frozen in an expression of terror. The hem of her skirt was pinned to the grave by the knife.[22]

The old dream-book lore seems to be gone. People who dream of a death no longer expect a wedding, and people who dream of muddy water no longer expect a death. Nor has a Freudian symbolism supplanted the old. Dreams that get into the family sagas are, like Mrs. Hornsby's, direct and obvious in their meaning.

A recent example concerns the Rust family, formerly of Ranger. As John Rust tells the story after hearing it from his parents "a countless number of times," his mother awoke one morning and said, "Jim, we'll never sell this little farm. Regardless of what happens, we'll hold on to it as long as we live."

He said, "Why, Mary, do you feel that way about it all of a sudden?"

She said, "Last night I had a dream. Look out this kitchen window, up here at this side of the hill, will you, just a hundred feet away? See that old live-oak tree out there, the largest tree on our place?"

He said, "Yes, what about it?"

"Well, right there under that tree is where we will find our fortune, because in my dream last night it was very vivid—the picture of that tree— and our fortune will be found right there under that tree. Now in what form my dream did not let me know, but I know . . . that that dream was more than a dream—it was a vision."[23]

In 1915 a neighbor of the Rusts named Jim Baker, "who had become famous in that section of the country for locating water wells with a peach-tree limb," came to the Rust home and said he had always had a feeling that there was silver upon the hill, and asked permission to prospect there. Jim Rust told him to go ahead—he could have half of all the silver he found. Baker cut a fork from a peach tree, tied a dime to it and began walking over the farm. The peach fork turned down and came to rest under the tree of Mrs. Rust's dream. Baker showed up the next day with an auger and began boring by hand. At about a hundred feet, however, he gave up hope and quit.

Two years later oil was discovered on the adjoining McClesky farm, and the Texas and Pacific Coal and Oil Company leased the Rust farm. Two days later workmen came and cut down the big live oak in order to make room for the drilling rig. The well came in, making ten thousand barrels a day.

"I guess there might be something in dreams," concludes John Rust. "There was something in that dream. The fortune was there just like the dream told my mother years before."[24]

There can be found in Texas, however, a considerable number of families whose total wealth is less than a million dollars. Of these a considerable number sometime in the past have barely missed getting rich. If it was in this century, the fortune would have been made in oil. Father or grandfather had a farm or a ranch or some timberland a mile or two or three from a newly introduced wildcat well producing X thousand barrels of oil a day. Various producers wanted to lease his land. They bid the price up to X thousand dollars an acre. But father or grandfather held out for more. In the meantime a well was going down between the discovery well and his land. It was dry.

Or, a small independent wildcatter was poorboying a well. At fifteen hundred feet his last dollar was gone. He went to father or grandfather and offered him a large interest in the venture for enough cash to drill another five hundred feet. Father or grandfather had the money idle in the bank, but the proposition looked too risky. He declined. The wildcatter found the money somewhere else and struck oil before be had gone another hundred feet.

If it was in the nineteenth century that the ancestor missed the fortune, he missed it by failing to find a lost mine or buried treasure. This was the experience of Adam Lawrence. In 1833 when he was living on a ranch west of the Brazos, an old Spaniard walked up to his cabin one day and said he was sick and needed help. Lawrence cared for him until he was well. Then the Spaniard told him that he had been a member of Lafitte's pirate crew, and that when his master was captured, he and two others were guarding the treasure on Galveston Island some distance from the scene of surrender. They placed the treasure in two small cannon, the gold in one and the silver in the other, and buried them in the sand 703 varas from a hackberry tree. They took an oath that none of them would try to recover the treasure unless all three were present. They made their escapes, going in different directions.

The Spaniard had recently learned that the other two were dead. Released from his oath, he was on his way to dig up the cannon. If Lawrence would go with him and help him, he would give him half the treasure, and if he would take care of him the rest of his life, he would make him his heir.

On their way to Galveston Island, they camped on November 3. That was the night the stars fell on Texas. In the bright moonlight Lawrence observed the old Spaniard asleep with his shirt open. There was a great scar on his chest. His relaxed face looked inhuman. An owl hooted in a nearby bottom; a timber wolf howled. Lawrence began to wonder. Maybe the old man was the devil leading him to destruction.

All at once the heavens seemed to be on fire; shooting stars were falling all around. Lawrence sprang on his horse and fled for home. He reached it late the next day, exhausted.

About a month later a man came hunting Lawrence. He said that the old Spaniard had died at his cabin a few days after the stars fell, and had given him a package to be delivered to "Señor" Lawrence. The package contained a map of Galveston Island, showing a hackberry tree and a line leading from it marked 703 varas. This Lawrence gave to his wife Sallie, telling her to put it away carefully. He then wrote his brother-in-law, Lindsay Rucker, a surveyor, to join him. But when Rucker arrived Sallie had forgotten where she put the map. They proceeded without it, but found nothing. Many years later a cannon filled with silver was washed up during a storm. The gold must still be there.[25]

If your name is Duarte or Guerra, your family saga will bear a resemblance to those of the Smiths and the Lawrences. There will perhaps be more emphasis on the supernatural.

It might well include a tale about how the jumping about of the stove led an ancestor to suspect the presence of a ghost; how he consulted his *compadre* as one more learned in such things than he; how the *compadre* concluded that without doubt a ghost was trying to reveal the hiding place of a treasure and that whoever found it must pay the debts of the deceased so that his spirit might have rest; how when the two men were digging under the stove, a voice said, "Whoever takes my fortune takes my debts also"; how they uncovered a chest full of gold; how the *compadre* took it all, promising to pay the ghost's debts and give the other man half the remainder; how when a week had passed and no debts had been paid, the *compadre* was found dead, his mouth full of mud; and how when the chest was opened it contained nothing but mud.[26]

Or your family saga might include a story, as that of the Guerra family does, about the Texas Rangers, *"los rinches"* of the Mexican Border ballads. The Guerras stood for law and order during a long period of international banditry—a banditry in which citizens of both republics were involved, and one which reached a climax during the Civil War and Reconstruction. When Texas was readmitted to the Union, the Ranger force was reorganized and sent to the Border with emphatic orders to suppress crime. Using methods other than passive resistance, they were largely though not wholly successful.

It was during this time that Uncle Pedro Fulano was living on a ranch he had established some miles from Buena Vista, the Guerra home. One day Uncle Pedro missed some horses. He followed their tracks and about nightfall came to a camp where three men had them in their possession. When he demanded his property, they opened fire. Unhit, he fired back. He killed one man and the other two fled. He took his horses home and the next day rode to the county seat, reported what he had done, and demanded a trial. He was acquitted.

About a month later two Rangers stopped at the Guerra ranch and asked how they might find Pedro Fulano. They said they wanted to congratulate him upon the bravery he had displayed in the protection of his property. Their host, somewhat suspicious at first, became convinced of their good faith, but he knew that Pedro would probably be alarmed. He told one of his sons to saddle a horse and ride immediately to Uncle Pedro's and prepare him for the visit. In the meantime he insisted that the Rangers stay for supper.

When they reached Uncle Pedro's ranch, he was not there. Two weeks later his wife got a letter saying that he was safe in Mexico. He had found a suitable location, and she was to sell the ranch and join him.

Uncle Pedro's story is told on the Border. It shows how the barbaric *"rinches"* terrified even honest men.[27]

I have attempted by examples to indicate the kind of folklore found in the family saga. Since most of these stories exist in multiple versions and are attached to more than one person, they cannot all be true. A study of the migration of specific stories might be undertaken when more versions are available.

In the meantime the fact of their migration from place to place and from person to person is not difficult to account for.

Listeners, especially children, often confuse narrator and actor. When I was a child, for example, my mother told me the story of the trapped corn thief. This tale concerns a man who, seeing that corn was being taken through a crack in his crib at night, set a steel trap and chained it inside the crib. The next morning he saw a neighbor standing with his hand in the crack. "Good morning, Mr. Blank," he said; "come in and have breakfast."

When I told a neighbor boy how my grandfather had caught a thief in a steel trap, he said it wasn't my grandfather at all. The tale was old hat to him. I questioned my mother and she explained that she had said her father *told* the story. She had not said that he was the one who set the trap. Later I was to find the story widely diffused.

Again, characters who are vivid for whatever reason attract stories. One has only to recall such historical personages as Andrew Jackson, Sam Houston, and Abe Lincoln of Illinois —or Peter Cartwright, also of Illinois, who once complained that "almost all those various incidents that had gained currency throughout the country, concerning Methodist preachers, had been located on me."[28]

Finally the very art of narration encourages attribution to persons the narrator knows or knows about. One cannot say, "*A* told me that *B* told him that C told him that D told him that E went on a turkey hunt." If the age and known experience of the narrator are such that he can plausibly say, "I went on a turkey hunt," that is what he is likely to say. Or if he is too young, "My father [or Uncle John, or Grandfather] went on a turkey hunt."

I have chosen my examples from Texas because that is where my work has chiefly been done. But I should like to suggest to folklorists all over America that in the family saga we have an important source of living folklore—a folklore that can be collected with relative ease. Each generation produces a few collectors and raconteurs of the family lore. These can be found and encouraged to talk, sometimes into microphones. Teachers in colleges and universities can put their students to work. Young Americans, like their elders, are searching for a past. They will bring you much chaff but more than enough wheat to compensate for it. Some students get a keen emotional satisfaction in questioning elderly friends and relatives and writing their family lore. If they feel secure in their status they will be honest. They will even tell you the Illinois equivalent of why great-great-great-grandfather came to Texas.

"The Family Saga as a Form of Folklore" (1958). In *Mody Boatright, Folklorist: A Collection of Essays*, pp.124–144. Ernest Speck, ed. Austin: University of Texas Press, 1973. (Published for the Texas Folklore Society).

End Notes

Note: Originally published in *The Family Saga and Other Phases of American Folklore*, pp. 1–19 (Urbana: University of Illinois Press, 1958).

1   From the number of genealogists who clutter up the Barker Texas History Center, where I sometimes work, I estimate that a million people are at work on such histories.
2   Homer Croy, *Jesse James Was My Neighbor* (New York, 1947).
3   Martha Warren Beckwith, *Folklore in America*, Publications of the Folklore Foundation, no. 11 (Poughkeepsie, 1930), p. 3.
4   Nathaniel Benchley, *Robert Benchley: A Biography* (New York, 1955), p. 21.
5   Andrew Forest Muir, "The Skeleton in Robert Benchley's Closet," *Southwest Review 43* (winter 1958): 70–72. To point out the inaccuracy of the story is not to convict Nathaniel Benchley of anything more serious than failure to verify what he set down as fact.

6 Mody C. Boatright, *Folk Laughter on the American Frontier* (New York, 1949), pp. 1–15.

7 Samuel Adams Hammett, *A Stray Yankee in Texas,* second edition (New York, 1858), p. 4.

8 W. B. Dewees, *Letters from an Early Texas Settler,* compiled by Clara Corlelle, second edition (Louisville, 1853), p. 135.

9 Ibid.

10 Angelina Smith, "Dandy Jim Smith," unpublished manuscript. This is largely a collection of tales gathered by Floyd Smith from "various relatives and oldtimers," that is to say, from oral sources.

11 T. B. Thorpe, "The Big Bear of Arkansas," in *Tall Tales of the Southwest*, edited by Franklin J. Meine (New York, 1930), p. 16.

12 Adam Lawrence came to the Red River Valley in 1815 and joined Austin's colony in 1822. Stories about his adventures were written, some in the first person, by W. S. Wade, before Lawrence's death in 1878. A typescript of Wade's work, entitled "Tales of Early Texas," has been furnished me by John Poindexter Landers, a great-grandson of Lawrence.

13 The elk were evidently thrown in for good measure. They are not native to Texas.

14 Two versions of the "The Panther on the Roof" and five versions of "The Panther in Pursuit" may be found in J. Frank Dobie, *Tales of Old Time Texas* (Boston, 1955), pp. 181–94.

15 J. D. Brantley, "Reminiscences of a Texas Pioneer," unpublished manuscript.

16 On whether the event happened before or after the family moved from Tennessee to Texas in 1822, Sarah Glimp's descendants are not agreed.

17 Dobie, *Tales of Old Time Texas*, pp. 183–84.

18 On Lawrence, see note 12. John Duval has a version of this story in *The Young Explorers*, first published serially in 1870–1871, and in *Early Times in Texas* (Austin, 1892), pp. 150–54. His principal characters are Uncle Seth and Bill Shanks, rather than Lawrence and Jones, and his mule is not hit by the Indians' arrows.

19 The story as told by Wilbur C. Gilbert, a grandson of Josiah Wilbarger, was tape recorded July 23, 1953. Gilbert mislocates the Hornsby ranch by about twenty miles, a fact that would indicate that he had not recently read the published version.

20 J. W. Wilbarger, *Indian Depredations in Texas* (Austin, 1889), pp. 2–13.

21 Gilbert, see note 19.

22 Maurita Russell Lueg, "Russell Tales," unpublished manuscript.

23 From a tape-recorded interview with John Rust, Borger, Texas, September 15, 1952.

24 Ibid.

25 Wade, "Tales of Early Texas."

26 Guadalupe Duarte, "Around the Fire with My Abuelitos," unpublished manuscript.

27 Fermina Guerra, *Mexican and Spanish Folklore and Incidents in Southwest Texas*, M.A. thesis, University of Texas, 1941, pp. 36–38.

28 Peter Cartwright, *Autobiography* (New York, 1856), p. 109.

1.
From the Old Sod to the New World

A family saga usually begins in the Old Country. When families search for their roots, their satisfaction increases the farther back in time they can go. In the Bible, the Jews go back to Eden and their beginnings. Most Texans are happy to trace their families back to Virginia or the Carolinas. Finding roots on the Old Sod and the stories that go with them is a bonus.

Consider this example. The first Lincecum ancestor that we know anything about was an English common soldier named Linseycomb who went to France on a military expedition and was left behind as an unexchanged prisoner. He married a Frenchwoman who was a Huguenot, and their son Paschal chose to flee the country rather than violate his faith by swearing an oath to support the Catholic monarch. When Paschal and his wife reached America, they refashioned the spelling of their name to reflect the French heritage: Linseycomb became Lincecum.

The point is, there you have the beginning of a family saga that one can hand down to succeeding generations with pride. The family has no documents to back it up and it may well be inaccurate in some (or all) of the details, but it sure makes a good story.

The Old World legend might be about an ancestor's involvement in the wars or it might be concerned with his relation to the land. It usually illustrates a character trait that the family is proud of. I married into a very large and close-knit family of Welsh-Irish who pride themselves on their aggressiveness and egalitarianism, and the stories the Sheltons tell illustrate these qualities.

Maud Shelton was a Welsh cousin to Anne Boleyn, Henry VIII's second wife, and she was also her attendant in court. Thomas Shelton was Maud's son and was in the household of Queen Elizabeth, Anne Boleyn's daughter. Thomas might have prospered and kept the family in England, but his sense of egalitarianism made him insist on eating at the Queen's table. He lost favor in court as a result of his impudence and was forced to come to America. Thus, in one legend the Shelton family can boast of its ties to royal blood at the same time that it touts its democratic spirit.

When you consider the immensity of the sea voyage from the Old World to the New in the seventeenth or eighteenth century, you can understand why so many families have kept a story of this trip among their legends. The John Cherry family, which eventually settled in the blacklands of northeast Texas, tells that three Cherry brothers stowed away in empty barrels and landed in Virginia in the early 1700s. The Cherrys were my mother's family, but I have always found the barrel story a little hard to believe. The first question that always came to my young mind was where did they go to the bathroom! I still wonder how a story of that sort got started. However, I've told the same tale to my own children because it makes a good story.

Most of us in Texas and the South descend from the scrapings off the bottom of the English social barrel or from religious or political nonconformists. English reform movements of the seventeenth and eighteenth centuries consisted of shipping debtors, indigents, and criminals to Virginia and the Carolinas in long-term indenture, a form of temporary slavery. This came to be such a profitable practice—cleansing the British landscape of undesirables while providing cheap labor for the Colonies—that people were shipped in indenture to the Colonies for all sorts of reasons. They were sent because of their religious or political beliefs and in many cases—as with the Scots after their loss at Culloden Moor in 1746—because they lost a battle.

Daniel Defoe's fictional characters Moll Flanders and her equally larcenous Lancashire husband were transported to the Carolinas in lieu of being hanged at Newgate Prison. They prospered in indenture, bought their freedom with proceeds from their earlier thieveries, became rich, and returned to England to end their lives in Christian penitence.

The first Colonial Robert Abernethy was deported from Scotland to Virginia in 1648 and was indentured for five years' servitude. According to family tradition, Robert was one of over 1600 Scots Royalists who were deported by Cromwell during the English Civil War.

Hazel Shelton Abernethy tells of the coming to the United States of her maternal grandfather's family, the Morrises of San Marcos and Austin.

ᥫ • ᥫ

WILLIAM AND CINDRILLA
by Hazel Shelton Abernethy
of Nacogdoches

My grandfather's grandfather came to this country in the 1820s. His name was William Morris, and he and his parents and brothers and sisters sailed from Scotland to Virginia. His parents died of "ship's fever" on the voyage, and William and his brothers and sisters, because they had no place to go, were bound out in servitude to pay for the expenses of the trip.

My grandfather, James Emmett Morris, told me this family story, but the facts that I remember are few and I have no knowledge of dates.

The family who owned the services of William Morris eventually moved to Mississippi and took William with them. He was their property until he was eighteen years old.

William's family were kind people who treated him well and let him hire out to work for pay. He used every bit of money he made to buy land. When he turned eighteen and ended his term of servitude, he had considerable land of his own.

William Morris married a fellow bond servant, whose only known name was Cindrilla. William and Cindrilla had a large farm, owned slaves, and sent five sons to fight for the Confederacy. Two died in the war, one lost a foot at Gettysburg, and two survived the war intact. One of them, my great-grandfather, Charles Wesley Morris, came to Texas in 1872 and raised seven children, who were born in Ellis, Wise, and Fisher Counties.

ᥫ • ᥫ

BEN JAMES COMES TO AMERICA
by Mary M. Aikman
of Kilgore

Exactly why Ben James, a Welshman and British subject, came to America in 1863 was a puzzle to his descendants for quite a while. He never gave a reason and it is only through a letter from his brother in Wales that his descendants know now.

According to the letter, an old friend of Ben's, a tailor, had been announcing to the countryside the cause of Ben's hasty departure: "Ben was a good shot and a quick runner, but he shot Sir John Lewellyn's pheasants

Leopold and Clara DeMuynck Lams on their wedding day. Clara is wearing her dress of mourning for Emile, her recently deceased husband and brother of Leopold.

Clara's Belgian immigrant brother-in-law, Desire Lams, and her brother, Peter DeMuynck

once too often and had to take the next ship out." In later years, Elizabeth, David's daughter, would ask, "Grandpa, are you ever going back to Wales?"

"No, child," he would answer, "too much deep water, and deep water make me so sick." What actually would have made him sick, we know now, would have been the warrant there waiting for him.

Arriving in America, Ben turned down an offer of one thousand dollars to fight in the Civil War because he "thought he was worth more than any thousand dollars."

ᑌᕮ • ᕮᑌ

SAILING IN A LITTLE BOAT
by Laurette Davis McCommas
of Whitewright

"Sailing in a little boat,
Sailing in a little boat,
Sailing to America."

I learned that song from Grandpa Leopold Lams. I can still hear him singing it, even though he died in 1957. He sang it whenever he was rocking a baby.

It was 1902 when Emile and Clara Lams, a young married couple, were living in Belgium. Times were hard, and one of Clara's younger brothers had died from starvation. When the small portions of food were given to the children, this brave little soul would always say, "Mama, divide my portion, and give it to the rest. I'm not hungry."

Emile and Clara couldn't stand this way of life any longer, and they decided to go to America, the promised land, the land of opportunity for all.

They had a toddler, named LaSalle, and Clara was expecting again. Clara's younger brother, Peter, and Emile's two younger brothers, Leopold and Desire, would also go.

Then the unthinkable happened. LaSalle died suddenly. Plans changed, and the men went ahead to prepare the way for Clara and the new baby. They were determined to send money back so she would not need to come across by steerage. This took two more years.

Finally, Clara and the new baby, named Gillian, came to join Emile in Minnesota and eventually another child, Albertine, was born. By now Gillian, who had been born in Belgium, was nine years older than Albertine. In 1915 tragedy struck again. The whole world was beginning a series of terrible flu epidemics, and Emile died of flu at the age of 39. Clara was devastated, but only after the funeral did she feel she had time to cry.

Everyone had left the house except Emile's brother, Leopold. He put his arms around Clara to comfort her. "Have you ever wondered why I never married?" he asked.

"Yes, many times," she said. "You're such a nice, handsome young man."

"I'll tell you now," he continued, "because the love of my life was married to my brother."

"Oh! You never told me."

"I'm telling you now, and I want you to marry me. I love you so very much."

She cried even harder, "Oh! Leopold, I have Gillian, and he's eleven years old. Albertine is two, and I'm pregnant."

"Then we'll need to get married right away, before you don't fit into that beautiful black dress you're wearing."

Albertine was my mother, and that is how Leopold Lams became her stepfather and my grandpa.

⁓ • ⁓

THE VOYAGE OVER
by Martha Baxley
of Denison

In one of my family lines, the Arners, there is a legend that has been handed down by word of mouth for generations: In the early 1800s, two teenage boys lived somewhere in Europe, probably southern Germany, because they told their descendants they did not live in the mountains but could see the mountains from their home.

They had heard many stories of the New World and had reached the age to want to see it for themselves. So despite having no money and their parents having no idea what they were about, the two brothers packed their few belongings and walked to the nearest seaport. They were able to slip aboard a ship bound for America. They hid in the hold and foraged for food during the night when the other passengers were asleep. When the ship reached America, they managed to get off undetected.

They were in America, and it was like a dream come true! For a time they stayed together and worked. Then one brother decided to try his luck in Canada, while the other settled in Pennsylvania and had a large family. Genealogical research has told me that *Arner* can be either a Swiss or German name. I have traced my line back to Pennsylvania but have not found records of the brother who went to Canada.

Mattie Wood Courtney Anderson, the wife of the "lost" Miles Courtney and mother of Joseph Patrick Courtney

Joseph Patrick Courtney, the only son of the "lost" Miles Courtney of County Cork

OUR LOST GRANDFATHER
by Frances B. Vick
of Dallas

Our great-grandfather, Miles Courtney, has been lost to us. The children of Miles' only son, Joseph Patrick Courtney—Maurice, Aileen, and Bess—heard the story and relayed it to their children.

Miles Courtney came over from Ireland, County Cork, born there in 1838, if we are to believe what he reported for the 1880 census. We have no idea where he landed in this country as we can't find him in any records before the census of 1870. We know that he worked as a laborer in Houston, that he married Mattie Wood of Galveston in 1876, that they had one son— Joseph Patrick Courtney—our grandfather, who was born in Galveston in 1877. Miles and Mattie divorced when our grandfather Joseph Patrick was very young, and Miles apparently continued working on building the railroad out of Houston, ending up in Shelby County. Our great-grandmother remarried and had children with this new husband.

Miles was lost to us, but we do have one story that is told about him. He also remarried, but never had any other children. When our grandfather was a grown man Miles sent word to him to come visit him. Big Daddy, as we called our grandfather, rode on the train to Shelby County and was met at the station by his father. Miles told him that he had no other children and that he wanted to leave whatever possessions he had to Big Daddy. Big Daddy turned down the offer, which my cousin Evelyn has jokingly said was probably our family's only chance to fortune, and that the land was no doubt in the middle of the East Texas oil fields.

ↄ • ↄ

COMING TO THE COLONIES IN A PRESS GANG
by Jean G. Schnitz
of Boerne

My ancestor Enoch Fitzhenry was born May 19, 1752, in the city of Armagh, County Armagh, Ireland. When he was thirteen years old, on his way to school one day, he was captured by a press gang and carried on board an English merchant vessel which sailed to the West Indies. There were several other young boys, also prisoners, along with the crew.

While at sea, the crew members fell victim to yellow fever and nearly all died. Enoch and the other boys were pressed into service to sail the vessel and carry out other duties. He served mostly as the ship's clerk, though in other respects he was a prisoner. When the ship arrived in New York, the boys were allowed to go for a walk, which turned into a wild run for freedom.

Enoch Fitzhenry arrived in New York in 1765 and later served in the Revolutionary War. After the war, he married Abigail Hart and they had fifteen children, one of whom, James Calder Fitzhenry, came to Texas. James Fitzhenry (1814–1854) is buried under a lone oak tree on Peck Branch, where the Counties of DeWitt, Lavaca, and Victoria join.

∽ • ∽

GUSSIE GETS HER MAN
by Laurette Davis McCommas
of Whitewright

Augusta, or Gussie, Pell lived in the village of Posina, which was in either Poland or Czechoslovakia. The people of the village had a joke among themselves. They asked, "Which country do you think our village will be in tomorrow when we awaken?" The border between Poland and Czechoslovakia had changed so often that no villager could keep up with it. There were no young men left. They had all been conscripted into the army by one country or the other, or they had run away. Gussie's own brother had escaped to Berlin to find work. Not one young man was left to marry any of the girls of Posina. This was a disaster, because in 1875 every young lady was expected to marry.

Gussie finally borrowed some money to get to the United States of America. She wanted to become a citizen, and of course she wanted to find a husband and have a happy marriage and children.

The trip by ship was so terrible and Gussie was so seasick that she decided she would never sail back home again, no matter what.

She worked hard in a poultry market in New York City for about two years, but none of the young men that came in paid her any personal attention. All they wanted to do was buy a chicken or a duck, which Gussie would have to kill and clean for them. The smell of boiling water and wet feathers was bad, but not as bad as the people and sickness aboard ship. Gussie reasoned that she must be too tall, too thin, too poor, or too plain for any young man to want to marry. She was also now in her thirties, past the good marriage age.

Gussie wanted to get her citizenship papers, but for that she had to be married. If she ever lost her job, she would be deported. One day two women came into the shop. They were talking about Herr Bredlow. "He's looking for a maid. Since his wife died, he needs help to care for that huge house and lots of help with his four children."

"I think she wore out and died," the other one said. "You know the saying: the first wife plants the potatoes, and the second one eats the gravy. Maybe he'll find a new wife soon."

Gussie decided she would be that maid, and maybe Herr Bredlow would fall in love with her and marry her. She was sure she could learn to love four little children.

When she knocked at the door of the gingerbread trimmed house, her knock was answered by a tall handsome young man. Loud voices could be heard screaming in the kitchen. Carefully she asked if this was the house where a maid was needed.

"Yes," she was told, "but that's my father. I'm Carl, his oldest son, and those are my sisters screaming at each other. They can't cook anything. Ella has burned the potatoes again. Last week I heard Emma ask the neighbor lady how many hours does it take to soft boil an egg? Wait here, and I'll send for my father to talk to you."

The first thing Herr Bredlow asked was, "Can you cook?"

"Yes," Gussie answered.

"You're hired," Herr Bredlow said.

One morning after she had been there a few months, Herr Bredlow seemed especially sad, and he told Gussie that they should be married. He told her that he didn't want to be a lonely old man in a big empty house. He said that if she would marry him he would leave her enough money to live on after he died, and she would never be poor.

That solved Gussie's problem.

Annie Bredlow Ginsky was born to this union of Gussie and Herr Bredlow. Annie was my grandmother, and Gussie was my great-grandmother. Yes, cooking can be the way to a man's heart. That's how Gussie got her man.

❧ • ❧

"MADE IN AMERICA"
by Elaine Brown Ascher
of Denison

My father's mother escaped from Russia in the 1890s by hiding under a bale of hay in a horse-drawn wagon. Crossing the Russian border, she eventually made her way to America. Having lived on the border of Russia and Poland, she never knew how to answer the question of her nationality.

"One day I was Russian. The next day, Polish. It all depended on who won the war that day."

Grandmother came to America by boat. She sailed steerage on the *Rotterdam*. One day, while she was standing on deck looking at the vast expanse of water surrounding the boat, an American sailor approached her. He was holding an unknown object in his hand.

"Banana," he said, offering it to her. She shrank from him, shaking her head no. It was her first encounter with the object in question. "He's trying to poison me," she thought. Again he offered her the banana. Again it was refused. Slowly he peeled it, broke off a piece, and put it in his mouth. He smiled and once again offered it to her. This time she accepted.

"Ba-na-na," he repeated, slowly enunciating each syllable.

"Pa-na-na," Grandmother repeated. And forever after, the banana became the "panana." It was her first word of English.

Grandmother was the first of her sisters and brothers to arrive in America. Their first stop was Ellis Island. Her father had preceded her. Together they managed to set aside enough money to pay the passages for the remaining family members. Then the unexpected happened. Her mother caught pneumonia, died, and was buried in the fatherland. The children arrived without incident, and it became Grandmother's job to care for them.

"I was never a girl," she would say. "I was always a mother."

Grandmother adapted to the ways of the new world. Refusing to speak her mother tongue, she learned English in short order. She changed her Russian name to Fanny Barnett. She also learned what was fashionable. The babushka was thrown out, and the modern American hat took its place. Dresses were no longer made-over burlap bags. They became homemade copies from pictures found in the latest fashion magazines. Grandmother became more American than the native born. She discarded the old and reached for the new, expecting her family to follow suit.

"You're in America," she would say. "You do what Americans do." And she did. Only English was permitted to be spoken in the house. She was the original "Made in America" label long before it became fashionable.

This strong woman would not have appreciated the definition of "grandmother" in Webster's Dictionary: "standing in the second degree of ancestry or descent." To her way of thinking, not only was she first in the line of descent, she was a very important first. After all, it was she who contributed a new generation of males. Five sons, no less. This made her Queen

Bee of a dynasty. She was the focal point of the family. It was she who raised and nurtured an entire generation of male offspring.

I cannot remember any part of my life which she did not try to dominate. I was the daughter she didn't have but was so anxious to conceive. I was her first born's first born. Could one aspire to any higher level than that? Certainly not in Grandmother's eyes.

Margaret Coakley Hurley, who sailed from Bantry Bay with the bonfire burning

THE BONFIRE OF HOME
by Joanna Hurley
of Denton

As beneficiaries of those who had the courage to leave their homeland and start a new life in America, my husband and I have long admired our Irish relatives. Many of them had no illusions about the physical stresses they would face traveling steerage or the loneliness and bewilderment they would endure getting started in a land so far away from home.

Probably the most admired among them was my husband's mother, Margaret Coakley, who was born in Bantry, a town in County Cork on the southern tip of Ireland. Margaret had repeatedly looked on as three of her brothers, many of her cousins, and several of her friends set sail for America. She too had made up her mind to set out on her own, but unfortunately a family tragedy interrupted her plans.

During a visit to Ireland several years ago, we met a cousin in Cork City who told us this story about my husband's mother that we had never heard before. He described the home where she was born, a house built by her father which was located on a cliff at the edge of a peninsula that jutted over the Atlantic Ocean. Our cousin also described the traditional farewell of his family. Whenever one of their kin emigrated, the custom was for the family to prepare a bonfire on the cliff beyond the house, a fire visible in the bay below as the ship headed out for America and passed by the peninsula, that could be seen until the ship went over the horizon. We have thought of those lonely emigrants, leaving all they knew and loved, watching that bonfire grow smaller and smaller.

He then finished his story about my mother-in-law Margaret Coakley, a story that brought tears to our eyes then and has done so ever since. The story began seventy years before, just as Margaret Coakley was about to sail to America. Her dream of leaving Ireland to start a new life in a land where the streets were paved with gold (or so our ancestors believed) was suddenly interrupted when her brother John's wife died in childbirth. The baby survived the delivery, however, and since her brother had vowed not to marry again, Margaret put her personal life on hold to care for the baby. She stayed until the child was five years old. Realizing when she reached the age of twenty-four, that this was her last chance to fulfill her dreams, she packed up once again for the voyage to the United States.

As Margaret sailed past the farewell bonfire the family had prepared for her, little did she realize how desperately lonely her first year in America would be and how she would long for that child she had to leave behind. The storyteller, Jimmy Coakley, said he remembered that day when he and the rest of his family lit the bonfire to say goodbye to his "mother."

ও • ঔ

MY FRUGAL DAD
by Henry Wolff, Jr.
of Victoria

It was only in recent times after I began doing some Wolf family research that it became apparent to me that frugality is a family trait stretching back to my ancestors in the Old Country. I began to see some family connection to being frugal, if not downright tight about money, when a distant relative gave me a letter that my grandfather Henry Wolff (The second *f* was added in Texas.) had sent from Burton, Texas, to his brother-in-law and sister, John and Emilie Stroh of Karnes City, on November 28, 1905.

"John," he wrote, "this deabo (depot) agent call me today to the deabo and sead I mus pay 50 cts more for Freight of the grave ston and he shoese me the bill ab Freight and den I pay hem 50 cts more and I sent you the Duplicate Bill. You can see it an the Bill your seaf I sent you the Bill. I received your and the Post Office Monny Order and I tank for you too."

The way I read it, there was a difference of fifty cents in freight on the tombstone, likely for my great-grandfather Christian Wolf (original family spelling) who had died at Shelby, Austin County, on June 3, 1901, and my grandfather wanted his brother-in-law and sister to pay their fair share.

While visiting the small ancestral village of Zinse in northwestern Germany during the summer of 2001, I learned that not all the frugal Wolfs had immigrated to Texas. When my great-grandfather Christian Wolf and a brother, Frederick, left for Texas in 1851, another brother, Wilhelm, remained in Germany and a story is still told there about him or perhaps one of his sons confirming my belief that frugality is a family trait.

This Wolf was a wholesale dealer and insurance agent who also operated a small pub in his home. He received a lot of mail. While the postman waited for him to answer the mail, he was obligated to supply the man with drinks. To solve this expensive problem, he subscribed to a newspaper from Berlin and had it delivered to a location at the far end of the village. This provided him with time to answer his mail while the postman was delivering the newspaper. He would have his replies ready to be picked up when the postman returned on his way out of town.

The frugal Wolf would later send a child to get his newspaper. It cost him less than the drinks and he had a newspaper to read as well.

◖ • ◗

THE STANGLIN FAMILY
by Carol Hanson
of Cedar Hill

The Stanglin family recalls this story passed down. This is about the first members of our family who were coming here from the "Austrian/German Empire" in the early 1880s. The two brothers, John and Paul, had already arrived in the United States. Then, some of their sisters (there were seven) also wanted to come over. The father agreed to pay their passage, but insisted that the family come in pairs, because he did not want to lose the entire family if the ship should sink.

The oldest, Susanna, decided to stay in Hungary with her husband and family. Everyone else, including the parents, emigrated according to the family's requirement of sailing in pairs. As far as we know, there was no shipwreck—so everyone arrived safely.

ILLEGAL ENTRY
by Lucy Fischer West
of El Paso

My father was born Martin Franz Jockisch in Hamburg, Germany, in 1891. At sixteen, much to his mother's chagrin, he ran away from home and joined the German Navy. In 1912, while on a fishing vessel in the North Sea, he cut his hand so severely that he was put ashore and admitted to a naval hospital. While there he struck up a friendship with a Russian sailor whose dream it was to come to America, where the streets were paved with gold. The Russian sailor's dream became my father's dream.

The Russian told my father that it was a piece of cake to get off the ship in New York and not report back. Assigned to the passenger ship *Königin Luise* after recovering from the gashed hand, my father crossed the Atlantic. He packed his sea bag with all his possessions and tried sauntering casually past the guard after they'd docked in New York Harbor. It didn't work; that day's leave was canceled, and he was sent back to his quarters.

The following day, December 12, 1912, he put on multiple layers of clothes, left the sea bag behind, walked past a different guard, and succeeded in jumping ship. He spent several weeks sleeping on benches huddled under a blanket of newspapers in Central Park in the dead of winter. My father's first job was as a "pearl diver" in a restaurant, washing dishes twelve hours a day for seven dollars a week plus two meals each day. His first week's pay went for English lessons; the second for better lodging than a park bench. Four years later, tired of having his last name *Jockisch* mispronounced to sound like *jackass*, he changed it to Frank Fischer. Many years later, he went to Canada and then returned to the U. S. legally, becoming a naturalized American citizen in 1934.

The Jockisch family in Germany around 1912, Frank Fischer (Martin Franz Jockisch) standing center in his naval uniform between his sisters Martha and Bertha. Seated are Martha and Franz and Karl, Frank's mother, father, and brother.

The *Königen Luise* on which Frank Fischer (originally Martin Franz Jockisch) sailed to America

2.

Gone to Texas

The stable and conservative elements in the settled Eastern part of the United States generally believed that if anyone pulled up stakes and moved out west to the new frontiers, he was doing so because he was down and out, in debt, or running from the law. That very well might have been the case. If our ancestors were doing well in Georgia or Alabama, they certainly would not have pulled up stakes to go to the unknown wilderness frontier of Texas. Most of those who went to Texas were down to their last chance, and Texas was it.

In the South when a man left his house to pioneer in the west, he sometimes scratched GTT on the door: "Gone to Texas." Sheriffs frequently closed out their books on a man by writing "GTT" on his file. Our ancestors left there and came here for a lot of reasons, and the family stories still told give some of the reasons. Many of the family tales say that the first one that came to Texas was one jump ahead of the law. But of all the tales I have ever heard, I never heard one that cast his ancestor Texan as a villain. He might have killed somebody, but the fight was always fair. Whatever the circumstances were, they were extenuating. And whatever he might have done, it wasn't what you would consider "low."

A DELICATE CONDITION
by Elaine Scherer Snider
of Conroe

Charles Tindol, the great-grandfather of Paul Hancock of Whitehouse, came to Texas as an *indirect* result of the Civil War. A resident of Coffee County, Alabama, Charles Tindol was an ardent Southerner and joined the Confederate Army as soon as the War started. During Grant's campaign against Shiloh, he was captured at Island Number Ten on the Mississippi River. As was usual during this time, because of cost and lack of facilities, the Yankees paroled Tindol on his honor and told him to return home and never again take up arms against the Union.

Charles Tindol, a man of his word, returned home to his wife in Alabama. The disgrace of abiding by an oath given to Union soldiers, however, caused Tindol to keep his return home a secret. And because he feared the Home Guard, a local "draft board" that saw that every able-bodied young man served in the army, Charles dressed in his wife's clothing when working outside of his house and doing chores. Being a small man, the deception was successful. After six weeks, however, he could resist the call of battle no longer. He broke his parole, re-entered the army, and served in the Battle of Atlanta against General Sherman.

After Appomattox, Charles openly returned home, only to find himself in a delicate position. His wife was six months pregnant. *He* knew he was the father, but his neighbors could only assume otherwise. No overt incidents occurred, however, until the baby was born. A neighbor called and asked to see the baby with a remark similar to, "I want to see who she looks like." Charles, although accustomed to sideways looks and whispered conversations, could not withstand such a bold slur on him and his wife, so he attacked the man. When the fight was over, Charles Tindol had slashed the man's throat.

To escape a court summons, Charles came to Texas. After the situation had cooled off in Coffee County, he returned for his wife and child. On their way back, they stopped to sharecrop a season in Louisiana, then continued to Texas and settled in Shelby County. As the war must have altered everyone's life in the South, so did it change the life of Charles Tindol and his descendants.

Mr. Hancock remembers his great-grandmother Tindol, who lived to be a hundred years old. Grandmother Tindol described her husband as "one of the meanest men I ever knew." Mr. Hancock's own father always told his son that Great-Grandfather Tindol had been guilty of the crime through circumstances which he never told his family, or he would not have left Coffee County in such a rush. Mr. Hancock believes that the story does not include all the facts. He says, "I think he was guilty enough to have been hanged pretty quick, so he left and came to Texas. The story, however, is the one always told when anyone asks how the Hancocks came to East Texas."

The truth of Tindol's flight to Texas will probably never be known, but one fact is certain. Says Mr. Hancock, "If it hadn't been for that parole, my grandmother would never have been born."

৶ • ৶

CAPTAIN JACK NASH
by Carole Hensley Bergfeld
of Midland

This legend involves a tale told by a lady now living in Tyler, Texas. Mrs. Caroline Nash Bergfeld tells about her great uncle, Captain Jack Nash, who lived in Kentucky and was on the move to Texas. He was later to settle in San Augustine.

Captain Nash traveled to Texas by means of wagon train. One day their train was overtaken by a great herd of Indians. After much reasoning and fast talking, the people of the wagon train persuaded the Indians to settle for a hand-to-hand combat between each group's ablest man. The victorious group would hold the other group as captives.

The wagon train party elected Captain Jack Nash, while the Indians chose their chief. The battle was long and hard fought, with Captain Nash being the victor. It was the custom of the Indians to give an article of the slain person's possessions to his slayer. Captain not only acquired many captives, but was given the war jacket of the slain chief. The jacket was made of leather and had many colorful beads and pieces of turquoise strung with leather straps and horsehair. Today this jacket is among the collections of a San Antonio museum.

৶ • ৶

THE LEGEND OF BILLY HICKS
by Dorothy Kennedy Lewis
of Ore City

The year was 1845. The wagon train was ready to travel. The group of twenty-four wagons would soon leave the small Georgia community for Texas.

The families had been ready for several months, but had been waiting for a capable wagon master. At last great-great-grandfather Stewart reported to his family that a Mr. William Hicks had arrived and was willing to take them through on a new route, one that was not as well known and was shorter.

Laden with as many personal possessions as possible, the families began to board their wagons for the long trip. The head of each family placed his bank roll in the hands of the wagon master, who had also been chosen by the group to be the banker. Mr. Hicks had a reputation for his bravery, his wit, and his intelligence. He loved to read, and this was a part of his activity each day when the train would stop for the night.

According to great-grandmother Gandy, who was five years old at the time, there was one such night that would never be forgotten.

The campsite was somewhere in south-central Louisiana, in the notorious Neutral Ground, about a week from the Texas border. The trail had wound its narrow way through the thick woods for days and camping had been difficult, but about noon on this day, a slight ridge on the edge of the woods appeared. There was a spring on the southern slope. The wise Mr. Billy Hicks decided to stop and make camp for the night.

The wagons formed a semi-circle in the clearing from one edge of the woods to the other. The camp's central fire was built on the edge of the woods from a huge tree that had been cut by the axmen. It had been trimmed by the families for their individual camp fires and plenty of brush had been piled behind the log to feed the fire for the night. Fire was still one of man's sources of protection from the wild animals of the woods. Each night, guards were chosen to watch for animals and Indians, to keep the fire fed, and to care for the camp in general.

On this evening, with supper over and the men securing their wagons and livestock for the night, Billy Hicks was sitting near the main campfire on the huge log reading. Suddenly from out of the woods came a band of renegades whose noisy entrance caused the men folk to rush from their wagons. They were immediately forced to line up to be searched. The robbers were looking for the "banker" for the train.

In the confusion and excitement the quick-witted Mr. Hicks had moved down the log until he was in front of the brush pile where he dropped the money belt and carefully eased it in among the branches. Being dismissed as they were searched, the men were held captive by a part of the group of robbers some distance away from the group being searched.

After the search was over and no large sum of money was found and while the men and older boys were kept under guard, the raiders began to slit open sacks of staples and seeds. This was a horrible sight to see. Why were they wasting their supplies? They had already given up the coins in their pockets, their jewelry, their small food stuffs, and their life savings to these robbers, so how could the renegades be so cruel as to waste their valuable food and seed supplies? Only Mr. Hicks knew why. They were searching for hidden money. At last the thieves left. They were convinced this was just a poor wagon train that had no money.

Now, the long hard job of cleaning up of the camp began. The women and girls began to mend the sacks, and the men and boys began to pick up the wasted food and seeds, especially the corn and beans. They needed every seed they could find if they were to be able to plant their crops in Texas. It was almost an impossible task. The settlers were in despair to think that after the robbery they had no money for tools that needed to be replaced or livestock that was to be bought or for supplies to last until a crop could be made.

Next morning, the activities around the wagons were much as usual. When all the family heads were present, Mr. Hicks called them over to the brush pile where he removed the money belt from its hiding place. You can imagine the elation of these men to see that they still had their estates. They could go to Texas now in good shape, thanks to the quick-witted and very intelligent Mr. Hicks.

In his honor, someone in the party made up the following jingle that followed Mr. William (Billy) Hicks most every place he went.

> Old Billy Hicks
> Full of his tricks.
> Throwed his pocketbook
> Over in the sticks.
> And when the robbers came 'round
> It couldn't be found
> So they were left well fixed.

◅ • ▻

THE BEAR AT THE SPRING
by Patsy Johnson Hallman
of Nacogdoches

Patman Freeman Paschall was born in 1821 in North Carolina, where his parents were reared. In early life, however, they began their westward move that eventually took them to East Texas. For a while they were in Alabama, but they soon settled in western Tennessee, near the Kentucky border. Patman's father, Jesse, and his grandfather, Alexander, took advantage of the U. S. Homestead Act and claimed two hundred acres of Tennessee land.

Alexander had first seen the land in 1825, when he was searching for a homestead. During his search he spotted a bear drinking from a spring. He shot the bear, and he decided to claim the land around the spring. Thus began the history of the Paschalls in Tennessee, while they were on their way to Texas. Today the spring is on the Beecher Finch farm and continues to bubble with gusto.

Patman Freeman Paschall (1863), who settled by the bear's springs in Tennessee on his way to Texas

THE RAWHIDE FIGHT BROUGHT US TO TEXAS
by Frances B. Vick
of Dallas

I assume I was read to as a child since I read at an early age. Or, it could be that I learned to read because I would not stay with Mabel, our maid, while Mother went to teach school at Pennington. As soon as Mother left for school I would strike out for the courthouse where my father officed in his capacity as county school superintendent. It apparently created a lot of disturbance to have this two- or three-year-old wandering the streets of Groveton, so Mother just took me with her to school. I sat in the back of her or some benevolent teacher's room and I suppose I learned whatever was being taught along with the legitimate students. In any case, instead of re-questing to be read to at night, I would climb into my father's lap and de-mand, "Daddy, tell me some bull." The expression came from my mother telling him to quit "telling that child all that 'bull,'" she being insightful enough to leave off the second half of the word that is usually applied, since I picked up with gusto any expressions that were used in the family and my father took issue with some of my mother's saltier sayings.

My father's "bull" consisted of family stories such as the ones about Grandpa Walker (Andrew Jackson Walker from whom my father got the Andrew in his name) being released by the Indians when he was captured during the Civil War guarding the salt works on the coast; or about Aunt Polly's husband (Carl August Johnson from whom my father got the Carl in his name) being shot and the buggy dragging his body home. But one of my favorite stories from the "bull" collection was the one about how my great-great-grandfather, Lewis Dial, swam the Sabine River in the 1850s to avoid being killed by irate citizens in Louisiana.

According to my father, Lewis lived near Sugartown, Louisiana, with his wife Harriet Sweat, and nine children. A feud developed between two factions of the settlement over a dispute about the school. The factions met at the schoolhouse, with the rivalry so intense that they squared off with drawn guns and waited for someone to make a move. Just at this instant, Lewis rode up on his horse and taking in the situation decided to try and arbitrate. His first spoken words sparked the super-charged at-mosphere and the shooting began. When the smoke cleared there were so many dead and wounded that they were laid out on some raw cowhides stacked at the train station awaiting shipment, thus the term "Rawhide Fight."

The feud was now so bitter that Lewis loaded his family in his wagon and headed for Texas. He was middle-aged with boys old enough to help in a gun battle but he was not enough engrossed with his faction to want to stay around and maybe get himself and some of his boys killed.

When he first crossed the Sabine, he went down to Castroville, where there were some friends and relatives, and changed his name to Jenkins so he would be harder to track. That name lasted at least until the Civil War, when his son, Ephriam Dial, went into Company M of Hood's Brigade as Ephriam Jenkins. So, as late as the 1860s the family was still using that name, or at least Eph was using it, perhaps because he would be going through Louisiana to join Longstreet's Corps in Lee's Army of Northern Virginia.

Part of the story continues in Castroville where Lewis joined a posse to recapture a baby that had been stolen by the Indians. The story goes that by the time the posse caught up with the Indians, they had built a campfire where they had boiled the baby and were preparing to eat it. One of my aunts by marriage who was raised in Yoakum, Texas, said that she remembered the story very well as one told in her family about Indian depredations, and added the information that the men in the posse never did tell the mother of the baby what had happened to it, to which one can only respond, "Thank goodness!"

When he felt it was safe to do so, Lewis returned to East Texas and bought land there in Trinity County in 1854. And there the story ends, according to my "bull" sessions with my father.

All of this made perfect sense to me since my family were all involved in the school business and they were indeed serious about it, down to fistfights, if necessary, to control unruly boys in the school or their irate parents who protested the punishment. And altogether, those stories made for some wonderful "bull" sessions between father and daughter.

_ॐ_ · _ॐ_

THE FERGUSONS TRAVEL TO TEXAS
told by Mary Ann Long Ferguson
transcribed by Odessa Hicks Dial
and Alice Dial Boney
of Forest

One night in 1857, Mr. Ferguson came in and announced that he had made up his mind—we were going to Texas! He said, "That's where I started when I left home, and I'll never be satisfied until I go. Bill keeps writing about the wonderful climate and the rich soil, so I'm going to farm. I've always wanted to be a farmer, and I'm going to take the chance in Texas!"

I knew it would be futile to argue, and it never entered my mind to do anything other than go with him. What was his life was mine to share, for better or for worse, although for a time I was heart-broken to leave all my people in Mississippi and all the comforts to which I had been accustomed and strike out on this long trip to Texas. We had lost our first child, Henry J., in 1851 when he was little more than a year old, but we had two others now—Nelson Foster, born April 28, 1853, (the only boy we raised to be grown), and Harriet Ellen, born October 10, 1855. In no time at all everything we had had been disposed of, and a covered wagon, oxen with which to pull it, and needed supplies had been purchased. We did manage to make room for a beautiful walnut marble top dresser Mother had given me when we married, some bedding and linens, clothes, and the family Bible. Mr. Ferguson's favorite saddle horse was tied behind the wagon, and we were off to Texas.

Mary Ann Long Ferguson with her father, Thomas Jefferson Long, ca. 1855

This trip to Texas was long, as oxen are much slower travelers than horses, and we never hurried them. If we saw a good fishing place, we both would fish until we caught a good mess. We stopped to talk a while at most every farm house we passed. The entire family would come out to meet us, anxious to get the news from other places. They would often beg us to stay over night, and sometimes we did if the weather was bad or if Mr. Ferguson particularly liked the people. As a rule he was a very good judge of people when he had talked with them a while. Families lived miles apart in those days and grew so hungry for companionship. Many of them offered all kinds of inducements if we would settle near them. Very often they gave us fresh meat, milk, butter, and other things to eat that we could not prepare over a campfire.

Mr. Ferguson did most of the chores when we made camp, even the cooking, as I had the children to bathe and feed. Mother taught me how to do everything about running a house as she always said a mistress could not train a servant unless she knew how to do things herself, but I dare say she never thought the day would come when I would really be doing these things myself. I really had had very little experience as we had servants at home, and when I married we continued to live at the hotel where I had a personal maid and a nurse maid for the children. I don't know when Mr. Ferguson learned so much, but it seemed to come natural for him, and every day I marveled at the foresight he had when he purchased supplies for the trip for it seemed that anything we needed he could produce it from somewhere.

Naturally we did grow weary of travelling sometimes, but for the most part we had a wonderful trip and none of us were sick the whole time—not even a runny nose! To me the most wonderful part about it was the fact that we had time to talk and plan and really get acquainted with each other and with our children. We learned to lean on each other and confide in each other, a lesson that was never forgotten and one that so many modern couples never take time to learn.

Did I ever tell you about the time I fell in the Red River? Well, that happened on our trip to Texas also. Torrential rains had washed the planks off the only bridge crossing the Red River on the route we took, but the good Lord had seen fit to leave the large timbers spanning the river. As usual Mr. Ferguson found a way. He measured the distance between the timbers, which were rather wide, and found that the wheels of our wagon would just fit, so he said to me, "If you can walk across the middle timber and hold the wagon tongue up, I think I can push the wagon across, then I'll come back and swim the oxen over." Well, there wasn't any other recourse as the stream was too deep to ford, so off we started.

Everything was going fine, and we were more than halfway across when one of the front wheels hit a nail or bump of some kind. This made the wagon tongue wiggle-waggle, and into the river I went! As luck would have it the wheels stayed on the timbers, or all would have been lost. It never entered my mind to be afraid for myself even though I couldn't swim a lick, for I knew Mr. Ferguson was a champion swimmer and would get me out, but I did fear for the two little children in the wagon—afraid the commotion would frighten them and they might fall in too.

In due time we were out of the water and had the wagon across, but by this time it was so cold that our clothes had frozen stiff. I found a little wood while Mr. Ferguson swam the oxen over, and we soon had a roaring fire going. We got into fresh clothes and dried the wet ones by the fire before continuing on our journey. As I have always said, the Lord will look after his own.

I think I mentioned earlier that we brought the family Bible along; in fact, in those days no family felt complete without one. We both were reared in Methodist homes and were Christians, but like so many Christians of all times, we hadn't spent much time reading the Bible ourselves. If for no other reason I think our trip to Texas was worth while for we spent many hours each day reading aloud from the Good Book. I feel it helped to fortify us for future trials, and one thing I know—by the time our journey was complete, we were both Baptist, but Mr. Ferguson never joined a Texas Church.

We settled in central Texas in a little log cabin near Kosse, Texas. The community was called Old Eutaw, but our nearest neighbor was about ten miles distant. How easily I could have become frustrated, but I had to think of my babies, and hard work never hurt anyone. Our furnishings and tools were meager, and this was a far cry from the farming Mr. Ferguson had known in Virginia with plenty of tools, animals, and slaves to do most of the labor.

ဆ • némeaux

BROTHERS
by Patrick Mullen
of Beaumont and Columbus, Ohio

My grandmother, Lillian Terry, grew up on a farm near Waxahachie, but she lived in Beaumont for most of her adult life, and it was in Beaumont that I heard Nanny tell about how her father first came to Texas. She said that he was always fighting with his brother on the tenant farm their father worked in Alabama. They fought so often that their father gave them an ultimatum: "One more fight and you'll both get the whipping of your life." The brothers were peaceful for a while, but one day they were working together out in a field and got into an argument that led to a fistfight. Bloody and bruised, Nanny's father realized he could not go back and face his father. He dropped his hoe and started walking west and didn't stop until he was in Texas. He never saw his family again.

◞ • ◟

THE RED RIVER CROSSING
by Jean G. Schnitz
of Boerne

Edgar Weston tells a story about Columbus Addison Lee's trip to Texas. At the Red River Crossing, a trading post stood on the Texas side of the river. An old Indian guided the wagons over the river, a trip which required following the sand bars for quite a distance until the wagons were able to

The Columbus Addison Lee family in Seymour around 1891. The parents, Columbus and Permelia, sit in the front row center. In the back row are Dora Bell Lee, Cora, Amos, Ida, and Luna. In the front row are George Lee, Daniel Addison (the small child), the parents, Elbert, and Mary Tennessee.

reach the Texas side. The wagon carrying my great-grandfather C. A. Lee was among the first to cross the river.

The slow and tedious crossing of the river took almost all day, so C. A. was getting angry and impatient. He commented to someone, "That old Indian is taking much too long to get these wagons across the river. I'm not going to pay him when everybody gets here. Let's just go on."

The trading post manager heard the comment and told Addison, "Mister, I don't know who you are or where you are going, but I can tell you one thing for sure. You can't go far enough or fast enough to get away from that old Indian. If you don't pay him, you are going to wake up some morning without any horses and probably without any women."

C. A. Lee paid the Indian.

✥ • ✥

TENNESSEE TO TEXAS
by Barbara Pybas
of Gainesville

Kenneth Monroe Pybas made a mistake in the 1870s in Bedford County, Tennessee. He took a chance by helping out a friend. He had returned from the war in 1865 and with a good business head had managed to hang on to his farm. He later became the manager for the S&F Tollpike, putting four of his sons on the payroll, and accumulated enough money to put in successful crops.

One of his neighbors desperately needed a responsible party to co-sign a note so that he could secure and pay for his farm. K. M. Pybas made the mistake of signing that note. When his neighbor ultimately could not come up with the money, Pybas became legally responsible. The Pybas clan had increased by that time, with four married sons and several grandchildren, three younger siblings, two girls and a boy as well as the eldest son, who was unmarried.

Ultimately, Pybas was forced to sell his holdings to pay off the note he had unwisely signed. However, there was still some money left, and all the family was gathered in and made the important decision to move to Texas. He sent the oldest son, Jordan Cain Pybas, riding a good horse to find a location, and the family moved to north Texas. The tax records show that K. M. Pybas paid taxes on property near Grapevine in Tarrant County in 1879.

The Pybas family began their trek in the spring of 1878. Seven wagons carried the families, with four pregnant daughters-in-law. The story is told that the girls walked most of the way because the wagons jolted and jarred

Kenneth Monroe Pybas, Jr., and his sister, Emily Evaline Pybas (Boy and Missie), who made the seven-wagon trip to Texas with the rest of the Pybas family. The picture was taken in Gainesville in 1886.

Kenneth Monroe Pybas and his wife Eleanor Cain Holt Pybas, who came with their children and grandchildren to Texas in 1878 and to Gainesville in 1881

56

them. As they began to get settled, and the babies were born, tragedy struck. Three of Blair Pybas' children died in one week of typhoid fever, and another became desperately ill.

K. M. Pybas resolved, "We are going to leave this unhealthy climate on this [Trinity] river." Again, he sent his sons to find a new location. They found a "Tennessee Colony," a few settlers from Tennessee, northwest of Gainesville, Texas, very near the Red River in Warrens Bend. They came to Cooke County in 1881. There the family established a gin in 1885, and farmed cotton in the fertile river bottom. Two of the brothers served as County Commissioners, one was a Road Overseer, building roads for the county with horses and slips and dynamite.

Today there is a long row of Pybas graves in a country cemetery, Barehead Cemetery, in Cooke County. The patriarch parents, four of the sons and wives, and several of the children are buried there, the first stone being for a baby born in 1881.

୬ • ୬

LOOKING FOR LAND
by Henry Wolff, Jr.
of Victoria

Thousands of German immigrants came to Texas looking for land, and afterwards one generation after another continued to migrate throughout the state, still looking for land.

When my dad was eighty-five years old, I sat down with him to do an interview for my newspaper column in *The Victoria Advocate*. He told about his family moving from near Brenham in Washington County to Rosebud in Falls County, near Waco. Dad's father was a first generation Texan who had grown up at Shelby in Austin County, where his parents and many other Germans had settled in the mid-1800s.

In the early 1900s, first and second generation German-Texans moved out of the overly crowded communities of their parents and grandparents in search of land elsewhere. They first moved to the central part of Texas, and from there they continued their search for land into west Texas and the Panhandle.

As was customary, at the time that my grandfather Henry Wolff's family made their move to Falls County, personal belongings and livestock were shipped in a freight car, and the family went by passenger train. My dad, the second Henry, remembers they left a haystack behind that some old fellow came and hauled off with oxen.

His oldest brother, Walter, had gone ahead on the train and had every-thing in order when the rest of the family arrived at their new farm. Dad was six years old at the time, having started school only a few days before they moved. The second youngest of four girls and four boys, he was soon enrolled in a school near their new home.

"We had to walk about two miles," he recalled, "and often it was cold and muddy." Sometimes when it was raining, his father would take the children to school in the family buggy.

Within a couple of years, the tenant farm they lived on was sold to a new owner, and they moved south to Burlington in neighboring Milam County, where several families farmed in an area with a community pasture. Dad remembered when the doctor would come riding across the pasture to call on one of the families, he was on a little dun pony and always riding at a gallop.

"A lot of times when I'd see him coming," he said, "I'd go open the gate for him."

They later moved to near Westphalia, back in Falls County, in three wagons and stayed there a year before moving to the nearby Ocker Com-

Henry Wolff at 85, the writer's father and the carrier of the tales of looking for land

munity in Bell County. My dad hadn't been to school for a year because the school at Westphalia was Catholic and charged for books.

"Dad didn't see any use in buying the books if we were going to move anyway," he recalled.

There was a bit of excitement when they had previously moved from Burlington to Westphalia. They had already moved their corn and other feed for their livestock and had the three wagons loaded with all their personal belongings. One of the older boys, Irvin, was handling one of the teams while sitting on top of a wood cookstove that had been placed at the front of one of the wagons.

They came to a little creek where there was a crossing of cut timbers, and the mules bolted as the wagon started across the loosely laid logs. The team broke loose and pulled Irvin off the wagon, and one of the wheels ran over him. They took him to a doctor at Burlington, who determined he had no broken bones. Grandad laid Irvin on top of the family bedding stacked toward the back of the wagon, and he rode the rest of the way at his ease.

"I rode up there with him," my dad recalled.

Years later after Dad married and I came along, we moved farther west, out to Ballinger in Runnels County, and I particularly remember passing though the Santa Anna Mountains. Those mountains ever since have seemed to me like the gateway to west Texas.

One thing that was the same was that my family was still looking for land.

᪥ • ᪥

C. A. LEE ESCAPES TO TEXAS
by Jean G. Schnitz
of Boerne

In 1862, another event influenced Columbus Addison Lee's decision to leave Missouri to go to Texas. C. A. Lee's father-in-law, James Parks Yandell, (my great-great grandfather) was an avid anti-Confederate person who was not timid about speaking out against slavery and the Confederate cause. What's more, Yandell had opposed the marriage of C. A. and his daughter, Permelia Caroline, (my great-grandmother), causing the young couple to elope. There was continual conflict between C. A. Lee and Yandell until Yandell was ambushed in 1862. He fell from his horse at what is now the gateway to Corinth Cemetery in Lee Valley, near Cassville, Missouri, and was buried where he fell. James Parks Yandell, who had shot his own son-in-law years earlier in Illinois, which caused his own sudden move to Missouri, had thus been killed by his own son-in-law—which is another story.

All the Lee family in Missouri knew that C. A. Lee had been the trigger man in this ambush and that he had killed his father-in-law. All, that is, except his wife, Caroline Yandell Lee, because no one wanted to be the one to tell her. Family stories also say that after the Civil War, C. A. Lee decided to move his family to Texas to escape his reputation as a bushwhacker and murderer. His greatest fear was that his wife would leave him if she found out what he had done.

When the Lee family arrived in Texas, C. A. Lee was apparently able to change his reputation and became known as a family man, music teacher, church leader, and community leader.

୶ • ୭

GONE TO TEXAS, 1940!
by Marilyn Colegrove Manning
of Houston

It was 1939 in Midland, Michigan. I was three years old. My dad worked for Dow Chemical Company. We lived on Salem Street in a little two-bedroom brick house which my Dutch mother kept spotless in spite of a messy daughter.

I had no real understanding of world politics, of course, but the radio was always on in the morning with news and a variety of things. When my dad would come home for lunch he would pick me up, give me a hug, and ask me, "Well, Marilyn, what did the German High Command have to say today?" I would say something or other, I suppose, but I knew there was something important about the news and that my dad and I had an agreement that we would talk about it.

At the same time that Germany was in the news, Dad was sent to Texas to look for a new site for Dow Chemical to build a plant. He and his boss would explore the Gulf Coast and would be gone for a long time. When Dad was gone, I remember asking my mother if he was in Germany. She said no, he was in Texas. I couldn't really make any distinction between the two. Neither of them was in Michigan. I did know that.

In 1940, Dad came home with a new car: a red Oldsmobile. With a back seat for me. As I look back on it, I suppose the car was a necessity because we were going to have to make a trip to Texas in it so Dad could help Dow get the new plant off the ground in Freeport. We were only going for six weeks; then we would come home.

And off we went. It was a long drive, and singing in the car was a major way to pass the time. We learned, "Come Away with Me, Lucille, in My Merry Oldsmobile" to go with our other standards: "I'm Forever Blowing Bubbles," "The Band Played On," "My Blue Heaven," "I'm Always Chasing Rainbows," and "She'll Be Comin' Round the Mountain." Finally we arrived in Freeport.

Goodness, Freeport was a strange place. The only paved street was 2nd St. It was raining. We were going to stay at the newly constructed Dow Hotel, which had six rooms. It was hot. It was muggy. We didn't have a word for how uncomfortable it was. We had never been in such a climate before, and it was a shock.

The hotel was okay and we were to live there for six weeks. As the weeks passed, we ate in one or the other of the two restaurants in the town. We tried to take advantage of being in a different place and went to see what we could. Galveston beach was one of our outings. We went to Angleton to see the courthouse. There wasn't much to do.

Finally, when it was time to go back HOME, to Michigan, Dad came to Mom with the proposal that we move to Freeport. The company would be building some new houses—"Dow Houses"!—for the people who would be coming to work in Freeport at the new plant. The plant was going to be important because they would be making magnesium for what was to become our armed forces. It was becoming clearer and clearer that war was imminent and that Dow would be important to that effort.

Apparently my dad made a good enough argument for moving that my mom conceded, and we went back to Michigan to get our stuff together for the move to Freeport.

We moved into our house on Broad Street, and we hadn't been here long before a hurricane made its appearance. In 1940 they didn't name the storms, but my mother had several names for it. She was sure we had moved to Hell and didn't know it. We made our way to Houston to the Texas State Hotel to ride out the storm, but Dad had to stay in Freeport. It was a kind of a lark for me. Very exciting. When we returned to Freeport, my folks now had an investment in the place.

In spite of heat, humidity, mildew, bugs (We had never had bugs in the house in Michigan, and Mom fought them with all her might for the rest of her life.), we became Texans. None of our relatives ever understood it. They were sure that the Colegroves were demented and would perhaps one day wake up and come back to "God's Country," but they couldn't have been more mistaken.

On December 7, 1941, we were in our house in Freeport when the word came that Japan had bombed Pearl Harbor. We were going to go to war, and Dow would be a major source of materials for the United States. Dad would oversee the building of a housing development called Camp Chemical to accommodate the influx of people to work at the plant, and it would be built in record time (about six weeks). Camp Chemical became the largest "town" in the county!

Lots of Michigan people moved to Freeport to work for Dow. The Yankees had invaded and that quiet little place would never be the same. Nor would we.

3.

The Civil War

⌘

Nothing looms greater than the Civil War in most of our family histories. The violence of war came into the homes and lives of our ancestors of the 1860s with more intensity than we have ever known. The Civil War wrecked a nation, and some of the debris drifted to Texas.

Those settlers who came to Texas after the War brought stories and songs that are still having an effect on our culture and traditions. Grandad regularly whistled, hummed or sang the chorus from "Vacant Chair": "We shall meet but we shall miss him. There will be one vacant chair. . . ." Grandad's father, John Ware Abernethy, was a Confederate soldier, but told few tales about the battles he fought in. The only battle story he told stayed in my memory because Grandad told the story like a joke. He said that some soldier buddy of Great Grandad's told him that anytime they got into a battle, to find some brush to hide in and fire from. Great Grandad followed his advice, dove for the brush during his first skirmish, and soon came running out with a bear behind him.

And my maternal Grandmother Cherry would tell about how as a young child in Hunt County she saw this strange old tattered man coming down the lane toward the house. She ran scared and crying to her mother. The tattered man was her father coming home from the War.

Enoch Pitts, Mrs. Frances Pitts Norvell's grandfather of Kountze, made it through the War, but he never made it home. On his way back to Texas he stopped in a hotel in Richmond, Virginia, and that night instead of turning off the gas-mantle lamps, he blew them out.

The Yankees won the War but they did not win all the battles, as will be seen in John O. West's story of "Granma and General Sherman." I remember another Southern victory described in a story that Avie Williams told at a genealogical meeting in Timpson about the Yankees taking her ancestor's only remaining mule. This mule was the meanest mule the family had ever known—"He'd back his ears and wall his eyes/And Lord! that mule could kick!"—but he was their only plow animal. The Yankees confiscated him for their own, but that mule either got away or he was so mean that they turned him loose. The Yankees kept that mule only a week, after which time the mule showed up back at the farm, helped them make a crop that year, and a year later pulled the wagon that took the family to East Texas.

Granma Anna Narcissa Sutherland Watts (1840–1935), who gave General Sherman a lesson in manners

GRANMA AND GENERAL SHERMAN
by John O. West
of El Paso

The family legend I most often heard from my mother was about her grandmother. Born Anna Narcissa Sutherland in middle Mississippi, she married—probably at about fourteen—a Doctor Watts. Granma bore and raised a dozen children, all told, and never cooked a meal. Daddy said she couldn't boil water without scorching it. When I knew her, she was in her nineties and all of five feet, one-and-a-half inches tall. She dipped snuff very delicately, smoked a little clay pipe, and read without glasses in her Bible every day. When *Gone with the Wind* came out, I found out that Granma had borne a baby in Atlanta, just about the same time Melanie Wilkes had hers! But the story I always loved to hear happened a while before that.

Granma Watts had a run-in with the terrible General William Tecumseh Sherman, the one who marched to the sea with death and devastation in his wake—and she won! She stood up to him in her own backyard. This was after the fall of Vicksburg, and Sherman's men were foraging through Madison County, Mississippi, taking everything that wasn't nailed down, and they finally got to Granma's.

Granma went out into the backyard where the Yankee soldiers were gathering chickens. She was ready to discuss the matter. I can imagine that her remonstrations with those damn Yankees were anything but ladylike, but I doubt that they did much good. Yankees had already been called about everything in the book by then, even by little Southern ladies. Anyway, in the midst of all the ruckus and the squawking and blessing out Granma was giving the Yankees, a scroungy little man rode into the yard, slumped down in the saddle, with a cigar stub between his teeth. And although Granma didn't know one rank from another, she could tell from the way the men acted that here was somebody who was in charge—so she charged!

As Mother always told the story, Granma had on the front of her dress a sparkly pin with diamonds—possibly the Order of the Eastern Star, or something like that—but it was some ladies' order that General Sherman's mother also belonged to. Perhaps it was the pin that caused the general to order his men to turn loose the chickens that had somehow gotten stranded on their saddle strings, and put the feather ticks back together. That was the part of the story that I always enjoyed the most. It tickled me to visualize all those Yankee soldiers chasing around after the feathers to put back in the mattresses they had ripped open looking for gold.

In spite of her victory over Sherman and the Union raiders, Granma always hated Yankees. She believed all the wild tales that were told about Abe Lincoln, and she went to her grave believing that the South should have won the war.

There were some details of the story that bothered me: General Sherman was a powerful man even if he was small, and Granma was a frail little old lady when I knew her. Could it have happened? She lived on to be ninety-seven, and I got to know her pretty well, but I never dared to ask her if she had really faced General Sherman down. And as tiny as she was at that age, it didn't seem she could ever have been so fiery of spirit that she could have stood up to General William Tecumseh Sherman, the Scourge of the South!

But that was one of the wonderful stories that my mother told about my ancestors—and I always believed them—of long ago and far away, and of that event that some folks call simply "The War"—as if there could never have been another one. Maybe, as Daddy said, she couldn't boil water, but Granma had run the small plantation while her doctor husband was off doing his part for the Cause. And if she could do that, maybe she could have stood General Sherman down after all! I like to think so!

❧ • ❧

JAMES WARE'S HANGING
by Gloria Counts
of North Little Rock, Arkansas

[James Agnew Ware was a Baptist preacher in South Carolina, who in 1836 was sent by the church to Pontotoc County, Mississippi, to minister to the Chickasaw Indians. He was also a physician, and one of his daughters married my great-grandfather. —Abernethy]

Yankee troops literally blazed their way through the South during the Civil War. When they arrived at the Ware plantation [in Pontotoc County, Mississippi], there was snow on the ground.

"I remember hearing the old folks talk about that day," said Mrs. Shannon [who related the story to Mrs. Counts].

"They were all huddled around the fireplace when the Yankees came stomping in. But my Auntie Anna, who was always feisty, had hidden the silver in her clothes. When she moved, however, one of the soldiers heard the tinkling sound and demanded to know what it was. Auntie replied that it was the family silver and dared the Yankees to try and take it. They didn't."

Mrs. Shannon adds that when they demanded Auntie's grandfather's gold watch, "She [Auntie Anna] dashed it on the fireplace hearth and busted it all to pieces to keep the Yankees from getting it."

But though the house was spared a Yankee torch and the family silver was saved, Dr. Ware himself did not escape injury.

Acting on a rumor from an escaped slave, the Yankees demanded to know where Dr. Ware had buried his gold.

Dr. Ware replied that there was no gold. The slave had merely seen him the summer before when he was filling in a hole under the garden fence to keep out the rabbits.

"The Yankees did not believe this," said Mrs. Shannon. "They took him from the house and hanged him by the neck several times, up and down, trying to make him tell where he buried his money."

When their torture proved fruitless, the soldiers finally rode off after taking Dr. Ware's boots from his feet and leaving him lying in the snow.

He was never well again, and he died soon after, in April 1865.

૭ • ૭

A WOMAN'S STRONG LOVE
by Dianna Shull

My husband's great-great-grandfather, William Harris, died gloriously in battle during the Civil War. Upon hearing the news of his death, his wife rode forty miles from Eldorado, North Carolina, to Salisbury, North Carolina, in a wagon. She managed, by herself, to put the body in the wagon, then returned to Eldorado so that he could be buried on the homeplace. Such a journey, lasting several days, for a woman alone is quite a feat, but loading the body in the wagon and traveling several days with it shows just how strong a woman's love can be.

૭ • ૭

SWIMMING THE SWOLLEN STREAM
by Lottie Guttry
of Longview

Sarah Browning stared out the window of her plantation home, desperate for a sign of her husband, Alexander. The defeat of the South in the bloody Civil War had ended Alex's tour of duty as a Confederate soldier. Why had he not come home to protect her and their five children? Was he dead? Perhaps he lay in some unknown hospital recovering from injuries he had suffered in the conflict.

Five years had passed since Alexander's regiment had returned, but the memory of that day remained vivid in Sarah's mind. She and her children had run all the way into the square in Clearwater to welcome him, expecting that he would enclose her in his arms and then turn wide-eyed toward his children who had grown three years' worth since his departure. He would

have lifted each of them on his shoulders and called them by their names—
Lula, Minnie, Lena, Sally, Tom.

Her fantasy had turned to anguish when she had failed to find his face
among those of the returning soldiers. "Did you see him?" she asked each
man of the regiment. Most had shrugged and turned away. One soldier,
however, thought that Tom had certainly died in battle. Bitterly, she had
trudged homeward, unable to respond to the children's unrelenting questions about their "daddy."

She continued to look out her window over the fields, damp and shiny
from recent rains, toward the roaring creek that bordered the property.
She felt spent and tired. For three years she had stretched the monthly
stipend—eleven dollars of Confederate money—to keep the children fed
and clothed. During the war money from crops had kept the plantation
solvent, but now debts consumed her like a voracious pack of dogs. Even
though her slaves had remained loyal, she couldn't pay them. Rampant
inflation had swallowed her stipend. Shoes for the children cost $225, and
flour was seventy-five dollars a barrel. A neighbor had reported that "carpetbaggers" were coming. Carpetbaggers! Even the word caused her to
shudder. Many of her neighbors had already deserted their land in fear of
these Northern intruders. Even her homestead, her last asset, was in jeopardy if they seized her land in lieu of money she owed in property taxes.
Closing her eyes, she prayed, "Lord help me. Deliver my dear children
and me. We have no one to turn to but you, Lord, in this time of our deep-
est need."

She opened her eyes to see the white canvas tops of covered wagons
inching across the flat green land on the opposite side of the creek. At the
same time she heard someone pounding on the front door. She bounded
down the stairs and through the sidelights saw her neighbor standing on
the porch pointing excitedly at the wagon train across the creek.

"Sarah," he said breathlessly when she opened the front door. "That
wagon train's headed for Texas. Get your children across that creek and be
quick about it!"

Without hesitating, Sarah ran back up the stairs and wakened the children. As they dressed, she packed a few belongings in a suitcase and herded
them toward the creek. "Thank you Lord for sending me a sign," she prayed.

Although the wagon train had camped less than a hundred yards away,
it may as well have been a hundred miles. Between Sarah and her "deliver-
ance" swirled the muddy, swift-flowing waters of the stream, swollen by

recent rains. But she would not let the high waters hold her back. She picked up three-year-old Minnie and dove into the swirling waters, and lifting Minnie's head above water, swam across to the other side. One by one she carried the five children across.

The wagon train carrying Sarah Ann Browning and her five children wended its way westward to East Texas where the travelers made their home near Kilgore in a small community known as Cross Roads. In time Sarah met a handsome, personable young man named Erastus Parr, who had served in the Union army. Despite the "Yankee" stigma, Erastus soon won over the children and their mother.

The marriage of the spunky young widow and the handsome gentleman from the North seemed a happy ending to an unhappy tale. After their marriage, Sarah and Erastus had three children—Margaret, Elizabeth, and George Parr. Sarah seemed to have forgotten her past problems and the husband she presumed to be dead. Sarah often told her first five children that their father had died in battle, but their persistent questions about how it had happened and where he was buried left Sarah wondering whether she even believed he had died.

The healing passage of time eventually eased their doubts, and a generation later Tom, Lula, Sallie, Lena, and Minnie told their own children about their father, a Confederate hero, and their courageous mother who "swam the swollen stream." Tom became a circuit-riding Methodist preacher who settled in Houston. Lula's marriage produced seven children. One of those children, Asbury Alexander, had a close relationship with his Uncle Tom and a special affinity for stories of his grandfather—stories that would soon take an eccentric twist.

One day when Tom, the minister, returned to his office, he found a frail, old bewhiskered man with a withered arm waiting for him there. The stranger revealed himself to be Tom's long lost father, Alexander Browning. The old man told his middle-aged son about his capture in Spotsylvania, his imprisonment in Elmira, New York, and his exchange as a prisoner. His experiences as a prisoner-of-war had undermined his health and a badly set fracture had left him with a deformed left arm. He had applied for a pension and returned to Florida where he had asked one person after another about his wife and children. The neighbors knew nothing except that they had gone to Texas. Finally, reaching a dead end in his search, he resigned himself to their disappearance and remarried. Later when travel was more feasible, the old urge to restore the family unity led him to resume his quest. This latter-day Odysseus told how he had tracked down clue after clue until at last he had found his son. Old, ill and soon to die, he yearned to see his wife and children before his death.

Tom told his father how his mother had swum the swollen stream to save her children and about their life in Texas. He then informed him that Sarah and his sister, Lena, had already died. After his Texas visit, Alexander returned to Florida to his second family and died there a few months later. He is buried in Clearwater, Florida.

SOURCES OF INFORMATION

Eaton, Clement. *A History of the Southern Confederacy.* New York: Macmillan Co., 1954.

Carter, Myrtle King. Letter to Lottie Guttry, March 31, 1974.

King, John. Conversations with Lottie Guttry, 1974.

King, Tom. *Genealogy of King and Browning Families.*

Smith, Jo Ann. King Genealogy.

Speck, Nancy Carter. Conversations with Lottie Guttry, 1974–2002.

᭢ • ᭢

MY GRANDMOTHER'S TRIP
by Louise Martin
of Garrison

My grandmother, Nancy Elizabeth Jones, was born in 1857 to John Robert Burns, a blacksmith, and Lucinda Caroline Folsom in Chattahoochee County, Georgia. Lucinda, Nancy's mother, died on April 16, 1862, and Nancy and her two brothers were sent to live with their grandparents. Soon thereafter, on May 4, 1862, Nancy's father enlisted to fight in the Civil War.

During the term of John's service he did not contact his children, and when he was discharged in 1864 he did not return to his home in Georgia, but went to Texas. He resumed his trade as a blacksmith in Taylor, in Williamson County.

Nancy lived in Georgia with her grandparents until she married Clarence Edgar Jones in 1879 and moved to San Augustine County, Texas.

In the early 1930s Nancy's married daughter Ninnon Jones Cartwright, lived in Santa Ana, Texas, and invited her mother for a visit. On the train to Santa Ana, Nancy met a lady by the name of Effie Burns Kennedy. During their conversation, Nancy told about her family life in Georgia and how her father, John Robert Burns, had left her and her two brothers after her mother's death. Effie Burns Kennedy told Nancy that she was also the daughter of a

John Robert Burns and that he came from Chattahoochee County, Georgia, to Texas. After comparing events Nancy and Effie discovered that they were half-sisters. A correspondence between the two began and lasted for several years.

Nancy Burns Jones died November 27, 1939, and Effie Burns Kennedy died in 1949.

Grandmother Nancy Elizabeth Jones, who discovered her half-sister on a train trip, with her son Elton

ᏗᎣ • ᏪᏇ

UNCLE LEVI
by Patsy Johnson Hallman
of Nacogdoches

[Patsy Johnson Hallman interviewed Mr. Anderson in 1964, when he was eighty-five years old. He was then living near Miller Grove in Hopkins County.—Abernethy]

My uncle was just a boy when the war broke out between the states. Our family lived in Georgia and even the young boys went off to fight. They put Uncle Levi in the navy. Around 1865 his ship was down at Galveston Island (he pronounced it Gal <u>vest'</u> ton Island). And one day word came that the war was over. They just put them boys off the ship there on that island and told them they could go home. They started out on foot—no horses, wagons, or any other way to travel.

At first Uncle Levi was with a group. They walked north and east. And when they got way up there in the deep pines of East Texas they run onto a settlement of Indians. By that time the boys were nearly starved, and the Indians took them in, fed them, and let them rest there for several days.

After a time they left the Indians, walking on toward the north. In a couple of weeks after they had left the village, one after another took sick. Uncle Levi and the two boys he was with all come down with the same ailment. They were feverish, vomiting, and breaking out in big, itchy sores. You see, those Indian children had had the pox, and the boys did not know enough about it to be afraid of it. Both boys with Uncle Levi sickened and died. After Uncle Levi buried them, he kept going, sick as he was.

One evening about dusk he thought he could not go any further. Just when he was about to give up, he saw a light ahead of him down the dirt road he was following. The light gave him the hope and strength he needed to go a little further, and finally he made it to the door of a cabin where the light shown.

He knocked at the door and it was opened by a man who held a lantern high up to see the night visitor.

"Can you help me, Mister?" asked the young sailor. "I'm awful sick."

The man held the lantern higher, peered at the stranger, and said, "Boy, you have smallpox, and I have a house full of children. I can't let you come in."

Uncle Levi bowed his head in despair and turned to leave, but the man continued, "I do have a ginhouse out back; I could put you up in it."

And so he did—he led the boy to the outbuilding, brought sheets and pillows and quilts from the house and made him a bed. That first night he stayed with the boy all through the night bathing his face and arms as the fever rose and he neared convulsions. In fact, for days the man nursed the boy and got him safely through that terrible disease that killed so many folks.

That morning after his fever broke, the man brought a bucket of water, a washpan, soap and clothes for bathing and cleaned off the filth of war and travel and sickness. The lady of the house burned the old clothes, and they dressed him in some of the man's shirts and overalls. Uncle Levi said the woman's soup that came three times a day was the best food he ever ate— before or since.

When he was well, the family took Levi into their home, and he rested and ate with them, and regained his strength.

When he was well enough, he started out again. This time he had directions, food, and a bed roll. He made it all the way home to Georgia. His sweetheart had waited for him, and they were married, and started a family. But he could never forget that place where the light in the window saved his life. In a few years he and his wife and children and two brothers and their families moved to that place—the community in northeast Texas called Miller Grove.

"Mr. Anderson, who was the man?"

"Why, it was old man Ferguson. You know, Patsy Ann, the Fergusons have been here since before Texas was a State. They've always lived on the land next to ours. His grandson is Clyde Ferguson; his great grandson is John Ferguson at the Methodist Church. You know they're always a part of the community; guess they just started out that way when the first one come to this country."

ↂ • ↂ

LETTERS FROM EZEKIEL COBB
from Fran Nolan

[Copies of the following letters were brought to my folklore class in the fall of 1975 by Fran Nolan, then a student at Stephen F. Austin State University. They were part of an assignment in the study of the family legend. They were the property of Mary Clark of Beaumont, a descendant of Ezekiel Cobb.—Abernethy]

Mrs. Amanda Cobb
of Burkville, Texas

Camp near Chaneyville La November the 8th 1863
Dear Wife I write you a few lines to let you no that I am in beter health than I have ben in Sence I Saw you I am improving fast as a man can and I hope this Wil find you all Well I have no news to Write you more than our men are fighting ever day or two and taking a grate meny yankeeys Prisners they braught 550 by here this morning and they pas With Some ever day We have orders to march in the morning but I dont Whare We Wil go the yankees are returning and I think we Wil follow theme I cant tel what wil be don I cant tel you whare to Write for I dont know Whare I am going Wil let you no Soon as I can the Boys is all well and in good hart and redy to fight and dont think they can be Whipped I want you in good hart and do the best you can the War cant last long I think it will Stop in les than one yeare. . . .

Camp Virmilion, 1863
. . . Nathaniel Martha Ann Louisa Elizabeth Sarah Ezekiel Sicley my dear Children I Want to See you all so bad I dont no What to do all I can Say is good by and be good children until I come So no more good by Ezekiel Cobb

Sabine Pass Texas Feb. 3 1864
Mrs Amanda Cobb

I seat myself this morning to write you a few lines I cannot Say with pleasure . . . it becomes my Duty to inform you of the Decease of your Husband he died yesterday morning few minutes before Eight Oclock the 2ⁿᵈ Feb. he Died with the Conjestive chill . . . I will send by Mr. Wm Fuller who will leave here tomorrow for Newton Mr. Cobb pocket book containing 26 Dollars 21 in confederate notes which was all he had at the time of his Death there is Due him 4 months wages & twelve month comutation which I think I can Draw I will use my utmost endever to get it for you. I Sign myself Your friend truly
J. T. Ramsey

᪥ • ᪥

AN OLD TINTYPE AND A FADED JOURNAL
by Eleanor Monroe
of Sherman

Isaiah Jefferus Kimberlin, the brother of my great-grandmother, was just a name on my family tree until his great-granddaughter, Helen McGee Ludlam, showed me an old tintype of him when he was a soldier in the Civil War. She told me a story about the unusual picture.

Isaiah was a spy in General Joe Shelby's Brigade. In the winter of 1862, Shelby made a raid into Missouri; and he sent Isaiah, disguised as a cripple, into the town of Sedalia and through the enemy's camp to obtain information about the movement of their troops.

That night, Isaiah started back to join his brigade and to pick up his firearms that he had hidden in a hollow log. When daylight came, he decided to stop at a house and ask for something to eat.

While waiting for the food, a Federal scouting party passed nearby. A Negro, who had seen Isaiah go to the house, told the captain of the group that he thought there was a "Reb at dat ar house." The soldiers charged up to the house and captured Isaiah. Since he was not in uniform, they thought he was a bushwhacker (a non-enlisted man who fought behind enemy lines), and the captain ordered him shot. But Isaiah convinced him that he was a Confederate soldier, and the Captain agreed to take him back to headquarters for trial.

In Sedalia, the officer in command questioned him. Someone recognized him as the cripple that went through the camp the day before, and there

Isaiah Jefferus Kimberlin, captured by the Yankees and condemned to be shot as a spy

were shouts of "spy, spy!" The guard took him to a blacksmith's shop and had a twenty-four-pound cannon ball and a draft chain riveted on his ankle and put him in prison under heavy guard.

He was tried by a court-martial and sentenced to die. But before the order was carried out, the guards took him to a photographer to have some tintypes taken: Isaiah with ball and chain and the guards with their guns drawn and aimed at him. They wanted to show the penalty for being a spy.

When they were through, the guards stepped outside; and the photographer went into his darkroom. One of the pictures was left on the table. Isaiah decided to destroy it, but changed his mind and held it in his hand under his ball and chain.

The soldiers marched him back to the prison. On the way, he saw an old lady that he knew coming toward him, and she recognized him at once. He tried to let her know that he wanted something. As they passed, he rubbed up against her and gave her the picture. She took it without speaking a word to him, or he to her. Later, she sent the picture to Isaiah's wife.

Every night, while he was in prison, he worked to get his ball and chain off and to tunnel through two walls. The night before he was to be shot, he managed to escape.

His brigade had left the area, so he traveled 250 miles through the woods, over prairies and across rivers to General Hindman's headquarters in the Confederate army. By the time he reached his destination, he was ill. Hindman ordered him to enter the hospital and receive medical care. Later, he sent Isaiah to the home of one of his friends in Sherman, Texas, to recuperate.

Isaiah spent several weeks in Sherman. He liked the country, he liked the people, and when the war was over, he moved his family to North Texas. In Sherman, he became known as a cattle baron. He raised Durham cattle, including a bull named Sargent, who was declared an international champion.

๛ • ๑

EPHRIAM DIAL IN THE CIVIL WAR
by Frances B. Vick and Andrew Brannen
of Dallas and Saron

Andrew Brannen always talked of Ephriam Dial with great admiration, as though he knew him, which he couldn't have since Eph died in 1890. So it was the stories told about him that made him a legendary figure to my father. Daddy said that Eph was quite a reckless and adventurous individual and would do many things which no average person would do. He butchered cattle and sold the meat. When slaughtering a cow he would fill a cup with the blood then turn it up and drink it. Or, he would place the cup on the ground and on horseback approach the cup at a full gallop, reach down, and grab it and upend it and drink down the blood.

Eph's exploits went beyond the family stories, however. D. H. Hamilton wrote a couple of stories about Ephiam Dial in a pamphlet he published entitled "The Activities of Company M. First Texas Volunteer Infantry, Hood's Brigade, Army of the Confederate States of America, from the View Point of a Private in the Ranks, During the Civil War, 1861 to 1865."

This company was first organized at Sumpter, then the county seat of Trinity County, located about four miles east of where Groveton now stands. In preparation for leaving, the company drilled during the day and attended balls and entertainments every night. They marched out of town in double file to the tune of "Dixie," played by two fiddlers at the head of the column.

The youngsters in the group continued partying at camp at night and for several nights, until one morning they found one of the "kids" was

Ephriam Dial, who single-handedly captured a squadron of Yankees

gone—Harvey Pinson. The captain sent Eph Dial and Willoughby Tullos back to get Harvey. When they overtook him and started back with him they managed somehow to get a bottle of whiskey and all three of them got drunk. During the spree Willoughby Tullos shot off a portion of the end of the trigger finger of his right hand. His finger was so badly wrecked that they decided it was necessary to operate on it. The only surgical instrument available was a dull pocket knife, which Eph used to perform the operation by unjointing the finger at the second joint. They decided they needed to dress and bind up what was left of the finger, so Eph went to a house nearby to get some sugar and turpentine to put on the finger. But when he got there the people had neither sugar nor turpentine. So he decided to use salt, which they had and gave him. He bound up Willoughby's finger in the salt, using cloth torn from his shirt.

After taking another drink they all went to sleep and did not wake up until the next morning, when they resumed their march to overtake the company. Hamilton reports that Willoughby's finger got well and he made a gallant soldier, using his second finger to pull the trigger, which he did many thousands of times during the course of the war.

Much later in the war, Company M was in the vicinity of Richmond, Virginia, at Fort Gilmer, where they then moved a mile and a half to a fort to meet the Federal troops there. The fort, which had been thought to have only a small squadron, was in fact fully manned. Company M was lying behind breastworks in front of the fort, and batteries of guns opened upon the Yankees with grape shot. The smoke was so dense that no one could see anything, but it was perfectly quiet after Company M quit firing.

When the smoke cleared no Yankees were anywhere to be seen. Eph Dial, always a daredevil, jumped up on top of the breastworks and said he was going down to see what had become of them. So he went down in the direction of where they had last seen the Yankees approaching and found a squadron of them lying down in a depression. He walked right up to them and boldly ordered them to surrender, which they did. Eph then commanded the officer to form his men in a line, leaving their weapons where they were. This was done, and Eph marched them to the rear, about a half mile and turned them over to the Provost Marshal, from whom he demanded and received a receipt.

After the surrender Eph Dial started walking toward home in Texas. He got as far as North Carolina where he met and married a girl. Three children were born of this union before she died.

Eph then headed again for Texas, where he arrived after an absence of about ten years. To say that his family was overjoyed to see him is putting it mildly. He was a favorite of Aunt Polly and Grandma Walker, his sisters.

꿍 • 꿍

THE CIVIL WAR AND THE SCUDDER FAMILY
by Jean G. Schnitz
of Boerne

My great-grandfather, George Troupe Scudder, enlisted May 8, 1862, in Co. F., 55th Regiment, Georgia Infantry under Gen. Joseph E. Johnston. He first served as a prison guard at Andersonville. Later he drove the brigade supply wagon until he was captured by the Union Army at Cumberland Gap. He was held as a prisoner at Camp Douglas, near Chicago, Illinois, for most of the Civil War.

Conditions at the prison camp were so bad that George Troupe Scudder nearly died of starvation. He probably would have frozen to death had it not been for a young man named William Ira Scudder, editor of a newspaper in New Jersey, who came to the prison to interview some of the men. William Ira Scudder heard of a prisoner by the name of

An unreconstructed Rebel, George Troupe Scudder (c. 1905) with his granddaughter Leatrice Green.

Scudder and asked that he be allowed to see George. After his visit, the young newspaper editor sent George a big box of warm clothing. Without this warm clothing, George Troupe Scudder would almost certainly have frozen to death during the severe winters of his imprisonment. George named his first-born son, my grandfather, William Ira Scudder, in honor of his benefactor.

According to George Scudder's stories, the food served to the Confederate prisoners at the Union Army prison camp consisted of the scraps left over after the Union Army was fed. Sometimes nothing at all was fed to the prisoners for more than a day at a time. The meager scraps of food were put in buckets and served to the prisoners in the same manner that farmers feed hogs—that is, by pouring the mixed bits of leftover food into wooden troughs and providing no utensils with which to eat.

George Scudder told tales about his friends and fellow Confederate prisoners being beaten and sometimes killed if they made any effort to obtain better food or to complain about conditions. He said that shooting and bayoneting were the consequences of any action by the prisoners that did not conform to the desires of the captors. George Troupe Scudder remained a prisoner until the end of the Civil War in 1865.

Until his death in 1916 George Scudder remained a "Yankee Hater." Family stories say that he would not sit on the front porch of his home in Graford, Texas, which was across the street from the local post office, because he could not stand to look at the American flag flying there. So he sat on the other side of the house until the flag was removed at sundown. He never would accept visits from my grandmother, Dora Lee Scudder, because her father had been in the Union Army.

My aunt, Esther Scudder Orton, remembered that when she was a small child, she spent many hours sitting on her Grandpa's lap listening to his stories. Kittie Scudder would call from the doorway, "George, are you telling that child those awful stories again?" George would reply, "Yes, I am, because I want her to hate Yankees, too."

ↄ • ↄ

THE LAST HAM
by Barbara Pybas
of Gainesville

Jordan Cain Pybas was fourteen years old, the man of the family, in Bedford County, Tennessee, while his father, Kenneth Monroe Pybas, was serving in the Confederate Army. His mother, Eleanor, and five younger children as well as several Negroes still on the plantation, were his responsibility.

The family had already given almost all their foodstuffs to help feed the Confederate soldiers. After the Union soldiers raided the corncribs and smokehouse, there was barely anything left to eat. Jordan, fortunately, was a crack shot and kept the family from starving by killing wild game.

On one bright moonlight night, Jordan heard a noise at the smokehouse. He could see a Union soldier prying open the door. Inside was only one ham, the only meat that remained and that they had been hoarding, keeping it as security, a token that would keep them from starving. He could see the Union soldier had a gimp leg and watched him as he limped off, swinging the valuable ham as he walked.

After the war, Jordan became of age in Tennessee, then migrated to Texas. That country was opening up, Jordan became prosperous in farming, and he bought a gin near Grapevine, Texas. In 1883, he mounted his horse and rode to Ft. Worth to purchase insurance on his business investment. Returning, he could see the smoke rising. It was the gin. Jordan was left with nothing but his horse, his rope and his saddle.

Starting over, Jordan ventured into Indian Territory. There he leased grassland from the Indians on Walnut Creek, near Purcell, Oklahoma. When the Oklahoma Territory was opened with a Land Run on April 22, 1889, Jordan Pybas was fortunate to stake his claim and to homestead in the territory near Purcell. His only son was born in a dugout, June 4, 1888, when Pybas was forty years old.

Adding a last chapter to this story is a story told by Jordan's son, Jordan Cain Pybas, Jr. He said he remembered when he was about five in 1904, riding with his father in a wagon pulled by his only team. A man with a gimp leg was walking along the road, and his father stopped and gave him a ride. After a few minutes of conversation, his father found that the man was also a homesteader and had come from Arkansas to the Indian Territory for the Land Run. He also found out that he had been with the Union forces in middle Tennessee in 1863. His father yanked the horses to an abrupt stop and angrily told the man to get out.

Before his death in 1922, his father told him the reason: He had suddenly realized that this was the same man with the same limp, the Union soldier, that had stolen the precious ham, leaving the Pybas family destitute.

Jordan Cain Pybas, who never forgot the Yankee that stole the Pybas family's last ham, and his wife Lydia

CIVIL WAR CASUALTY
by Eleanor Monroe
of Sherman

The young woman whose picture was in our family album smiled at me from out of the past. The soft curve of her mouth and the gentle look in her eyes gave no hint of the stern, critical woman I remembered as my great-grandmother.

Ma Burrus, as I knew her, had suffered a stroke that paralyzed her left side, and she lived with my grandmother, one of her five daughters. Early on, I learned to give her wheelchair a wide berth. If I came within her reach, she gave my head a thump with her silver thimble. Was it because I misbehaved—or was it because my mother was a Yankee from Kansas? Ma Burrus had no use for Yankees.

She was too old and I was too young for us to communicate; and when she died, my childhood memories were of a strict and prejudiced woman. Years later, I was told my great-grandmother's story.

In the days when Ma Burrus was young and she was called Arminta Jane, she lived on a farm near Blue Springs, Missouri, with her parents, Samuel and Eliza Kimberlin, and five brothers and two sisters.

In 1861, the talk in Blue Springs turned from cattle and crops to politics and rumors of war. Missouri was a border state and its people were divided. Distrust separated lifelong friends as each took his stand for North or South. Neighbor turned against neighbor; brother turned against brother; and Missouri, torn with hate, made war upon itself.

One by one, Arminta Jane's brothers left the farm to fight with the Confederate Army. Isaiah, the oldest, became a spy for General Joe Shelby's Brigade (See "An Old Tintype and a Faded Journal" above in this chapter).

One day, the dreaded news came: Isaiah had been captured by the Union Army; and he would be shot as a spy. But even as the family grieved, news spread that Isaiah had tunneled his way to freedom and escaped under the very noses of the Union soldiers. The chagrined officers combed the countryside to capture him.

A group of cavalry men descended upon the Kimberlin farm. The commanding officer demanded that Samuel tell them where Isaiah was hiding. Samuel refused. Angry and frustrated, the soldiers dragged Samuel to the barn; they threw a rope over a rafter; and they hanged him.

Eliza and her daughters looked on in horror. The officer-in-charge then turned to them and ordered them to leave. He allowed them to collect a few personal items while the soldiers readied one of the farm wagons for their use.

As Eliza drove down the dirt road away from her home, Arminta Jane and her sisters huddled in the wagon bed. The smell of smoke permeated the crisp, autumn air. Arminta Jane looked back. The farmhouse was ablaze. The officers were making sure that no one was left alive, hiding inside. The flames that pierced the sky that day kindled a rage in Arminta Jane's heart—a rage that smoldered for the rest of her life. Now I felt her anger, I shared her grief; and I understood her outrage.

Again I studied the face of the young woman in the family album. My great-grandmother smiled at me from out of the past—and I smiled back at her.

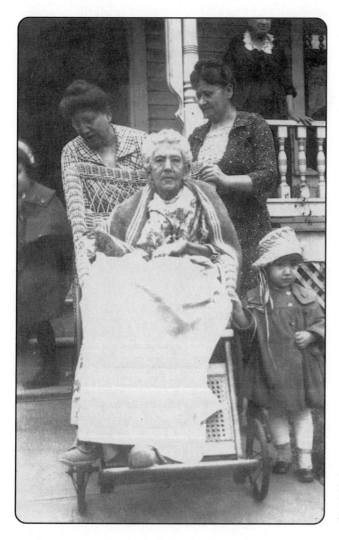

Arminta Jane "Ma" Burrus in wheelchair with little Eleanor Monroe by her side, a casualty of the Civil War

THE AFTERMATH OF THE CIVIL WAR
told by Mary Ann Long Ferguson
transcribed by Odessa Hicks Dial
of Forest

As you know the war came on soon after we settled in Texas and Mr. Ferguson was gone so much, but of course in war times we couldn't have traveled far anyway. When the war was over, my brother Jeff, who had been in the army, was somewhere in Louisiana and he walked most of the way to Texas to see us before going back home to Mississippi. After he got home I had a letter from my mother saying that he had arrived safely, but everything they had had been destroyed during the fighting in Mississippi and they were in Louisiana with my father's people, the Longs. Also they all were dying with yellow fever and I would never hear from them again. I never did hear anymore from them, so they must have died and were buried somewhere in Louisiana. Of course this made me very sad, but this old world is full of sadness, and we can't let it get the best of us. I had my children and husband to think of, so with chin up and a smile on my face, I'm ready to face the future.

John Ware Abernethy, seventy-seven years old and he could still button up his Confederate uniform

4.
Indians

❦

A part of the romance of the Texas frontier, as we look back now in our families' histories, were the Indians who occupied the land long before our ancestors ever thought of going to Texas. For that first wave of frontiersmen who occupied the edge of westward Anglo expansion, the Comanches and the Kiowas and the Apaches, among other tribes, were a real and constant danger. For the second wave of settlers, soon after the Civil War, the families looking for new farms and new pastures, the Indians were retreating, but they were still a threat to their lives and livestock.

By 1875 the Indians had been defeated and driven to the reservations in Indian Territory. The tens of thousands of Indians who had occupied the whole of Texas had been reduced by sickness and hardships to a few thousand, and those few that remained on the fringe of Texas civilization were pitiful creatures indeed.

Because of the fierceness of those final struggles, the Indians of West Texas are remembered heroically. Most of the Indians of East Texas, under the pressures of early Texas settlement by both Spanish and Anglos, had disappeared or were eased out of the Pineywoods into Indian Territory. The only major conflict was the expulsion of the Cherokees from East Texas in 1839 after the Battle of the Neches. So we have fewer stories about conflict with Indians from families east of the Trinity.

One of my grandad's favorite tales was of taking a herd of Dan Waggoner's Triple D cattle across the Red River at Doan's Crossing in the late 1880s and being waylaid by a band of Comanche Indians demanding beeves. The boss paid them off and there was neither a battle nor a stampede. This brief encounter with Indians was a vivid episode in Grandad's cowboy days, and his family still tells the tale—but not as vividly as he used to tell me when I rode behind him on old Shorty.

And every cowboy who worked in the Panhandle or nearby claimed to remember seeing, sometimes meeting, Quanah Parker, the last of the Comanche warrior chiefs.

A sketch of Quanah Parker by Jim Snyder of Nacogdoches. Chief of the Quahadi Comanches, Quanah Parker continued to lead the Comanches when they moved to the reservation. He was a hero to most Anglo settlers, those who did not have to fight him.

Waggoner's cowboys in the late 1880s, when they were still herding cattle into Indian Territory

∾ · ∾

JOSEPHUS AND FRANK BROWNING
by Karen McDonald

The Browning Ranch on Hubbard Creek, not a great distance from its mouth, was a well known place during the pioneer days. This ranch was near the present town of Crystal Falls, in Stephens County.

During the middle of June 1860, Josephus and Frank Browning, sons of William Browning, my great-great-grandfather, were out riding the range in search of cattle. When the noon hour arrived, these boys were below the mouth of Hubbard's Creek and about one mile from the Clear Fork, in a mesquite and live oak flat. Since they were tired and it was extremely hot weather, they decided to stop under the shade of a tree and let their horses graze.

A short time later, they heard Indians coming. So the Browning boys hurriedly cut the hobbles from their ponies and started away. Since Josephus had more difficulty with his horse, he was soon overtaken by Indians and killed. Frank, being badly wounded, fell from his saddle when he crossed

Hubbard's Creek. Frank's pony, with two arrows sticking in his body, ran to the ranch.

William Browning instantly knew Indians had attacked his sons. So he, in company with others, took the back trail of the pony. When Frank was found at a crossing of Hubbard's Creek about one and a half miles east of the present town of Crystal Falls, he was still conscious and able to relate the story to his father. Frank stated, "I stayed with Joe until he was killed; then I ran away from the Indians."

He also told his father the feathered warriors attempted to grab his bridle reins, but when he shot two or three of their number, the Indians fell back. William Browning then sent to the ranch for a wagon, and after Frank was carried home, the relief party brought in the body of Josephus.

Frank was wounded about seventeen different times and at least two or three arrows passed completely through his body. But under the care and treatment of a doctor summoned from Fort Belknap, he recovered. His death, however, about twenty years later, was largely attributed to the old wounds. Frank Browning was my great-grandfather.

A few days later, nine of the scalps of the Indians who murdered Josephus were brought back to the Hubbard ranch.

❧ • ❧

LYE SOAP
by Elizabeth Stanley Pope
of Bluff Dale
as told to Janet Jeffery
of Austin

One night during the Civil War, Elizabeth Baker was making soap inside the cabin, stirring it with an old gourd dipper. She heard a noise and turned to see what it was. A Comanche had dug a passageway under a log in the cabin wall and had slid his body through the hole. She saw his head poking out of the floor and into the interior of the cabin. Without taking time to think, she scooped up some hot soap and flung it at him. His screams woke her children. She shushed the children so she could hear what was going on outside. The family relaxed some when the intruder's companions carried him off, and his screams faded in the distance.

Mary Baker was one of those children. She was about eight years old when this happened, around 1864. She told it to her daughter, Elizabeth Pope. Mrs. Pope, my grandmother's cousin, passed this along to me in the fall of 1985. She was ninety-two at the time.

Elizabeth Russel Baker, who scalded the Comanche. Elizabeth lost an eye when she was run over by a wagon when she was a child.

ᴓ • ᴓ

A NIGHT TO REMEMBER
by Eleanor Monroe
of Sherman

In 1829, Sarah and Josiah Williams were newlyweds. Josiah had inherited land in Scott County, Illinois, from his parents and had received additional acres from the government for fighting in the Black Hawk Indian War. He built a log cabin on the property, and it was to this home he brought his new bride. In due time their first child was born. Josiah ran a large stock farm. He was also a teamster for the government, hauling supplies to western forts. He was often gone overnight, and Sarah was left alone with their infant daughter.

One night while he was gone, she heard noises outside the cabin. She could see a small group of Indians prowling about the livestock. She kept very quiet and hoped they would leave. When they tried to force the front door open, she picked up her sleeping baby and escaped out the back door. Still holding the baby, she managed to crawl up on the roof.

The baby began to fret. Sarah could hear the Indians eating, talking, and rummaging through her things in the house below. She knew that they would be able to hear the baby if she cried. To keep her quiet, she began to nurse her, and she nursed her all night long.

The next morning, still unaware of Sarah's presence, the Indians left. Sarah and the baby survived. If she had not, I would not be writing this story: Sarah was my great-great-grandmother.

ANOTHER INDIAN STORY
by Myrtle Oldham Ham
of Erath County
transcribed by JoEllen Ham Miller
of Stephenville
with original spelling

[Grace Myrtle Oldham was born on April 5, 1886, in Navarro County, Texas. She was the daughter of Louis and Margaret Hunter Oldham. According to her stories she moved with her family to Alexander, Texas, Erath Co., before she was one year old. Later the family settled on a farm on Alarm Creek a few miles north of Alexander. She married Robert Edwin Ham on May 7, 1905, and they were parents of eight boys and two girls. Myrtle and Ed lived most of their lives on farms in the area around Alarm Creek and raised all but one of their children there. One boy died in childhood.

Myrtle told many stories about Indians, and panthers, and rattlesnakes—some she had heard as a little girl and some she had experienced herself. Sometime after her last child left home and after Ed died, she wrote some of her stories down. Never having the chance to attend school on a regular basis, Myrtle had to make her own rules of punctuation and spelling; but she wanted to "set" her stories down so others could read them. She died June 8, 1963, and is buried beside Ed who preceded her in death on April 24, 1950. They lie in Johnson Cemetery in sight of the Oldham family farm on Alarm Creek.

I am JoEllen Ham Miller, one of Myrtle and Ed's numerous grandchildren, and I happen to be the one who found the stories Grandma Ham wrote and carefully stored in her quilt box with her most prized possessions. I was born on the other side of Alarm Creek from the Oldham family farm and have lived most of my life in the same area raising my own four children there. Now that they are grown they love to read Grandma Ham's stories to their own children. I know Grace Myrtle Oldham Ham would be very pleased to know her great-great-grandchildren are enjoying her stories. She wanted everyone to be able to hear about the way things were in the "old days."—JoEllen Ham Miller]

Just west of my home is a place known as the old orr tank, one time there was a bunch of indians camped over there. My childrens Greatgrandady Keith was out hunting for his stock and come up on them. So he hid and watched them, he could tell they ware cooking meat. As they had it strung up on poles over the fire, and was mending theire mocons,

Robert Edwin Ham and Grace Myrtle Oldham Ham. We are richer for the stories that Myrtle "set down" and for the granddaughter who rescued them from the trunk

didient have but one horse and it was an old sore back horse that drug theire food on a kind of sled made out of poles tied to gather with strips of cow hide, he watched them untill they broke camp. He said they all got up and wrapped up theire blankets and marched off single file, wasent any thing but men. And they ware off on a hunting trip, he went back home got his old rifle and followed them untill they crossed the Bosque river, there he turned back he found a moxoin, said it was baddly worn. He said they ever one looked just a like, the finest speciement of man kind he ever did see. Said he could heare them laughfing and talking. There was an old camp place there for a long time, the indians met there often. This happened over close to the old silver mines.

There was a story told, about a woman who wrode a fine race horse. that the indians wanted very bad, so one day she rode it away from home. and on her way back home she ran in to a bunch of indians. and they tried to run her down, but as she was rideing the best horse (but they all most caught her) she allways said her horse hadent jumped a big tree that had fell across the road and the indains horses couldent jump it & had to go around it then was when she gained on them. she said the indains pored the whip to theire ponies but couldent catch her. they wouldent shoot at her for fear of killing the horse, and they wanted her horse, she told us she could heare them screaming and laughing just like it allmost tickel them to death, but she finely came in sight of her home and they turned around and left her alone. (she was old Moze Hurleys wife).

(The last Indian raid in Comanche County as remembered by a daughter, Mrs. Savanah Leslie Hurst. I have heard the storie told by Aunt Jane Keith) Mrs. Hurst wrote in her letter:

I was borned in a log cabbin. A one room cabbin chinked and daubed with mud. But the chinking and daubin had fallen out in places. Often they would heare noises around the house at night and knew it was inians and would look through the cracks and watch the indians prowling around the yard Those inians ware looking for horses to steal. They wouldent fight unless forced to. The raid when my father was killed was an exception. He went out to drive in his horses & ran into the indians. About 2 miles from our house and they killed him. We lived about 7 miles north of Comanche town and my father oprated a mill, for granding corn & wheat. Into meal and flour for the settlers.

The inians that killed my father was followed by a large company of men. but the inians ware so far ahead of the men thought they ware so far ahead they stopped and made camp but there pursures kept on following them. got so close to the camp. that the indians ran off and left most of theire camp equipment. the white men brought back a lot of stuff such as blankets and Indian bows and arrows. She said she had often wished she had kept some of those things. as it would be so interesting. this day and time. said she and her brother and sister would gather up arrow heads and other relices for their play house. the arrow head the indians carved out of the flint was very beautiful. all kinds of decorative carveings on them and was very sharp on each edge. had to be as they depended on them for theire food as well as use in battle. now I ve heard this story told from severel different people.

about the year 1862. the people was allways runing from the indians so one day a boy come runing on a horse down the creek giving a warning to all the settlers that there was about 300 Commanche indians. coming through the co. on the war path. so ever body gathered togather ever thing they could carry and got on theire horses and run for Dublin and stayed severl days, so when thire scare was over all went back home, wasent any indians come so they called the creek Alarm Creek on the account of the false alarm. Grandma Keith said she was scared allmost to death. she went through several bad indian scares.

ೞ • ҩ

EXPERIENCES OF CALVIN AND NANCY FISHER
by Grace Fisher Porch
granddaughter of Perlina Bolton White
of Old Greer County

At seeing and hearing the name of Uncle Colonel ("Colonel" was his given name, not a title.) Bolton, I am vividly reminded of some experiences Dad and Mother had and used to tell us about. They decided to go "way out west" (from Whitley County, Kentucky, to what had been Greer County, Texas, and was in 1900 in Oklahoma Territory), so in a covered wagon they struck out alone. This was in the year 1900. Mom was 22 and Dad was 24.

One evening after they had reached "out west" in Texas they stopped to rest and stay overnight at a place with a stream nearby. A perfect place, they thought. Dad went to catch some fish within a stone's throw of the wagon, and Mamma, worn from traveling, and with my sister Eunice, lay down in the wagon to rest. They had not heard of the recent uprisings and killings of white people by some of Quanah Parker's renegade Indians. Quanah had made promises and agreements in good faith, but there were some of the Indians who were bent on revenge and retribution and would not comply.

Dad had been gone only a short time when Indians suddenly surrounded the wagon. They did a lot of pointing at Mamma as they milled around the wagon and talking, but all Mother could understand was "paleface." Dad had caught a few fish and started back to see about Mamma when he saw the Indians.They had moved so stealthily that he had not heard them. He ran for the wagon. Simultaneously, the Cavalry from Ft. Sill arrived. They were on patrol because of recent scalpings, and miraculously arrived just in time to save Mom and Dad. They also escorted them to safe territory and gave them advice and directions for the rest of their journey. While being escorted, they saw along the way, several grim reminders of what could have been their fate—scalps hanging from trees.

A. J. WALKER AND THE INDIANS
by Frances B. Vick and Andrew Brannen
of Dallas and Saron

We were always told that Grandpa Walker's father, Thomas, was from Alabama, born there in 1792. Grandpa Walker is A. J. Walker, Andrew Brannen's grandfather. Grandpa Walker was born in Texas in 1844 in Tyler County.

When Thomas was seven years old, back in Alabama, he went to school and did something that made the teacher give him a severe whipping. We never did know what Thomas did that was so terrible. Anyway, when he went home that evening he begged his parents not to make him go back to school. The next morning he was sent back as usual but instead of doing as he was bid he ran away.

After wandering about for several days, Thomas fell in with a tribe of Choctaw Indians, who were on their way to Arkansas. They received him kindly and took a great liking to him, as he was one-quarter Indian himself. He traveled with them all through Arkansas and Louisiana and mastered their tongue. He said they were very good to him and treated him the same as they did their own children. He remained with them for ten years. Grandpa Walker said that Thomas Walker never whipped any of his children.

That Indian blood came in handy years later. Grandpa Walker was herding cattle from Columbus on the Colorado River to Abilene, Kansas. They were four months making the trip and underwent many hardships, including some with the Indians, particularly the Osages and Comanches.

According to Grandpa Walker, there was something singular about an Indian. An Indian can tell at a glance if you have a drop of Indian blood in you. The reason he knew that is that every Indian he chanced to meet, who could speak any English at all, told him he had Indian blood in him, and if he denied it they would say he lied.

One day while on his way to Abilene, he and his friend Jim camped for dinner. The cattle were all grazing nicely and everything seemed lovely. They ate their dinner and prepared to get their horses when to their astonishment they found the horses were gone. They had an idea which way they went, so they started in search of them. They traveled until they reached the top of a mountain about three miles from camp, where they could command a good view of the surrounding country.

When they reached the top of this mountain, there just before them they found one noble red man with their horses. They swooped down on him and took possession of their horses, and held a council as to what they would do with the Indian. They finally decided to take him to the foot of the mountain and kill him. They talked the matter over in his presence, not dreaming that he could understand a word they were saying.

When they reached the foot of the mountain they ran into thirteen Osage Indians. Their prisoner was an Osage himself and these were a party he had been with. Imagine their surprise when he told them all the conversation they had had and what they intended to do with him. He spoke English as well as Grandpa Walker did. It looked rather blue for them, as they stood no chance at resisting the Indians and escape was impossible.

Grandpa Andrew Jackson Walker on the far right with the Brannen part of his family in 1909. From the left: Aunt Polly Johnson holding Ophelia Brannen, William Jefferson Brannen, the father of aforementioned Ophelia, and Carl Andrew, Leo Bergman, Herschel Sampson, Vera, and Evelyn. William had just lost his wife, Lottie Walker Brannen, whose clothes had caught fire from the kitchen stove and she had burned to death. Aunt Polly, whose husband had been murdered in 1901, came to live with them and help raise the children. Herschel is the Brannen who remembers that when he was born, his parents kept him warm by putting him in the oven (see Ch. 12). Leo is the Brannen who was named after his mother heard it called at a courthouse witness roll call (see Ch. 12). Grandpa A. J. Walker shows up again chasing mustangs in chapter five.

After parlaying among themselves about two hours the chief of the band asked Grandpa Walker in plain English if he did not have Indian blood in him. He acknowledged as quick as possible that he did, and would have gone farther and told him he was a full blood if he had thought it would have done any good. After holding another pow-wow with themselves they allowed Grandpa Walker and his friend to depart. After this little episode Grandpa Walker never again denied the Indian blood in him.

୬ • ୭

A FAT MAN'S MISERY
by Jean G. Schnitz
of Boerne

In 1883 George Troupe Scudder with his sons Ira (my grandfather) and Charles were camped near Mineral Wells when they heard that Indians had come into the area and had stolen several horses.

As told by my aunt, Esther Scudder Orton:

The Indians were escaping with their stolen horses when some of Papa's (Ira's) cousins, the O'Rear boys among them, got their guns and went after the Indians in an attempt to recover the horses. After following them quite a distance, the cousins came up over a hill about sun-up and saw that the Indians were still lounging around, the horses were hobbled, and the fires were burning.

The boys made up their minds what they were going to do. The Indians were eating and didn't have their guns close to them. The boys put some space between them and came down the hill shooting. The Indians couldn't get to their horses and they couldn't get to their guns, so they scattered like blazes and the ones that couldn't get on their horses ran away. Several of the Indians were killed.

The cousins recovered the stolen horses and started back toward Mineral Wells. They stopped for the night near a place called "Fat Man's Misery," which was a place where there were many huge rocks so close together that only slender people could squeeze between them. One of the cousins was hiding in the rocks standing watch when he saw an Indian climbing high above him on the rocks. The Indian was coming at him with a big knife, and he had his gun in his hand. He shot the Indian, who fell on top of him in such a way that he could not get up. He nearly drowned in the Indian's blood before the other cousins, alerted by the sound of gunfire, found him and moved the dead Indian so he could breathe again.

ᘉ · Indians · ᘍ

GRAMMA GARRETT
by Lucille Harris
of Denison

"Lucille, you shore do look like my Gramma Garrett," Grandpa Patterson would say and wink, "and Carol's got her temper."

With that one brief comment, Grandpa always got the results he was after. Carol's temper would flare and she would exit the room in a huff. Grandpa would laugh mischievously and tell me about his maternal grandmother who lived in Falls County, Texas.

"Gramma Garrett was a strong, raw-boned, red-headed woman with a hot temper. You didn't wanta git her riled up. Why, one time Gramma fought off Indians single handed. Yep, she shore did.

"Them young bucks was a tryin' to break in to her smoke house and make off with her meat. Gramma went a runnin' outta the house and grabbed up a stick o' fire wood from the wood pile. She ran a screamin' at them Indians swingin' that stick o' wood. They seen that mad, red-headed woman a comin' toward 'em, and they taken'd off. They high tailed it right outta there. Yep, they run fer their lives. Gramma Garrett saved that meat all by herself.

"Gramma was a strong, raw-boned woman. She had red hair and a temper to match it. You favor Gramma Garrett, but I tell ya, that Carol has got Gramma's temper."

ᘉ · ᘍ

SHE PUT IT IN WRITING
by Jennifer Curtis
of Sagedale

I grew up aware that a Catherine DuBois was one of the grandmothers of my family, but I did not realize that I could get to know this grandmother from the 1600s. It took a choir practice, some old papers, and research to discover the legend of her capture by Indians. However, it was in reading about her last will and testament that I came to understand that she was a woman who kept her word.

It was Christmas and the custom of my choir was to quietly share thoughts and sing during the hour before the Christmas concert. I was exhausted from the day and was enjoying relaxing when one woman shared a devotional story she had read by V. Gilbert Beers about one of his grandmothers, Catherine DuBois.

This Catherine DuBois lived in the 1600s, and she and one of her children had been captured by the Indians. The legend was that she and her child had finally been tied to a tree and were to be burned alive. Catherine asked permission to sing her death song. She had a powerful voice and began to sing Psalm 137: "By the rivers of Babylon, there we sat down, yea, we wept, when we remembered Zion." The Indians were so impressed that they asked her to keep singing. It was the sound of her voice that led the rescue party through the thick forest to rescue her.

I thought to myself, "Interesting. Same name but our Catherine DuBois lived in the 1800s." Later that week, I was going through old letters and found one letter from 1940 in which one of my ancient aunts related a story about our Catherine DuBois—but it was the Catherine from the 1600s and the same story as the one in the Gilbert Beers' devotional. The aunt related the genealogy, and I wondered who was this woman who could sing in the face of danger and death?

She was born Catherine Blanchan and married Louis DuBois in Mannheim, Germany, on October 10, 1655. She and Louis came from Germany to the wilderness of New York. There they built a home and had ten children. She remarried after Louis' death and Catherine died in 1702.

According to the *History of New Pultz*, her own will is dated September 22, 1702. Three items impressed me in her will: she restated that the letters of manumission and the freedom she had granted her slave women were to stay in effect, she provided money for a particular slave woman, and lastly, stated that the money was to be given before Catherine's own children should have their inheritance.

How many people even today make promises but never bother to put them into a legal document? How many people would ensure that a slave not only had freedom but also had the means to survive? How many people would place that obligation to a slave before their own children could receive any monies?

I found that Catherine DuBois was not only a woman of courage in her adventure with Indians, she was a woman of her word. She put it in writing.

◡◠ • ◠◡

A RENEGADE RIFLE
by Austin T. King
of Pittsburg

In the year 1910, my father Austin King was buying cattle in Texas and New Mexico for George W. Saunders Company out of Fort Worth. He was in El Paso and bought fifty head of heavy steers, and the owner put them in the loading corrals for shipment on the railroad. They had to be watered and fed for several days. Dad slept on a cot at the corrals but he needed help. An Indian man from Mexico came by and wanted to work, so Dad put him to work.

The man, Cipriano Bernal, a medium-size man of about thirty, was a very good worker, affable and friendly, and the two made friends quickly. Cipriano was from Socorro, had a wife sick with malaria, and was trying to get funds for her medical attention. Dad advanced him some money.

"You are a good man, Señor King, you have paid me well. Gracias. Since I may need more funds for my wife, I have something to sell you very cheap. It is a .45-70 rifle that belonged to my father in the Sierra Madre of Mexico. I will sell it to you for five dollars. I must sell because where I live it will be stolen from me. You will take care of it, and it will last you a lifetime."

Mr. King looked the rifle over, but not really wanting the gun so much as wanting to help this man, he said, "I will buy the gun, but I will pay you this twenty-dollar gold piece." He put the twenty in Cipriano's hand. Dad boarded the train carrying the gun and later brought it to East Texas where it still is, in my possession, in good shape. It has been used over the years for small game as it shoots a .410 shotgun shell as well as the large rifle shell.

"What is the story behind this gun, Father?" I asked him one day when I was ten years old, the year of the Great Texas Centennial.

"I have no way to verify this, but I can tell you what Cipriano told me."

"Cipriano was about five years old, he thinks, living in a small, crude village in the Sierra Madre of Mexico with his parents. Life was hard, food was scarce, and the winters were hard. But after the snow melted every year the Mexican cavalry came into the mountains from Chihuahua City and raided the villages of these mostly Indian people. They were always looking for gold, plundering anything of value, and always they violated the Indian women something awful."

"The Indians decided to fight back. They went high up in the mountains and came back with a good bag of gold. They took it to Albuquerque to a white man they could trust, and told him to go East and buy two hundred guns and lots of bullets. He did as they asked, and the Indians came to his house and took the guns.

"The white man decided to help the Indians, as he had had military training. He went with them, laid a well-planned trap, and sure enough,

103

the soldiers came and walked right into it. Something like ninety-eight were killed in the battle. Cipriano, only a kid, watched the battle from above on a large rock. His father used the rifle and claimed to have killed two of the soldiers with the gun. So, that is the story of the gun."

৩ • ৩

A TALE GRANDPA TOLD ABOUT INDIANS
by Ernest B. Speck
of Alpine

Before I tell you the tale Grandpa told, I guess I better tell you about Grandpa. He was George Washington Templeton, and he was born in Missouri in 1841. He came to Texas with his family in 1848. Between then and 1882 when he married, he had been a Confederate soldier and scout, he had gone up the trail six times, he had been a cowhand and freighter, he had spent winters trapping, and he had been a gambler.

About 1910 Grandpa saw a sketch in the *Dallas News* by an old friend, John W. Proffit, and he wrote an account of an Indian attack in 1867 that included Grandpa.

Grandpa and John and some other cowboys were all working for Newhouse and Johnson (the people he drove up the trail for), and Grandpa had been too sick to go with the others to help with the branding one day.

Later in the day he got to feeling better and went to go work with the others. As he told and wrote down the story in his rather formal nineteenth century prose:

"When within 200 yards of the pen I heard a war whoop and looking up saw between 80 to 90 Indians coming toward me. At first I thought they were Tonks (Tonkawas) and that they only aimed to scare me, but when they began to pull their lances I had no time to argue the case with them.

"Then I had about 80 to 100 yards to cover to reach a small thicket, and I got there with both feet, although looking over my shoulder as I went into a deep ravine and saw their lances raised, could almost feel the cold steel pierce my back.

"However I made my way to the center of that thicket by crawling on all fours. The green briars beneath and the June sun above and the perspiration standing out on me in huge chunks was a paradise to being out in the open.

"They circled the thicket several times. I could see them bat their eyes and hear them jabbering but couldn't understand them. Finally, they abandoned the thicket and made for the pens where the boys were at work.

"It is generally believed that the boys saw them coming and made for a clump of trees when they met their sad fate. There was about 100 shots fired. The boys, having only the bullets in their pistols, had no chance to protect themselves. I could hear the battle raging and seemed to realize their fate.

"Between sundown and dark I heard the voice of John Cockran tell some of the boys that Indians had killed George Templeton, that he saw the Indians lance him.

"On hearing this I left my position and went to where the boys lay weltering in blood. The moon was shining by then and the battleground presented the most ghastly sight I ever witnessed, the Indians having taken their scalps and all clothing except one sock on one of the boys."

5.
Animals, Wild and Domestic

The Spanish explorers and settlers who came to Texas in the eighteenth century found huge herds of deer, antelope, elk, and buffalo. These animals grazed the grasslands by the thousands. Preying on them were wolves, panthers, and bears. Feral hogs, left over from Hernan de Soto's visit two centuries earlier roamed the eastern woods. The rivers were filled with fish, and the sky was filled with edible birds. Texas was a land of turkeys, bears, and honey for the Spanish and for the Anglos who followed them a century later. It was a hunter's paradise, and for two hundred years, between 1700 and 1900, Texans slew the wildlife as if the supply were never ending.

Just as the early settlers competed with the Indians for territory, they competed with their fellow predators for the meat on the hoof that abounded around them. Many of the stories that families remember and pass down are the tales of their hunts and their dramatic encounters with wolves, panthers, and bears—or with equally dangerous snakes and alligators.

Our ancestors' lives were also involved with domestic animals, with horses, cows, sheep, goats, and hogs, on whom they depended for food and clothes and transportation. Most families remember in their stories the horses they rode as children and the teams that plowed their fields and that were a part of their families—like Old Shorty the cowhorse, and Kit and Kate the mule team. We remember for generations the stories of dogs that we have hunted with or dogs that have been companions to our family. I still remember Ring the greyhound snake killer, and Jack who always trailed the pack and was christened "the hind leader." Some folks even remember cats in their family tales.

∾ • ∾

BEARS AND WILD BEASTS
by Myrtle Oldham Ham
of Erath County
transcribed by JoEllen Ham Miller
of Stephenville
with original spelling

Borned in 1886 a girl child to Lewis and Emly Oldham. they named the child Myrtle. she was the oldest girl of a family of 6 children. her first home was a little log cabin in the Trinity river bottom, among pin trees, and where the Negro could be heard singing and whistling as they went about theire work. her first nurce was an old Negro mammy—she was known as ole Crecy—when Myrtle was 11 month old her father sold his Trinity botton home, and loaded all his possessions in two wagons and started for the golden west. after several weeks he landed in a small western town, (Alexander, Erath County) and there this little girl really began life. she allways wanted to be a real pioneer, all tho she was raised on a farm. she cravd to travel, her father finely bought a sandy land farm. close to another pioneer town, and there she grew up. and married. so now the storys will began. I do hope some day there will be some one who will enjoy reading them, for ever one of them is true. I have picked them up as I've gone thro life.

[For Myrtle Ham's biography and the story behind these stories, see her "Another Indian Story" in chapter four, "Indians." Editor]

* * * * * * * *

In the year about 1832—a [caravan] of several families Miller by name. left the Carolina and emergrated to Tenn–they ware my oun Great grand parents. My grand mother Avline Miller, was a year old baby. her older sisters often told us children of the long trip. of how they crossed the comberlin Mt. some on horse back others in wagons, drawn by oxen. How they went whole days with out watter, and how it rained so much they couldent keep fire at other times and met beares and other wild beasts. said thire only fear was the Indians. which they never did see.

After they finely got to Tenn they selected a camp and after severl weeks cleared off a place and built a cabbin close to the Tenn river. You see those days people had to be close to watter.

Myrtle Ham, sitting on her porch in Erath County, cleaning a chicken

My old Aunt told us 3 storries. first was about a panther, her mother was making soap, out in the yard all the children 5 of them. ware playing around. when they noticed the dog was acting very scared. and about that time thire mother. looked up from her work and seen a big yellow panther, creeping up on her. so she very quitely told the children to get the baby and get in the cabbin, and she said she had to think of some way of escape and that quick so she did, as she knew it was life or death with her. so she was using a goard, and she dipped up a goard full of the boiling soap, and as the panther come on she threw the hot soap right into its face—and turned it, it run off. And plenty fast, wasent seen any ways soon—my Grand mother said she could barely remember that narrow escape. But I had two or 3 real old Aunts that could remember it.so well.

And they told us a beary story—happened at the same place. one day they looked out the cabbin door, and seen a big brown bear. said it just passed on by the house. when well past it seemed to sit down like a dog, turned it head all most strit back and looked so funny. Made a noise sounded like a cow mooing to her calf. but got up and went on its way. They said they eat bear meat all the year round.

then they told us two more panther stories one happened while they lived in theire little cabbin home. the grass was real tall. one day while theire mother and the little boy and one or two of the girls ware out hunting wood, they noticed the grass movveing. seemed to be all in a strip or row. so they kept watching it, so getting alarmed, they started for the house but before they could get there they noticed it was a very large yellow animial, so it turned out to be a big panther, the grass was so high it all most covered it up. but it never payed them any mind, but theire father followed it. severel miles into the mt, and it wasent found, but it finely come back and killed theire stock all winter. so that ends the story.

then old Aunt Nancey. all ways said the only 1 lie she ever really told was when she told her father when asked her and her two sister about wattering the work horses, after severel years her father moved away from theire first little home. and settled severel miles up the river and improved a larger farm built a big new house. and cleared a real farm so he allways sent them with the work horses to the river to be wattered. After a days work was over—so on that night the 3 sisters has to ride the horses to the river, as just as they rode down into the river a big panther jumped across the trail, and scared the horses, and they bolted and turned and ran up the bank, so they wouldent go back to watter. when they got back home theire dady, asked them (as he all ways did) did the horses drink and they answered yes sir. So she said that was the lie she told.

I thought Id quit with that story but Ill tell this one and close this chaper, the same two old sisters told about how bad another panther scared them. said they allways raised fine watter mellons on theire farm. so one day the 3 sisters and Brother (Daniel) went after some mellons, just bout the time they started back to the house a panther sprang out and screamed. And of chorse they never lost any time leaving there on they ran some of them threw down theire mellons, but aunt Nancey said when she arrived at the house she still had hers and had stuck her fingeres clear through the rine of the mellon. And was just hanging on to it, and it would be a mistry all her life how she ever done it, for try as hard as she could never could do it again. They all tried it and they could not do it.

I remember a true panther story told by an old man from Kentucky. his home was in the mt of that state, it seemed he cut wood or big logs for his living. there was two little boys in the family so one day the oldest boy (Cade Logan) was sent to the woods to take his father a drink of watter. so just as he come to where his father was a big panther jumped out of a tree and landed on the little boy. nocked him to the ground. his dady grabbed his ax, and with one blow killed the panther on the spot. they skinned the big cat and also kept the claus of it. I remember seeing them. and I also have seen the scars on the boys body where it scratched him. he was a grown man before I ever knew him. he died close to where I was raised, for his people moved to Texas about the year 1894 or 95—old Mart Logan was his father. And Joce Logan was his mother.

I'll now tell a bear story that mother told, it seemed there was a old log cabbin on her fathers land, on the Trinity river. and the school teacher which was a widdow woman with one small by lived there, so my mother and her sister would take it time about spending the night with her—so that special nite was mamas to stay. So when supper time came they ware setting at the table, when they ntoiced the cat kept fighting something through a crack in the floor, so the ladie got up to see what was wrong, about that time it was heard smelling up through the crack in the floor. Mama said it would sniff and made a funny whistling sound. so they got up and began to barr doors and move bead steads against windows, she could heare it rubbing against the house, but couldent get in. said they never slept very much that nite, so the next morning it seemed to be gone. after a while that morning the woman had to have watter so she and mama went to the spring and there sat the bear. they got theire watter and never lost any time leaveing there, after they reached the cabbin, the woman blew a horn (the only way she had calling for help) 3 or 4 times, and in a few minutes there was severl men there to help her. one man brought his dogs, but there wasent a gun in the whole neighborhood, the dogs soon ran it off. it never did try to hurt any one. that was in Anderon Co, close to Tenn, Conlony (where my mother Emely Hunter was raised.)

Now this is a turkey story my father used to tell us. came very near turning out to be something else. he said he and a negro boy allways hunted Turkeys ever fall and winter, said they would take theire guns and go to the Trinity bottom, and call and go to gobblin like a Turkey, and in a short while a bunch of turkeys would appear. so that time he hid by a big tree while the negro would call from where he was hid, so about the time the Turkeys appeared. he heard something coming down the big tree behind him (said he was squatted down) he was so intent on watching the Turkeys he never even looked around. about that time a big linx cat dropped right smack down on him. said it was as surprised as he was, so he jumped out of the way. and the negro killed the big cat, but he got the scare of his life. he would laugh ever time he told it. but he told us they allways got theire Turkeys, lenx or no Lenx cat.

Another story Ed told us was a rattle snake scare they got at the little hut his dady built on Indain Camp Creek. one night his dady was away from home. and he and the rest of the children was around the cook stove where his mother was cooking supper. when the cat began spitting at something, his mother looked under the stove, there was a big rattle snak there, he got the shuvel and killed it. the snake was brought in the house in a stump. or at least they all way though that was the way it go in there . . .

I'll tell another snake story that happened. Around here. About the year 1880. A Mr. Sherrod settled in this neighborhood, got watter out of a spring close to theire house so as it was the custom in those days the children most allways carried the watter, so the daughter (Tillie Sherrod) went after the watter that day. and while at the spring a big rattle snake bit her on the ankle, she taken off her garter and bond her leg. but befor she could get to the house her leg was baddly swollen they put her leg in coil oil and give her whiskey she lived over it but was lame for severl years.

THOMAS AND THE RATTLESNAKE
by Waun Harrison
of
Jacksonville

On almost every occasion that my mother's family has held a reunion, I have heard some wild tale centered around my grandfather's brother, Thomas Echols. Since Thomas is no longer around to defend himself, I'm sure that the truth becomes farther and farther separated from the plot with each telling.

One particular incident with which I am familiar involves Uncle Thomas at the early age of sixteen. As a farmer's son and as a large boy for sixteen years, he was assigned the task of breaking a large piece of land with a two-horse disk. This particular southwest Texas meadow had not been planted the year before and was now about twelve inches high in assorted grasses, weeds, and snakes. On the morning that my great uncle was working, he had encountered several rattlesnakes, some hurrying from his path and one which had not moved soon enough to avoid the blades of the heavy disk. Needless to say, these experiences had made the young farmer more than a little apprehensive.

When fate chose to jam a large rock between the two disk blades and force Thomas to make repairs he stepped into the still unmolested high grass where the rock was riding with as much care and grace as an overgrown sixteen-year-old boy could muster. Now, according to Uncle Thomas' version of the story, as he bent down to pry the rock free, a small rattlesnake appeared from the grass and with no warning struck Thomas on the little finger of his right hand. Quickly he killed the snake but realized that it would take him too long to reach the farmhouse several miles away. So with legendary calm he placed his little digit in front of the nearest disk blade and firmly clucked to the waiting horses. That he did not die from loss of blood seems more incredible now than that he might have died from the bite of that particular snake.

If, however, we accept the more recent version of this tale as told by almost everyone except Uncle Thomas, we can discount the effect of the snake bite and concern ourselves solely with the bleeding finger. Because it is the major premise of the second version that Thomas never met a snake that morning. Instead, he spooked his team while removing the jammed rock and donated, by accident, the major portion of his finger to the fertility of the southwest Texas soil.

PAPA JOHN AND THE BULL
by Sue Wenner
of Waco

My grandfather's missing eye used to mystify me until one day I asked my mother how it came about to be that he only had one eye. That day she told me the story of how my "Papa John" has lost his eye and had proven his courage.

When he was very young, his pet pig got loose and wandered into the catch pen which held the herd bull. Papa John, afraid for his pig's life, jumped over the fence and ran after his pet. The bull, upset at this intrusion of his privacy by a boy and his pig, charged. Papa John caught up the pig in his arms and ran from the bull. Upon reaching the fence he turned to wave off the bull, but undaunted the bull came on. Papa John threw the pig through the fence at the last minute and sacrificed his eye in the process for at that moment the bull's left horn caught and ripped at his face. Papa John's one eye gave him a wise, brave look which he carried until his death.

"Papa" John, with missing left eye, and "Mama" Nora on their wedding day

DO UNTO OTHERS . . .
by Lillian Ellisene Rumage Davis
of Angel Fire, New Mexico

Grandaddy sighed. "The horses were always wild. I never knew why, until the boys were grown. Carl began to tell us about the times they played when Lillie and I went to town to funerals."

I knew the tales of the cattle pony. My dad and J. T. wanted a mount like the magnolia flying red horse. They tied a wagon sheet around her neck. The sheet flapping against her rump made her wild. Away she ran, the sheet billowing over her body. The mare cleared two six-foot fences before she finally accepted the contraption tied to her, and returned to the barn.

The children worked in the fields as men except when their parents went to town. On those days, the fantastic dreams of their childhood fantasy worlds took flight. The family owned a 1917 model truck, and the boys were learning to drive. Claude had stuffed the tires with tow sacks because he didn't have inner tubes. Driven by a flight of imagination the boys decided to create a super horse. They took the pony to the old truck, wrapped a wire around his ears, stuck it to the coil, and turned on the ignition. The electrical current was so strong, the horse reared up and fell backward. Such a commotion frightened J. T. and Warren. They jumped on the metal fender. The voltage knocked the boys to the ground, just like it had the horse. Grandma always said, "What you do to others unjustly, will eventually be done unto you."

◡◦ • ◦◡

CATCHING WILD MUSTANGS
by Frances B. Vick and Andrew Brannen
of Dallas and Saron

When Grandpa Andrew Jackson Walker lived with his parents and siblings on White Oak Bayou in the late 1850s, yellow fever broke out in Houston. It was brought from New Orleans and more than half of the population died with it. So the family moved to Mustang Bayou in Brazoria County and settled about where the town of Alvin now lies. The nearest neighbor was six miles distant. Most of the country between Buffalo Bayou and the Brazos River was a howling wilderness, except along the streams where there were a few settlers. It was a splendid stock range and the whole country was alive with both horses and cattle. Grandpa Walker said he had seen hundreds of deer scampering over the prairie at one time, and the wolves were almost as numerous as the deer. Mustang Bayou was the center of the stock range, especially for the mustang, or wild horse.

According to Grandpa Walker: "the finest sport to be had is catching wild mustangs. A mustang is a wild unbranded horse that belongs to anyone that can catch him. The way we used to catch them was to walk them down. They usually ran in herds or bunches and they had a certain range. Their range may take in one hundred miles or perhaps more.

"Four or five men would enter the expedition to walk down the bunch, for instance one man saw the bunch at a certain place, another ranger may have seen the same bunch fifty miles south from where the first man saw it, others may have seen it along the route between the two points mentioned, thus it would be concluded that their range lay along these places. A man would be stationed every twenty or thirty miles along the route, and then the bunch would be started.

"The first day the wild horses would scamper away, throwing their manes and tails to the breeze making a sight that would whet our desire to capture them, for there is nothing prettier in the world than a troop of wild horses at a distance. They look perfection when they throw up their heads and sniff the wind then scamper away. The man that first starts them follows them for one day on a pony, taking his time. His place is taken by the second man about nightfall, presuming we started the bunch in the morning. The second man follows them all night, for the hunt is made when there is a full moon, so that the bunch can be tracked at night as well as during the day. On the morning when the third man takes the trail, the stallion or master of the bunch is behind the herd biting and kicking the laggards along. The third day, or even on the evening of the second day, finds the bunch strung out in a straight line, each following the other in Indian file. Then they are becoming tired. They are allowed no time to eat or drink. About the fifth day the whole herd is at our mercy, and we close in and very easily take them.

"My first experience with them was extremely exciting. I was stationed at the last stand and the riders closed in on the bunch just before reaching my station. It happened that a mare got by them and tried to pass me. She was pretty well run down and the other boys had captured her colt. I thought this was the chance for me to show my skill with the lariat. I was riding a splendid horse so I tied one end of my rope around my horse's neck, and made my loop in the other end. The first throw I laid the coil around her neck, and the moment the rope tightened the fun commenced. She made straight for me and my pony, rearing, kicking and biting. She seemed to blame me for the loss of her colt. I would have been willing to turn her loose, but I had the rope tied to my pony and I had no knife. I was in a close place for I could neither make peace, conquer nor control her and I was sorry that I ever saw a mustang. I was about ready to give up when one of the other boys came to my assistance. He was older and more experienced than I, and we together made short work of her."

๛ • ๛

A SNAKE STORY FROM THE 1930s
by Barbara Pybas
of Gainesville

A family named Baccus lived in Cooke County near the Red River on an upper bottom called Blue Hollow. Not many sharecroppers owned cars during the 1930s, and they worked their crops in the river bottom with horses or used the land owner's tractor. The Baccuses had been a fairly large family with several children, but unfortunately for Mr. Baccus, his wife had run off and left him. He had to raise all those kids by himself.

One time they had scythed some hay, and Mr. Baccus came down and wanted to borrow a buck-rake off Dad to stack it. The buck-rake was behind a sand hill in the river bottom, grown up in weeds and grass, and hadn't been used for some time. The oldest Baccus boy, Marvin, was in there getting ready to hook the rake up to the team when a rattlesnake bit him. It was a pretty big snake and made a good hang on the boy's leg. It was a severe bite just above the ankle.

Mr. Baccus sent one of the boys to get Sam Poston, who was the pipeline walker and did own a car. Sam was held in high opinion because he had a steady job for the Empire Oil Company, looking after the pipeline all the way from Healdton, Oklahoma, to Gainesville. The Baccuses wanted Sam to drive Marvin to the doctor, twenty-five miles to Gainesville.

Mr. Baccus had heard that a good remedy was to kill the snake, split it open, and wrap the carcass around the wound. That would draw the venom out. So, that's what he did.

They finally located Sam and made the long trip to Gainesville. The boy was really hurting. They got Marvin to the doctor and carried him in with the snake carcass wrapped all around his leg. The nurse saw the snake-wrapped leg and ran away, hollering for the doctor and emptying the waiting room with her screams. No doctor or nurse would touch the snake carcass, and they finally had to get Mr. Baccus to come in to remove the snake carcass from Marvin's leg so they could treat him.

After a period of severe swelling and high fever, Marvin eventually recovered from the snake bite. The result of the wound was two fang holes in Marvin's leg that became the object of awe for his schoolmates.

ဆ • ဆ

THE BEAR KNIFE
by Florena Williams
of Sherman

When he was less than ten years old, my grandfather, B. E. Williams, was taken on his first bear hunt by his great uncle, Tom Van Hook. Instead of finding a bear, a bear found them and charged the boy. B. E. aimed and fired as he had been taught, but he only wounded the bear, which continued its charge.

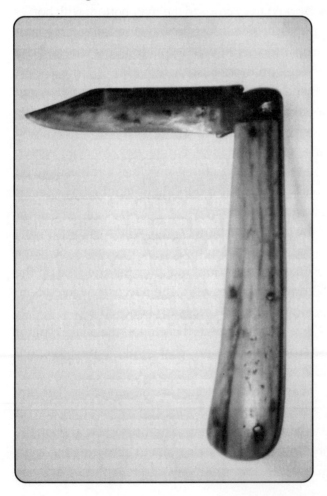

The pocket knife that Uncle Tom Van Hook used to kill a bear in a hand-to-hand fight.

There was no time to reload or even pass the gun to his uncle, but the more experienced hunter did all he could under the circumstances. Uncle Tom drew his hunting knife, and though it seems impossible now, in the wrestling match that followed, Tom managed to repeatedly stab the bear until he killed it.

The knife which great-uncle Tom Van Hook used has been passed down and is affectionately known as "the bear knife." It is now in my possession, and the blade is four inches long and three-quarters of an inch wide. The handle is brownish yellow, perhaps made of bone.

᠗ • ᠗

HOG STORIES FROM THE DAVIS FAMILY
by Kenneth W. Davis
of Lubbock

My grandfather Davis was a short man with an at times shorter temper. He and his second wife raised fancy chickens to show at fairs and to eat. Early one summer several of these chickens disappeared with no trace. Granddad Davis was mystified until one late afternoon when he took fresh water for the hog's wallowing pit and caught the sow that had recently farrowed eating one of the prized chickens. He gave the hog a mighty kick in the ribs and broke his foot; the sow died. This incident prompted a saying in the family to those who would act rashly: "Don't kick the sow!"

My great-grandfather Davis, a Civil War Veteran, was in his last years a really fractious individual who made life miserable for his wife. His son, my grandfather, said that the old man did his best to be a problem even when being cooperative would have been the easier course. This old man loved pork in any form and would glut himself on fresh sausage, and ham or shoulder meat. Once when he was in his late 80s his wife made a mess of hogshead cheese, a delicacy the old man favored. He began eating with gusto and soon had eaten far too much despite warnings from his wife and two of his sons who were visiting. The result of this gluttony was epic gastric distress that necessitated the scrubbing of the kitchen floor with lye soap. His wife of some 60 years declared that enough was enough and banished her husband from the premises. He left Granger, Texas, in a huff and never returned. No one knows for sure when he died, but he is buried in the Confederate Cemetery in Austin.

A story my father delighted in telling my sister and me as well as the grandchildren involved the always fat hogs a neighbor raised. This man and his wife had fourteen children, a dozen of whom finished college. The

Grandfather William Davis, who killed a sow with one kick and broke his foot in the process.

woman cooked excellent meals when the children were growing up. Peach cobblers were her specialty. From full flavored blackland cling peaches, she fashioned these traditional desserts using various spices and great amounts of sugar. A United States Department of Agriculture official from Belton, Texas, county seat of old Bell County, heard stories of this couple's heroically fat hogs and drove to nearby Holland, Texas, to try to learn the secret for growing such obese hogs. He arrived and found the man at the hog pen watching the creatures eat the last of the slops he had brought them. In response to the official's questions, the man somewhat reluctantly said, "Well, if you had et as much peach cobbler as them hogs has et, you'd be fat, too." The man's wife had never quite managed to cut back her cooking from what it had to be when there were at least ten children at home. Then, perhaps to make up for having been a tad surly to the official, the man gave him a gallon syrup bucket full of the purest white hog lard ever seen. The official later said that chicken fried in this lard from peach-fed hogs was the best he had eaten in his entire life.

SUSANNAH AND HER ANGORA GOATS
by Lora B. Garrison
of Utopia

Stories have been passed down about Susannah Auld's adventures as a pioneer woman: The care of the family's rare and experimental Angora goats became her personal project after her husband acquired a small herd in 1900. Susannah had to round up the Angoras every night and get them into a shed, to keep the varmints from getting them, since the grey wolves, mountain lions, and black bear were abundant. At that time there was no cross fencing, only fields with stone fences.

One day, in the middle of the afternoon, one of our blue northers blew in. Goats will always move into a cold wind, so very quickly the goats had traveled north over the next mountain range.

Susannah realized she had to find them and bring them back or they would be lost. She tracked the goats over thirty miles in rugged mountain country for the next twenty-four hours. She had some jerky to chew on and stopped at springs for water.

Susannah Lowrance Auld, who tracked her stray goats thirty miles in a blue norther with a four-month-old baby on her hip

The night was very cold, and she lay up under a bush to sleep for awhile. She pulled her long black skirts up over her shoulders for warmth and to protect the small bundle she was carrying. It was near Rocksprings that Susannah finally caught up with the goats and turned them toward home.

This was quite a feat for a woman alone, without a dog or a gun for protection. But what really made this an unusual experience, was the fact that Susannah was carrying her four-month-old baby son Marcus, and of course he had to be nursed, so she couldn't have left him at home.

Annie Lee Auld Davis, Susannah's daughter and pioneer rancher of Uvalde County

WILD GOOSE
by Palmer Henry Olsen
of Clifton

Uncle Kris owned several milk cows, among which was one named Wild Goose. She was a small blackish cow—probably a scrub jersey—with some brown hairs on her sides and belly, white foreshanks, and horns that curved inward. There was a good reason for her name. When the time came to calve, she always sought the farthest, wildest, most rugged and inaccessible spot in the pasture. It was an area of rocky cliffs and dense scrub brush. Hog plums, a few blackhaw, shin oak and sumac, together with briars and prickly pears, formed an almost impenetrable jungle.

The time came again for Wild Goose to have a calf. She failed to show up on two successive evenings. Uncle Kris hitched a horse to the buggy, and invited my cousin Lawrence and me to come along on the hunt for the new mama. We were also told that we had to stay in the buggy and keep quiet. We had already been told by Aunt Annie that Wild Goose was mean and would tolerate no one but Uncle Kris when the calf was young.

Irvin Parks, Lawrence Olsen, and
Palmer Olsen with Pat the dog in 1906

We followed the woods road up by the big hollow live oak and through the thick Spanish oak groves and the few cedars. We meandered along the branch past the wheat field; turned right into the narrow lane between the field and the hay meadow; and then slid and pitched over the ruts and gullies up the rougher, steeper road past the mountain tank. We weaved through the ever-thicker brush till we finally reached the end of the road. Uncle Kris tied the horse to a small live oak and told us again to keep quiet and stay in the buggy. After an hour or so—it seemed ages to us—he returned leading Wild Goose with her small calf wobbling along behind. We got back to the house and the cow lot about sundown.

It was just beginning to get dark when Uncle Kris started milking Wild Goose. Lawrence and I naturally wanted to miss no part of this wild cow operation; so, uninvited, we crawled up on the fence and sat down on the top plank.

We had hardly settled when Wild Goose spotted us. She was standing broadside, and when she wheeled to come at us, she rolled Uncle Kris completely over and off his stool, and she kicked the half-full milk bucket right in his face. Lawrence and I didn't stop to argue with Wild Goose nor to make a dignified retreat. We fell backward off the fence and hit the ground running for the house. We never had to be warned about staying away from Wild Goose again.

Uncle Chris and Aunt Annie Olsen in front of their house in Bosque County

THE GOAT ON THE COURTHOUSE SQUARE
by Mildred Boren Sentell
of Snyder

When Daddy began to work for the Gulf Oil Company, my sister was four and I was two. Soon my twin brothers were born, and though they were healthy, Mother thought they were too thin. The doctor told Mother to give them goat's milk to drink, and so Daddy bought two nanny goats.

Although we lived in "town," we had as many animals as most farmers ever did. In addition to the goats, we had Daddy's Bantam chickens, a cow, two or more horses, and sometimes a dogie lamb. I didn't know that this was odd; I thought everyone had neighbors who packed up and moved on a regular basis, sometimes even taking their houses along.

From the time that we got the goats, every time that we went out of town (which was always to Post), we pulled a trailer with a goat in it. We would drive off in my mother's Chevrolet with Daddy in the front seat, driving; Mother in the front passenger seat, reading; all four of us children in the back seat with our little dog; and trailing along behind, the goat.

On one trip, we drove up to the courthouse in Lamesa and parked so that Daddy could go in and visit his cousin Monte, who was in jail, waiting to be tried for killing two people. While Daddy went in, we four got out and sat on the grass on the courthouse square. Mother sat in the car, reading. Soon we looked up and the goat had joined us on the grass. Immediately we jumped up to put the goat back in the trailer.

The goat ran. We chased it. Some people on the square chased it too. Mother was oblivious. Someone ran inside to get the sheriff, who began to chase the goat. Suddenly Mother looked up and saw what was happening, but she did not get out to chase the goat; she sat in the car, staring straight ahead. Finally Jack Phinizy drove by in his pickup and stopped and roped the goat, which we put back in the trailer and tied.

When my brothers were about eight, they seemed fat enough, so Daddy quit milking goats and sold the nannies. We then stopped hauling goats, of course, but Daddy continued to pull the trailer, just in case.

WAGON YARD TRADES
by Ross Estes
edited by Robert J. Duncan
of McKinney

I was on my way home from tradin' in the wagon yard at Gainesville one day around 1917. I was in a wagon, leadin' a pony. A man struck me on the road, and he wanted to know if that pony would work to a single buggy. I told him yes, that when I'd traded for it, it had been hooked up to a single buggy.

He wanted to know if I'd swap it for a cow and a calf. I said, "Well, I might." Cattle was cheap back then, horses was, too. Well, he opened a gate and I drove into a pasture, and we cut across the pasture and went out a gate on the other side to his house.

We got there, and he called his wife out to look at the pony. He picked out a cow and a heifer calf and offered to trade. I said, "Don't you want to see her work?" Yeah, he'd love to see her work. He had a single buggy there, and we put her to it. I got in and drove her down in the pasture, turned around, and trotted her back. That woman was wantin' her to pull a buggy. I could tell that she really liked that pony.

They had some other calves there. I said, "I couldn't hardly give that pony for that there cow and calf." I had twenty dollars tied up in the pony, but I didn't tell them how much she'd cost me. I said, "If you'll throw in that little Jersey heifer right there, we'll trade." He took me up.

I didn't have no sideboards on the wagon. When we got her front feet up in the bed, I reached around and got her by the tail and twisted it, and she jumped up in the wagon with her hind feet. We throwed her down and tied her to the wagon bed.

I didn't get home 'til the next mornin'! Annie was puttin' breakfast on the table.

I was still way down the road and that blame cow had broke loose from the wagon. She was follerin' the wagon, draggin' the lariat rope, thirty-two foot long. She bawled a time or two, jumped a grader ditch, and took out across the field. I pulled over to the fence and took after that cow. It took me the longest to catch her. I took her back down there and tied her to the back of the wagon. And her calf would bawl. Oh, I didn't go a mile 'til she just rode the back of that wagon plumb in home.

I sold the cow and calf for forty dollars. I kept that heifer, I think, three weeks, and swapped her to a feller for a sow, and that sow brought me nine pigs. I kept the pigs for six weeks and sold them for five dollars a piece.

So I come out pretty good. I spent twenty dollars on the pony and wound up with the sow and eighty-five dollars.

Ross Estes at 88, horse trader and story-teller from Tioga, Texas

♘ • ♞

BIG BOY WHATLEY: HORSE TRADER
by Elmer Kelton
of San Angelo

I used to enjoy watching my father dicker with an old Midland horse trader named Big Boy Whatley. Dad enjoyed the challenge of trading with Big Boy. If you washed out even with Big Boy, you were in the big leagues.

One time Big Boy brought a young horse out to try to sell him to my father. He had a great story to tell. The horse was broke gentle as a dog. He knew how to watch a cow, and you could rein him with one finger. Pitch? No sir, he had never pitched a jump in his life. Why, even the womenfolks could ride him.

I used to wonder about Big Boy's womenfolks.

A cowboy named Happy Smith decided to try the horse. We've had space shots that didn't get as far off the ground as that horse threw Happy.

Dad chewed Big Boy out a little. "You told me that horse didn't pitch, when you knew damned well he would."

Big Boy calmly said, "That's the way I sell horses."

COOKIN' A POSSUM
by James Ward Lee
of Fort Worth

And speaking of possums, if you haven't ever seen one cooked, you may never have seen a veritable ocean of grease. A two-pound possum contains enough good grease to lubricate a gravel truck.

My cousin Hattie once cooked a boar possum for J. T. and their son Ray. After four hours of good solid baking and two quarts of run-off grease, that possum still had enough lard in him to grease the skids needed to launch the Queen Mary, who, by the way looked like she had her share of grease on her way to being the Queen Mum. Anyway, Hattie cooked the possum and my Cousin J. T. and his boy Ray sat on opposite sides of the table and ate toward the middle. I was the referee, so I only had to take one bite of the gray, greasy meat. Just to check. J. T. and Ray met in the middle—J. T. may have won by a greasy chin, but I don't recall, for all this was in a galaxy far away—Alabama.

After the possum was reduced to a pile of bones everybody in the room looked greasy—and queasy. J. T. rared back from the table and finished off the half-pint of Four Roses he had been using to cut the tallow of the possum as he went along. Ray was sticking strictly with Coca-Cola on the theory that the bubbles would melt the possum lard. J. T. drank of the cheap whiskey, smacked his lips, and said, "I God, I got that greasy sumbitch anchored." And he did. For about five minutes. After that he had a sudden urge to make for the backyard to relinquish possum and potion alike. A case of what Shakespeare calls "hide, fox, and all after."

~ • ~

HOG DROVERS
by Lora B. Garrison
of Utopia

The hog drovers on the Sabinal would mark all the male hogs and cut most. When a particularly mean old boar hog wouldn't stay in the bunch, he would be roped around the snout behind the tusks, before he was tied up, watching out he didn't thrash around and cut you with his sharp tusks. Then his eyes would be sewn shut so he would stay with the other hogs. These hogs would be three or four years old, and some of them had long tusks. They would cut hell out of those dogs if they could catch them. Those dogs had better stay out of their way if they wanted to live. It took a good dog to catch a mean hog.

Dave Huffman's son Jake recalled seeing Alex Auld catch a hog, "Mr. Auld used to get down and get an ol' hog to run at him, and he would catch it by the ear, and reach over and get it by the hind leg and flip it over and tie it up. Daddy told him he better use a rope, that he was going to let one of those hogs get him some day.

"It wasn't more than a week and one of those ol' boars caught him on the wrist and ripped it open. He was a tough ol' bugger, Mr. Auld was. He sewed it up with a spaying needle he carried all the time. The needle fit in a grooved piece of board and had a waxed thread wrapped around it."

ও • ৩

GRANDMA ANDERSON AND THE MILK COW
by Al Lowman
of Stringtown

Grandma Anderson of Staples was a remarkable individual of such formidable personality that her spouse scarcely existed outside her shade. Tom Anderson was once justice of the peace, but his main job was to sit on the front porch, rock, and look neat as a pin while grandma did all the work. For most of the day she gave him the sharp edge of her tongue as she bustled about. Then, at day's end, she would pull a stool up to his easy chair and sweet-talk him for a while before going in the house to fix supper.

A single episode in Grandma's long life became *the* watershed event in the community's history. Everything in Staples happened either before or after Grandma was gored by the old milk cow. As long as they lived—and as late as the 1980s there were a handful yet living—the witnesses knew exactly where they were and what they were doing when Grandma was gored. So many of them claim to have been "right there" when it happened that I am convinced that half the town was sitting around Grandma's cowlot waiting for it to happen.

This awful event occurred early on a weekday morning in the fall of 1911, as Grandma was trying to separate her milk cow from its newly born calf. The nervous cow unexpectedly charged Grandma, who was unable to swerve aside fast enough to avoid being totally disemboweled by one of the horns.

Jim Sherrill, who lived across the road from the Andersons, came running, and was the first at her side. Others heard the screams as well and never forgot them. Someone ran to fetch young Doctor Wilburn Williams, whose office was three houses away. Robert Lowman, Daddy's cousin, had been at the store only a few minutes when a distraught Ed Anderson, one of

Grandma's sons, appeared in the doorway. Ashen-faced and in tears, he implored the bystanders, "The old cow has just about killed Mama. Can some of y'all help us get her to the doctor?"

Instantly a half dozen men ran to assist. When they reached the Anderson cowpen they found the stricken woman, perfectly conscious, lying with her intestines strewn on the manure-covered ground beside her. Dr. Williams had already arrived. He now supervised her removal to a stretcher improvised from a barn door panel and led the way to his office. Robert Lowman told me he carried her intestines in his hands, as the litter bearers marched along. When they reached Williams' office Grandma was laid gently on the only feasible surface, which happened to be a diningroom table.

Years later Dr. Williams confessed to his foster daughter, Myrtle Tarbutton, "I was never so scared in all my life. There was the woman's husband and a couple of the big kids depending on me to do something. They sure as hell didn't know what to do and neither did I. So I washed the cow manure off her guts as best I could, stuffed 'em back in place as best I could, and sewed her up as best I could. There was no use saying a prayer because she didn't have one."

Robert Lowman remembered that when the doctor had finished, he remarked to onlookers in the jam-packed livingroom, "I haven't done a very good job here, but there's no way she could live anyway." At this time Grandma was in her late fifties, Dr. Williams in his early thirties. It was just like an Anderson to make a liar out of somebody. Grandma Anderson lived to be 105, surpassing the doctor by nearly a decade. Grandma was holding court at Staples reunions well into my lifetime.

Grandma Anderson of Staples at 105 years old. She was in her late fifties when she was gored by the milk cow.

6.

The Church, Preachers, and Religion

For years I listened to the telling of our family story about how my great-uncle Sam Abernethy, a Baptist preacher, had publicly debated and soundly defeated the Atheist in Old Greer County, Texas. I was always impressed with the story of this Herculean conflict until I learned—long after I was full grown—that the debate was between the forces of Sprinkling Methodists and Total Immersion Baptists. The Atheist, whom I had earlier pictured as a city-slick Satanic individual, turned out to be a Methodist Preacher—a Sprinkler!

Frontier religion was a tremendous social factor among Southerners, as their generations moved from Virginia and the Carolinas across the South toward Texas. Church was the gathering place on the frontier for all the settlers in a valley or along a woods road. The church house was the meeting place for area's political contests. It was the schoolhouse. And it was entertainment and enlightenment when the circuit rider made it on his appointed Sunday.

Seasonal camp meetings on the wilderness frontiers were the gathering places for settlers for miles around. They came together once or twice a year to camp for a week or two in reunion with family and friends. They came to sing their praises and their hopes to a God whom they prayed would not abandon them on this wild frontier. The chorus of an old Sacred Harp song says, "We'll camp a while in the wilderness, And then we'll journey home."

Camp meetings were places where trades were made and land was sold and new families had their beginnings. And preachers contested mightily for souls through songs and sermons.

Religion and the church house and outdoor summer revivals were large parts of frontier life, and families have not forgotten what happened there. They still tell the old stories of memorable preachers, and they still give their children the Christian names of John Calvin and Charles Wesley. I remember one old lady telling me how all the women in her family would spend days washing on their feet so that those members would not look so rusty when the time came for the Sunday's foot washing.

To provide a proper religious setting for this chapter, we will begin with a description of a fairly typical religious service. Josiah Bolton, who was editor Abernethy's great-great-grandfather, was a Baptist preacher who moved from Whitley County, Kentucky, to Piney, Arkansas, and eventually to Old Greer County, Texas. Josiah built the church at Piney and Mrs. Estella Wright Szegedin tells one of her family's stories about attending that church. Mrs. Szegedin begins her story, saying, "I was born at Piney one hot July night in 1897. Mrs. Josar [Josiah] Bolton officiated at my birthin.'"

Josiah Bolton (1822–1900) the Primitive, Hard Shell, foot-washing Baptist preacher at Piney, Arkansas

"We're gonna have singin' all day and dinner on the grounds."

༺ • ༻

THE CHURCH AT PINEY
by Mrs. Estella Wright Szegedin
of Fort Smith, Arkansas

It seems most of the Piney, Arkansas, people came from Kentucky and were neighbors there and attended a church called Concord. When the men at Piney, under the leadership of Rev. Josar [Josiah] Bolton, decided to organize a church, they named it West Concord in memory of their beloved church in Kentucky. The denomination was regular Baptist [I am not sure what a "regular" Baptist was, but Josiah and his wife Betty Bolton were in a long line of Hard Shell, Primitive, foot-washing Baptists that reached well into the twentieth century.—Abernethy]

The church house I remember was a large white building with a tall steeple and two doors in front. The steps were three long flat rocks. There was one time when they had 300 members.

Couples separated at the front; the men sat on one side of the building and the women on the other. The middle row of homemade benches was occupied by young people and children. The pulpit platform was some two steps higher than the main floor. The preachers sat behind a wide, waist-high pulpit that hid them from the view of the audience. In one corner, called the Amen Corner, were two benches. One was a good step higher than the first one that was a step higher than the pulpit platform. The deacons of the church occupied these benches and they could see well over the congregation. In the other corner on the first floor level were two benches where the leading ladies of the church sat.

Since the church was a "fer piece" for most folks, they came in wagons with pallets for the young ones. The teams were unhitched and tied to the wheels. There they stomped and rattled the harness. Mothers brought snacks for the little loved ones who would be hungry before church was over, sometimes as late as two o'clock. Pallets were spread in the aisles where the youngsters slept. If they had to "go out" it meant a walk up the bushy lane for there were no outhouses.

When the preacher began his sermon his voice would be so low one could scarcely hear, but as time crept on it rose in volume and each sentence ended with, "Hi, Yes, sir, ah." His voice would fall into his chest then explode like a volcanic explosion. The veins in his neck stood out like whip cord, froth worked from the corner of his mouth, which he was constantly wiping with a bandana handkerchief as his shoulders heaved up and down in convulsions.

Some of the young men preferred to loiter in the church yard. When there was a foot washing, which they always did with communion, the ladies would hang their aprons on the windows to keep them from peeping at the procedure. When the wine was passed, the women took tiny sips but the men in the Amen Corner took such big swallows, the glass would have to be refilled time and again. However, after communion the men out-sang the women. There would be so much volume to their voices, they rattled the windows.

It was at this point that Brother Len Nillams led the prayer, and he would send up an elaborate and appealing prayer for his aged father who also sat in the Amen Corner. His stepmother, Aunt Nannie, would nudge their neighbor and say, "He's goin to hit his pa up for some money, shore."

There was always a protracted meeting each summer and the old folks went after the young who had reached the year of accountability, which was age twelve. When they got the mourner's bench full of young people, the older members took over. They prayed, shouted and beat them on the back until they would have to "come through" in self-defense.

One man had a son called King David, who was outside the fold of safety. He prayed a fervent prayer for his son that would have melted a heaven of brass. He prayed, "Oh, Lord Ah, Take King David, Ah, by the hair of his head and the seat of his britches Ah. And hold him over hell Ah, until he squalls like a coon Ah. Then if he don't repent Ah. Just drop him in." Fortunately, King David got saved. It was well that he did, for he saved a few lives at the baptizing that followed.

A baptizing was a great event that followed every revival meeting. Wagons rumbled through the hills to the creek. Young men on horseback rode squeaking saddles that added to the sound. Neighboring communities always attended the service. There was always a tremendous crowd. Candidates for baptism would line up, holding hands. The preacher would lead them into water waist-deep which was necessary for proper baptism. The congregation on the bank would be singing lustily.

At this particular baptizing, the preacher forgot the towel he carried on his shoulder to wipe the faces as they came up out of the water. When he looked, his disappointment showed and someone said, "Throw him a towel" and someone did. The towel was wrapped around a rock, but the towel unwrapped in midair and the rock hit the preacher in the chest with such force he fell backward into the water. The line of candidates panicked. The thin ones changed ends and the fat ones sat down and went under. The twelve candidates were crying, and some of the women on the bank were screaming. But King David saved the day as well as lives. He waded in and soon had everyone right side up. The baptism was finished on schedule.

ꕤ • ꕤ

ICE
by Thad Sitton
of Austin

Thad Sitton interviewed the late Frank Ashby of Houston County on March 19, 1992. Frank Ashby related the following story about his memories of one phase of his church and religious life.

"You've heard of Hard-shell Baptists all your life, haven't you? Well, over there in Antioch I still own the old spring where they used to have their foot-washings. They had a big old blackgum tree, that's what they made their curb out of. And every summer when they got their crops laid by, they'd get up over there from around Ratliff, Colthorpe, all that Steed country over there, Stubblefield. They'd all come up there in their wagons, gather up, and have a week's preaching. They had 'em an old log shed thing over there with a split-board roof, a 'tabernacle,' I believe they called it. And they'd bring their wives and kids.

"Anyway, Grandpa said they were doing pretty good, he thought. He lived over there pretty close to it. [Frank once asked his grandfather if he had ever washed anybody's feet, and he said that he had—in this spring in Antioch.] Anyway, a pretty good bunch of them people—just old farmers, all of 'em honest people. Well, some fellow had been to Crockett. And he come back and said they're making ice in August. Said they're boiling water up there at Crockett and making three-hundred-pound chunks of ice.

"Grandpa said them old coons got to slipping off, three or four in a bunch, said 'That man's lying. He just flat lie—we ought to throw him out of this church. Get him out of here!' Well, grandpa and Uncle Billy Steed, Billy Campbell—he was a preacher, Billy Campbell was—Uncle Billy Steed wasn't no preacher. He's like grandpa; he's just a man. But they said, 'Well, wait a minute now. We don't know if he's lying or not. We ain't been up there.' 'Yeah [they'd say], you know they can't make no ice in August.' So, they appointed my grandaddy, Uncle Billy Steed, and Uncle Billy Campbell to go to Crockett to see before they throwed him out of church.

"Grandpa had a fine pair of horses and one of these surreys, had a little light on it. Both of my uncles stayed all night with grandpa, and they left at daylight and went to Crockett, twenty mile. And they went down there and looked, and sure enough, they was actually boiling that water and making that ice. They looked at it and felt of it and eat some of it. They stayed all night up there, and the next morning they went down there and bought 'em a three-hundred-pound block of it, rolled it up in some cotton seed and that old bag that went around the cotton, put it in the surrey, and here they come.

"He said there was 40 or 50 men gathered up around that tabernacle over there. They told 'em when they'd be back. They laid the chunk of ice out there. Course, a little of it had melted, but they had it pretty well protected. 'That man wasn't lying, they're making that ice. They're boiling the water, steam's coming off the top of the water, making that ice.'

"What tickled me, he said some of 'em they went to slipping off four or five in a bunch, you know, and talking. And said, 'Billy Steed and Tom Ashby froze that last winter when we had that big cold spell. They had buried it then and brought it over here trying to fool us.'

"Some of 'em told Grandpa and Uncle Billy and Uncle Billy Campbell, and Grandpa said it made him mad as hell. There's a big old stump there that they preached off of—big un—he said, 'You'll get up around here. I want to tell you something.' They all gathered up around there. He said, 'Now, I want to tell you. Y'all pointed me and Billy Campbell and Billy Steed to go to Crockett and see about this ice business, gonna throw a man out of church.' Said, 'We went up there and we looked it over good and we brought you a chunk of ice down here. We didn't freeze that damn ice last winter and keep it all summer.' And said, 'If that's the kind of religion y'all got, you can just take it and go to hell with it, I'm gonna go on to the house.'

"And said Uncle Bill Steed told him, 'Get off of that stump, Tom, let me talk to 'em.' Grandpa said he stepped down off the stump and Uncle Billy give 'em a cussing, and he went to the house. And Uncle Billy Campbell, he was a preacher, but he got up there and ground 'em up.

"And Grandpa said there wasn't a man in that three or four communities that didn't go to Crockett. They still wouldn't believe it. He said they went in buggies and ox wagons, horseback, footing it—ever one of 'em had to go look. They wouldn't believe nobody. Well, grandpa said that's the last foot-washing he ever went to! He quit. They never did have no more church over there. They wouldn't believe one another. Ignorant, that's all they was, just damn ignorant. Grandpa said he told 'em, 'You ignorant bunch of sons-of-bitches, if that's the kind of religion y'all got, I don't want no part of it.'"

Sunny Dell, the church in the Tyler County wildwood

GRANDPA AND THE PREACHIN' HOUSE
by Ruth Garrison Scurlock
of Beaumont

Grandfather Hartrick founded the first Baptist church in a big room in his house—later built a nice wooden church—mother and dad married in it. Grandpa got mad at his neighbor—a deacon named Chaffin—on adjoining property to the church. He jacked the church up on log rollers and moved it seven miles south to Little River—still on Grandpa's property—church is still there. I don't know what they fussed about. I doubt if they did in a few years, but we grandchildren thought "Old Man" Chaffin wore horns.

⁍ • ⁎

FERGUSON'S BOYS
told by Mary Ann Long Ferguson
transcribed by Odessa Hicks Dial
and Alice Dial Boney
of Forest

Mr. Ferguson, my husband, had really told me very little about his early life but as we sat around after the evening meal, Grandpa Ferguson loved telling me things about my husband and the family in general.

The Fergusons were Methodists; in fact, your great-great-grandfather with his slaves built the first Methodist Church at Union Level, Virginia, and according to the news we received from there, the old log house is still under the siding which was later added when the church was remodeled. Perhaps some Fergusons still attend this church.

Grandpa was very strict about church attendance, but once he let the boys (nine of them) beg off going. When he got home, not a boy was in sight. He found them on the river fishing. Naturally they got a lecture, and it was a long time before they were able to persuade him again to let them stay home again—all kinds of promises were made not to go fishing. That Sunday, about the middle of the sermon everything was thrown into such confusion that the service broke up. Every Ferguson boy, with his horse to a sulky and bells on, circled round and round the church. Grandpa almost beat them home, he was in such a fury, and every boy received the thrashing of his life. After all these years, even Grandpa got a big laugh out of the incident.

WATT MOORMAN AND THE METHODIST
by John F. Short
of Center

[The Watt Moorman tale is a story taken from the Short family reminiscences of the Regulator-Moderator War in Shelby County in the early 1840s. Watt was one of the most notorious participants. The story belongs to more than one Shelby County family because of tangled kinship lines.]

Watt Moorman of Shelby County was known for his temper and his wild ways. One of his favorite pastimes was teasing ministers. One day as he was going along a road he met a Methodist preacher. They stopped to talk, and soon began to discuss religion. Moorman acted as if he were much concerned. He asked the preacher to go with him into the woods so that they would not be disturbed. They went into the woods, knelt, and had prayer. Moorman began to cry, and he claimed his repentance and acceptance of the Lord. The preacher was shedding tears of happiness because he thought he had saved Moorman. Suddenly Moorman jerked out his knife and turned around to ask, "What party do you belong to?"

"Why, I am a Methodist," the astonished minister replied.

"Are you a dancing Methodist?" asked Moorman.

This really alarmed the preacher as well as insulted him, and he stammered—"Why no, I can't dance—I never dance!"

"Well, you converted me to your religion; now I am going to convert you to mine." He told him that he was going to make a dancing Methodist of him, and when the preacher tried to explain that he did not dance, Moorman threatened to cut off his head. Then Moorman began to clap his hands, and the preacher began to dance with all his might. He danced a good while, and then Moorman let him stop.

"Now you are a dancing Methodist," Moorman told him. "You may go now, but lest I forget this, I am going to take a piece of your coat tail." He then took his knife and cut off part of the coat. The minister was then allowed to go on his way, rejoicing that his life had been spared.

ᐳ • ᐸ

FATHER PARISOT'S SADDLE
by Gwendolyn Wingate
of Hamshire

[The two following stories are church-family legends. The stories have been passed down in the traditions of the St. Mary's Catholic Church in Hamshire. —Abernethy]

"One interesting case," said Father Kelly, "was that of Father Parisot, away back in '52 or '53. He was sent out on a mission from Galveston by a bishop. Not a red cent had he. Parisot made it as far as Port Bolivar, getting his passage over there by some means in a passing boat. He went to the Johnson home, . . . and worked them out of a horse, but he yet had not saddle.

"Parisot tried from all available sources to get a saddle but had no luck. He then announced to the Johnson family that he had decided to remain as their guest until someone did furnish him with a saddle. That brought the remaining paraphernalia together on short order. With the horse and saddle he was able to reach his assigned post."

****

After the Civil War, Fathers J. M. Guyot and P. A. Levy came from Liberty to bayou country. The South had just lived through the cruel days of Reconstruction, and the people were suspicious of strangers. Monsignor E. A. Kelly told the story of Father Levy's experience on one of his missions:

"On a visit to Orange County, Levy was met by a band of natives, made to dismount and led to a large tree on the river bank that was famous for its lynchings. They showed the nicks that had been cut in its bark that acted as a record of the number of executions. Then they told him to hit the trail afoot, which he did, of course. But he said to them, 'Boys, you have the drop on me now. I'll do as you say, but, remember this. I'll be back, and I'll make you line up together and say the Lord's Prayer.'

"They didn't know that Levy had formerly been a sharpshooter in the army. Levy came back into Orange County shortly after, was met again by the group of unfriendly greeters, and carried out his promise.

"'I can knock the eye out of a fly with this rifle,' he told them and proceeded to prove it. Then he suddenly turned his rifle on them and told them to line up. They were so astonished at his marksmanship just displayed that they obeyed orders, and it is said that they all gladly repeated the Lord's Prayer, besides delivering his horse back to him."

A baptizing in the Big Thicket

ᕦ • ᕤ

AUNT OCIE'S CHURCH STORY
by Patrick Mullen
of Beaumont and Columbus, Ohio

I'll let my Aunt Ocie tell her own story about my great-grandmother, who was my hero. This story was being told when Aunt Ocie was a child. Aunt Ocie told it all her life, and my cousins and I now pass it on:

"When I was just a baby, my grandparents and all of the brothers—my dad had these seven brothers and three sisters—and the whole family had gone to church. It was a little country church, just a meeting house for everybody. And these renegades from the Civil War were still just running wild and robbing; and they would come and rob people's smokehouses that held all their meat or steal a cow or a calf and just butcher it right there.

"And we had gone to church, and during the service—now, I don't remember it because I wasn't but eighteen months old, but they told what happened. This group of renegades came, and they called and called, and wanted to disrupt the church service, and wanted everybody to come outside. They didn't want any preaching in that part of the state, wasn't going to have any church in Arkansas. So some of the boys went out and tried to talk to them, and these renegades set up grindstones. Now, if you know what that is, you know it has a big handle, and they sharpened knives out there and let it be heard inside this old log cabin church. The renegades let the sharpening be heard all while the services were going on. So the people in church prolonged the service as long as they could and finally some of the boys came out and talked with them, but they would not listen to any talking.

"Everybody wore a gun in those days, never went without a gun. Now Uncle Monroe was just real hot-headed, and if he'd had a gun that morning he would have gone out there and probably just shot the whole outfit of them. Do you know that not a single boy wore a gun to church that morning. They wore them all the time, but not a single one of those seven boys wore a gun to church that morning. So when the brothers went out they just used anything in the world. They lit into the renegades with these knives, and one of my daddy's brothers was just cut all the way down. His belt was the only thing that saved him. I don't know how many stitches they had to take in the end.

"Then one of the renegades started for me in the wagon, and my grandmother, my daddy's mother, took a water bucket, which was a big old wooden bucket, you know, with bails around it, and she took this water bucket and let this fella have it over the head with this water bucket when he climbed in the wagon where I was. And they had to take him in and have so many stitches taken in his head.

"And it was months later that some of the boys were in the barbershop, and this man was in there getting a haircut, and he let out an oath that long, and he said, 'Oh, be careful. That's where that Mullen woman laid my head open with a water bucket.'"

√ • √

COUNTRY PREACHER
by Georgeanne Hitzfeld
of Helotes

"Country preacher" was the moniker given him by one member of our family who, along with the rest of the family, breathed the fine air of the Methodist Church. William Booth Evans had been born in Florida of Methodist stock, indeed his great-grandfather, Jessie Coe, had been a Methodist Episcopal minister and had built the first Methodist church in Norfolk, Virginia.

Our Grandpa Willie Evan's father, a combatant in the War Between the States, never recovered from the War or the reversal of fortune brought to

The Country Methodist Preacher William Booth Evans, who "stuck to scripture" but left his family

those who relied on slave labor. Willie's father died early and his mother followed soon after—"dying of a broken heart"—it was always said.

Willie and his sister were shipped off to East Texas where he eventually married Eponina Kyle, also of Methodist stock. An educated man, known for his propensity to sit under a tree reading Shakespeare rather than plow the field before him, Grandpa Evans took to plowing a different kind of field to reap a different harvest.

He became a "country preacher" and a Baptist at that. However, "his preaching was sound, stuck to scripture," said one of his daughters. Grandpa would hold a "preaching session" by ringing a bell to call people to church. It became family tradition that whenever ten or more people were gathered it was said "there was enough people for a preaching."

When passing the plate at the small black churches near home where he was allowed to preach and his meager farming efforts weren't enough to sustain the family, he would make a bigger circuit. Thinking it unseemly to allow his family to accompany him to the black churches, he did sometimes take them on the larger circuit.

Once he took them with him to Abilene where he was going "to save the cowboys." "The cowboys didn't care to be saved," reported one of his daughters.

Grandpa had been talking a lot about the farm workers' attempt to unionize and needing to help them when he took off for good, leaving his wife, five daughters and son to fend for themselves.

Grandpa Evans returned many years later, a broken old man. He did have the strength to hold another preaching session and arranged to hold a revival at the Edgewood Baptist Church in San Antonio. All of his children were there, some even accompanying him on the piano and with song. He passed the plate one last time.

ᗏ • ᗍ

REDEMPTION AND FRIED CHICKEN
by Georgeanne Hitzfeld
of Helotes

Sam Anderson, who learned early the need for moral virtue, plowing a rocky field

In the late 1800s my grandfather, Sam Anderson, then a teenager, was taken along with three cousins to see a prison near their home in Nashville, Tennessee. Papa's uncle was taking the boys to the prison to teach a moral lesson.

They were given a tour of the facility, and as it was mealtime they were taken to where the prisoners were having lunch. Each prisoner had a plate of greens and cornbread. Beside each plate was a pile of cockleburs. The warden told the young boys that because of the amount of greens eaten they were harvested with a scythe (by the prisoners) rather than picked by hand, and were, therefore, full of cockleburs. Cooked as they were harvested, the prisoners had to pick the cockleburs from the greens as they ate.

Seeing the meager fare, the boys innocently asked if the prisoners ever got to eat anything besides greens and cornbread. The warden answered, "When they go home they can eat fried chicken."

ɯɷ • ɷɷ

PA GUNN'S CONVERSION EXPERIENCE
by Sarah Zoda
of Sherman

My grandmother, Mama Hughes, told me that her father, Pa Gunn, was a circuit preacher who rode from church to church preaching the gospel. Sometimes he preached at the Methodist and sometimes at the Baptist because they were the only denominations in their surrounding Mississippi community. In later years, Pa heard that a Catholic priest had moved to Mississippi, built a church and was teaching Catholicism. He was very disturbed by the news, so he decided to visit the priest even though it would take him two days on horseback, one to go and one to return. He felt there might be a possibility of converting the priest to Christianity by introducing him to the Holy Bible. Then he hoped the priest could convert his church members.

When Pa met the priest, he was very surprised when the priest told him it was extra nice to meet someone who loved God so much that he spent his time traveling from place to place spreading the Gospel. Since Pa had heard that priests kept the Bible locked so people could not read it, that was the first subject he wanted to discuss. Pa told the priest, "Let's be real honest with each other. I'll answer all questions with truth and love and hope you do the same." It was mutually agreed, so their discussions got off to a good start.

Their conversation lasted all day, and Pa agreed to return in a week to continue the discussion. Their meetings continued for a year. Pa learned the Holy Bible was chained to the altar to prevent it from being stolen, not to keep the word from the people. The paper used for the Bible was so expensive that thieves would steal it, erase the Holy Scripture and sell the paper to be used again.

Pa became convinced that the priest was a kind and holy man who knew the scripture better than anyone he had ever known. It was clear to him that the priest's mission was to teach, preach, and guide souls to God through Christ. Pa was even convinced that Christ started the Catholic Church when he said to Peter, "I for my part declare to you: you are the rock and on this rock I build my church."

In short, Pa became a Catholic.

7.
Ghosts and the Supernatural

I have always felt somewhat limited because neither side of my family of Baptists and Presbyterians passed along any ghost stories. They just weren't the kind of people to tolerate any ghosts except the Holy Ghost.

But one time, soon after we moved into our present home, an old frame house built in the 1880s, something supernatural, or at least difficult to explain, did happen. My oldest daughter Luanna, then fifteen years old, told me that every night when she woke up that there was a light in the middle of the room where she and Deedy and Maggie, the two other girls, slept. The light didn't scare her, but to prove a point about light rays not bending, I set up a cot and slept in the girls' room one night.

In the middle of the night, the girls awoke me, and sure enough, there was a ball of light in the middle of the room. I checked to see if it was a street light. It was not. And there was no moon. So all three of the girls and I agreed that in the room there was a light for which there was no logical explanation, and we went back to sleep. Whatever it was, it was friendly.

When Robert broke his leg, Hazel stayed up with him that first night, and she said that doors opened and closed and the floors creaked and the house made groaning noises. Years later, when the old man who had lived in the house before us died, we heard footsteps all during the night—and we had not yet heard that he had died.

But, as I said, my family does not hold much with ghosts. So, if you have a family ghost or an ancestral experience with the supernatural that has been the topic for a many-times-told tale, get the details from the rememberers in your family and put them down on paper before the story evaporates. You might have a legendary treasure that surpasses anything your grandmother threw away when she and old Tom cleaned out the attic.

ᎧᏰ • ᎧᏰ

THE PENNINGTON GHOST
by John Artie McCall
of Crockett

This story concerns my great-great-grandfather Richard Pennington (1809–1891) and his wife Polly (1813–1895). Richard, by the way, was a grand-nephew of Daniel Boone, his grandmother being a full sister of Daniel. Richard and Polly lived a few miles west of Grapeland, Texas, and I think this event occurred in the 1850s.

Late one afternoon Richard was riding his horse toward his home, and tired of riding, he started walking and leading his horse. As he neared his home he noticed a man walking ahead of him. Richard walked faster to catch up with the stranger but could not seem to get any closer. Richard then looked down and noticed that the stranger was not leaving any foot-prints in the sandy road.

A huge oak tree stood next to the road with a large limb extending across the road, probably about ten feet above the ground. As the stranger got even with the big oak tree, he disappeared into thin air. Richard, being a sober and a religious man, was greatly mystified by the phenomenon, and he and his wife Polly discussed the episode long into the night.

The next day a stranger walked up to the Pennington house and said that he broke horses for a living. His size and stature were similar to that of the stranger Richard had seen on the road the day before. After he made a deal with Richard to break one of his horses, the stranger mounted the un-broken horse, which immediately started bucking. The horse broke out of the lot and headed down the lane in hard running-jumps. When the buck-ing horse passed under the large oak, the stranger's head struck the limb extending over the road. He was killed instantly.

Since the stranger had only mentioned that he was from the state of Tennessee, Richard could not find out who he was or what town he was from. Richard buried him a short distance west of the fatal tree, and that location was later to become the Pennington family cemetery.

For many years after, late in the afternoon, a ball of light was often seen moving back and forth on the fatal limb. If the observer happened to be on

Edward Gaines Pennington and wife Nancy Jane of Houston County, who inherited the Pennington house and haunt.

horseback or in a wagon, the horse or mules would always be scared and try to run away.

A Grapeland cousin, Clifford Pennington, told me that his father told him of seeing the ghost at least twice in the 1890s. One time the ball of light came down out of the tree and moved toward him. At another time the ghost moved across the road in front of him. Both times his horse tried to run away.

When I was a boy I used to get my grandmother to tell me the ghost story many times. I often wished that the tree were still there so I could see the ghost late some afternoon.

❦ • ❧

RESTLESS SPIRITS
by Elaine Scherer Snider
of Conroe

Two ghost stories haunt the family of Burley Lamb, a lifelong East Texas resident. The older one, told by his stepfather, concerns the restless spirit of a murdered woman. The second story is a childhood experience related by his mother.

When Mr. Lamb's stepfather was a boy, he and his friends played often near a spring that ran close to their property. Late in the afternoon, they would often see a woman with a bucket drawing water from the spring. She was a familiar sight and did not arouse much interest among the boys.

One night the woman's husband killed his wife by cutting off her head with an ax. The man was quickly caught and punished. Several days later, to the boys' amazement, the woman appeared as usual at the spring in late afternoon. Now, however, she was headless. Running towards her, the boys were astonished to see her slowly dissolve into emptiness. From then on, in the late afternoon, the headless woman continued to draw water from the spring, always eluding those who drew too near.

The oldtimers explain such an occurrence through the spirit's desire to have the body made whole again. Mr. Lamb does not remember whether the body and its head were buried together (which they probably were), but belief surrounding a mutilated body could easily develop into such a legend.

Mr. Lamb's mother tells this story about the night her father died. At that time her family lived in a house with a dogtrot. Behind the dogtrot was a room normally used as a diningroom but often used for sleeping quarters when needed. On the night of her father's death, Mr. Lamb's mother, who was about thirteen years old, gave up her bed to a visiting relative and slept on a cot in the diningroom. Her father's death from disease had been preceded by a period of confinement, so the young girl had not enjoyed the company of her father for several weeks.

Tired out from the day's sadness and the numerous visits from neighbors and relatives, she quickly fell asleep. Sometime during the night, she was awakened by a heavy pressure on her feet. She woke up to see her father, as healthy as he had been before his illness, sitting on the end of her cot. When he saw that she was awake, he began talking to her, although Burley's mother could not understand all that he said. When she reached for him, he disappeared. He never returned.

୬ • ଔ

BROTHER MURDER
by Timothy Lee Jones
of Allen

My grandfather told me, along with my cousin and other younger relatives, stories every time we got together at reunions, but there was one that always stuck in my mind.

Back close to the turn of the century my grandfather had two great-uncles only a year apart in age. They grew into young manhood on a small farm in central Texas and were always very close. But there came a day when that bond was broken, not by a difference of opinion but because of a common interest. Both fell in love with the same girl.

At first it started out as a couple of boys competing for the same goal, but as time went on it grew into a serious contest between two stubborn and determined young men, which was not helped at all by the young lady. Things were shaky, but one day the whole thing came to an abrupt and tragic end. Barney, the older, and James were both in the hayloft working. Both had been mad for quite a while but my great-great-grandfather had felt their working together would do some good. Well, it didn't, and finally they started to fight, not just arguing but an all-out fight.

Things might have been settled then and there, but James took a swing at Barney and Barney dodged, and James fell out of the hayloft into a pile of hay on the ground. Barney laughed at first, but when James didn't move he got down from the loft fast to see how he was. He reached his brother about the same time as his father, and there they found James with a pitchfork stuck in his chest, and he was already dead.

Barney went a little crazy and wouldn't talk to his father or listen and ran off across the field behind the house. The whole family was upset not only about James, but Barney stayed away and no one saw him for a couple of days. Finally, the third night my great-grandfather heard noises in the barn and went to investigate. When he went into the barn he found Barney hanging from the rafter with a rope around his neck.

Some people said that after he had killed his brother that the young lady would have nothing to do with him. His family however believed, and still does, that the agony and guilt of causing the death of his own brother drove him to kill himself.

After telling us this story my grandfather told me that the ground worn away by the toes of Barney's boots would not fill up, that no matter how much they tried, the marks of his boots were still there. He said that the grooves could be seen several years ago even. We asked him to show us, but he said that the old barn had burned down and the marks were buried under the ruins.

ᴥ • ᴥ

UNCLE FATE'S JEALOUS WIVES
by Lee Winniford
of Houston

Uncle Fate lived a long, busy, and procreative life. Three wives and several of his small children had been buried in his family plot before he finally

The Long Cemetery in Hopkins County, where Uncle Fate's wives slept uneasily in their graves

joined them there. (According to legend, at least two other wives had chosen other burial arrangements.)

When Uncle Fate's first wife was lying terminally ill, a young kinswoman was brought in to tend her. Love blossomed between Uncle Fate and his wife's attractive nurse, and the dying woman was bitterly aware of the affair.

Uncle Fate waited only a fraction of the "decent" mourning time before marrying his new love. But that marriage, too, soon came to a tragic end; that wife got milk leg after the birth of a child and died, and the baby died soon after. Although family and neighbors protested, Uncle Fate buried the second wife beside the first. He provided both wives with store-bought tombstones.

Strange things, however, kept happening to the succession of tombstones that he placed on the second wife's grave. The first sank into the grave after a heavy spring rain; a second fell from its pedestal and crumbled; a third disappeared completely. As other wives and additional offspring occupied more and more of Fate's time and energy, he eventually admitted defeat and marked the favored second wife's grave with a bois d'arc post.

What had happened to the second wife's gravestones remained a mystery, but many people believed they knew the answer. Surely it must have been the angry spirit of Fate's first wife, indignant that she must rest beside her hated rival for all eternity.

୭ • ଓ

TALES FROM MR. HATCHER
by Patsy Johnson Hallman
of Nacogdoches

Mr. Hatcher came to our small, rural community in 1939 to teach agriculture. Tall, well built, and handsome, he brought with him a young attractive wife and three small children. They came from Deep East Texas—from the land of tall pine trees, sandy lanes, and, if possible, areas even more rural than ours. During their first years with us they rented first one house then another, all in the vicinity of the school, and each one near our home. Not one of the houses had a storm cellar, so an early friendship with our family was assured because we had a good storm cellar.

The Hatchers and the Johnsons became friends right away. The terrible fear of storms that our father and Mrs. Hatcher shared brought the families together when the first spring storm brought pelting rains and wind-filled thunderstorms. And with each subsequent storm the relationship strengthened.

Our cellar, or "storm house" as we called it, was a good one, lined with rough logs and large enough for our family of six and neighbors who might want to come if there was a particularly bad storm. The Hatchers always came. We children were delighted! To us, a storm and a good time with the Hatcher kids came as a package. In their fright over the storm, Daddy and Mrs. Hatcher made us sit quietly on the benches in the cellar, but Mother and Mr. Hatcher were not so nervous about the storms, and we could usually count on their allowing a little storytelling and play.

If we were lucky, when we left the cellar after thirty minutes or so of waiting for the storm to subside, the clouds would still look somewhat threatening, and the Hatchers would go into our house to wait to see if the storm cloud would go around or if another one would come up making a return trip to the cellar necessary.

We would go inside the house, sit around the fire, and listen as Mr. Hatcher talked. He was a master storyteller. His ghost stories were the best we had ever heard. We children shivered as he related story after story while the storms raged outside our small frame house.

He said that the old two-storied MacFarland house in the community they came from had a ghost. The house stood on the county line between Marion and Cass Counties, and the neighbors believed the house was haunted.

Once a family of travelers was going through the community in a covered wagon, and they needed some place to spend the night. They asked at the country store if there was a place to stay, and the storekeeper told them they were welcome to camp out in the empty MacFarland house. The family got all settled in. They made a fire in the big fireplace, cooked their supper, lighted a kerosene lamp, and laid out sleeping pallets around the fire. Just as they were about to go to bed, the lamp light slowly faded away. The mother relit the lamp, and they continued getting ready to sleep. Again the light disappeared. This time, she relit the lamp and called to her husband to look at what was happening. As they watched, three fingers slowly moved down inside the lamp globe and pinched out the light! The father loaded his gun, pulled the pallets close to the fire, and sat in the rocker all night guarding his family. They made haste to leave at first light!

Another day one of the young men in the community decided he would find the MacFarland ghost, or "haint," as some people called it. He bragged to his friends that he would find out what was causing the haunting sounds that came from the house each night.

Taking a double-barreled shotgun the young man set up camp in the deserted house just at dusk. After building a big fire in the fireplace in the front room he pulled a rocker close to the fire and prepared to wait out the ghost. Soon, he heard a suspicious noise overhead.

"That's it!" he said to himself. "That's the ghost!"

As the scraping, wailing noise continued, he became too frightened to climb the stairs to find out what was happening. He sat petrified, trying to decide what to do. Then after an even louder noise, down the stairs came the biggest black cat the young man had ever seen.

The cat spoke. "Well," it said, "I see there are two of us here tonight."

"Yes," replied the man, "but if you will wait just a minute there will be only one."

Out of the house and down the road the young man went. He ran until he was exhausted, and thinking he was safe, he looked backward. The cat was right behind him.

"You run pretty fast," said the cat.

"Not half as fast as I can," replied the man, and away he raced.

That was the last time anyone ever tried to contact the MacFarland ghost.

৶ • ৶

DEATH OMEN
by Donna McFadden
of Beaumont

The supernatural has always been a favorite topic in folk tales. Lending an atmosphere of open-mouthed suspense, tales involving the supernatural have always been popular within family groups. This particular awe-inspiring tale of mystery took shape in Port Arthur, Texas, within the last decade; and it has never left that city's boundaries since the occurrence of the supernatural event from which the tale evolved. The story is told, as the truth, by Mrs. Renell Perron who has heard it many times from Mrs. P. W. Simonton, the only witness to the event.

Several years ago, Mrs. Simonton's first son, Paul, was working on a ship in Port Arthur, when he developed a serious respiratory infection. Since he had been placed under his mother's care by the family doctor, the Simontons decided that Paul's younger brother, Robert, should sleep in the same room with him. The boy had been ill only a few days when an unexplainable event took place in the Simonton household, an event that was to determine the fate of a member of that family.

One night, Mrs. Simonton was awakened from her sleep by a chilling breeze to find a woman dressed in black, standing just inside her bedroom. Being the realistic, down-to-earth person she was, Mrs. Simonton was more than ready to throw this nervy, midnight intruder out of her house—until she suddenly realized that the lady was not human. Instead of human features, the visitor had a bony, hollow-eyed face, and a mysterious, translucent appearance.

Out from her long, draped sleeves slid a ghostly white hand. Then, motioning with her spiny finger, the death image beckoned to the startled housewife. Speechless, Mrs. Simonton shook her head negatively, shuddered, then slid a little further under the bedcovers while the unwelcome caller stood waiting. Unsatisfied with this reluctance, the weird visitor slowly moved closer toward the bed. Before Mrs. Simonton could move away, this mysterious lady had pulled back the covers and turned toward the door.

Taking the woman's actions as a cue to follow, Mrs. Simonton got to her feet and followed the ghostly figure down the hall. The mysterious image kept moving until she entered the boys' room. Mrs. Simonton quickened her pace until she reached the boys' doorway. Just as Mrs. Simonton entered the door, the fading image pointed her long, bony finger at Paul and then disappeared. With the woman's departure, Mrs. Simonton, out of a mother's instinct, took each of her sleeping sons' hands into her own. Robert's hand was warm with life while Paul's hand was strangely cold! At that moment, Mrs. Simonton dazedly realized the full significance of the mysterious event. Paul Simonton's untimely death the next day supported Mrs. Simonton's heartfelt belief that a death omen had been revealed to her that night.

🙚 • 🙘

GRANDFATHER'S GHOST
by Gail Simon
of Angleton

The following story is that of a family ghost. It was told to Miss Gail Simon of Angleton by R. A. Dudley of Angleton, the grandson of the ghost.

About thirty years ago, his grandfather died in the house in which the family now lives. Mrs. Dudley, the daughter, worried about him for about six months after his death, for she feared that he might not have gone to heaven. So one night she asked the Lord for a sign that her father *had* gone to heaven. That night she awoke in the early hours of the morning for apparently no reason. There, across the room sat her father, calmly rocking in his old rocking chair. He did not speak to her or signal her in any way.

Since that time, the ghost has not been seen by anyone but Mrs. Dudley, but the light in his old room has flickered on and off and no one could be found there. Mr. Dudley, who now occupies the ghost's room, has upon different occasions been in the room when the light switch has been turned on and off and has seen no one at the switch. Also, upon different occasions, he has been awakened during the night by the weight of someone on his chest. He is unable to move, yet there is no one else in the room. Upon asking his grandfather to move, the weight disappears. The ghost had only bothered people in this one room until last year when he moved to the kitchen which he now also haunts by switching the lights on and off.

◡◠ • ◠◡

RETURN FROM DEATH
by Carole Bruce
of Jacksonville

When Grandma Bullock was a young girl of about thirteen, she became very ill with a fever. After several days she died. She was dressed in her best Sunday frock and laid out on the "cooling board." Before they were to put her in the coffin, an uncle decided to cut off a lock of her hair to have as a keepsake. When he bent down to cut it, the girl opened her eyes and said, "Don't cut my hair off."

After her recovery, Grandma Bullock lived to a ripe age in the seventies and during her life was in a sense an amateur doctor. My own grandmother remembers people coming to see Grandma Bullock when they were ill. Apparently some of the people believed that she had a special gift for curing since she herself had "come back from the dead."

◡◠ • ◠◡

THE LEGEND OF A DREAM
by Cynthia Lowry
of Coolidge

Mrs. Hately Lowry, whose mother was a Jinkins, told this story to Cynthia Lowry:

It was 100 years ago or more—Mr. Jinkins doesn't know the exact date—when his grandfather, a tall bearded man named Greenberry Jinkins, brought his wife and other relatives from Alabama to Texas.

They especially wanted good water, but when they made camp one night in what is now Cherokee County, they could find only muddy streams in the wilderness. Greenberry Jinkins was at a loss as to which way to turn to find better water.

They made camp that night on the hard ground, and Greenberry Jinkins was beginning to think that coming to Texas may not have been for the best after all. However, the next morning his wife rushed up to her husband and announced: "I know where we can go to find water." She then went on to explain that she had dreamed of a big, stooping oak tree leaning toward the east. Near its roots was a spring bubbling out of the ground. The location was north of the camp, she said.

Greenberry Jinkins scoffed at his wife's dream, but she persisted, and urged her husband to look for the oak tree: "It was too plain, it was as though I was right there looking at the water, and it was bright and clear like crystal."

As husbands often do, Jinkins yielded to his wife's wishes, and the party hacked its way northward through the underbrush. In time Mrs. Jinkins gasped and pointed to a large oak tree leaning eastward. Greenberry went to it, and there at its base he found a stream of fresh water bubbling from the earth.

With axes and a cross-cut saw the group cut pine logs to build a dogtrot house—two rooms with a hall down the middle. They smoothed the flat side of the split logs for tables and benches. They built a pole fence around the place to keep out wild hogs and Indians.

In one room of the house Greenberry Jinkins' son, Dolph Jinkins, was born, and he lived for 92 years in the same house and died there. And in this same room, Greenberry's grandson, Lonnie Jinkins, was born, and still lives there and he is now 64.

Lonnie Jinkins will sit today in the open hallway of the old house, on the same shaven log bench his grandfather made, and recall the legend of his grandmother's dream. And a few feet away, the spring still bubbles cool, fresh water, as bright and clear as crystal.

പ • ை

THE GHOST OF GHOSTY BRANCH
by Andrew Brannen to Frances B. Vick
of Saron and Dallas

My father, Andrew Brannen, told us about the ghost that lived about a mile from where he was born and raised in Trinity County. As he told it, the ghost haunted a branch about half a mile east of the Thornton Church and cemetery. Ghosty Branch was about two miles from Saron sawmill.

A prominent man in the community, while riding his horse across Ghosty Branch one night, encountered this ghostly thing. It was a white, grayish-colored mass which came floating through the trees and got behind him on his horse. It rode a short ways, grabbed him by the throat and choked him, cutting off his breath. Then it left and floated back through the trees.

The ghost caused many frightening incidents over the years. One man who was living across Ghosty Branch from the Saron sawmill had the ghost catch him and make him late for his job at the sawmill. Many romances were cut short because some girls lived across Ghosty Branch, and some boys were afraid to go to visit them at night.

༄ • ࿂

MYSTIC MAGNOLIA
by Herb Sanders
of Pottsboro

It was November 1969, and I was in Canton, Texas, for my annual opening day hunt with Bill, my brother-in-law and the closest person I have ever had to a brother. The day was perfect for a hunt. The day before there had been a weak norther and the temperature had dropped to the mid-sixties. To a bird hunter this means the birds will be flying, not staying on the ground and running.

Our destination was a 422-acre farm owned by Mr. Leroy White, a member of the church where Bill was pastor. We had been hunting on this land ever since Bill became pastor of the Starr Baptist Church six years before. Birds were plentiful here, but at times hard to find because of the heavy cover. We arrived at the Whites' house, and after a short visit and an assurance to Mrs. White that we would be back for dinner, we took off for our favorite section of the farm.

The day was right, the weather was right, the dogs were working like crazy, but the birds were not cooperating. We gave up on the open ground and headed into the heavy cover of pines, oaks, and shrubs to try our luck there. The birds were in the cover, but the trees and brush were so dense one shot was all we could get, and it had to be a good one.

The moment I saw the tree was after one of the covies had flushed and the bird I was on, for some unknown reason, had taken off almost straight up. I was on him as he was climbing, but the bird was spared because my full attention became fixed on the most magnificent magnolia tree I had ever seen.

The tree had to be one hundred feet tall. Seeing that tree, I felt the same way I had when I was a young man standing on the deck of a destroyer in the Pacific seeing my first whale. I knew a whale was big, but I did not

Herb Sanders, who has seen the Mystic Magnolia

know what big was until I saw that whale cavorting like a playful kitten. The tree had a perfect cone shape, with the bottom branches almost on the ground and extending from its trunk at least fifty feet in all directions. I suddenly became aware of the aroma. The sweetness was overwhelming.

Wondering why I had not taken the shot, Bill followed my eyes and was now as mesmerized as I. We approached the tree with a feeling that was close to reverence. I cannot tell you how long we stood and marveled at this specimen of flora, but it was a while. Our main question was why had we not come upon this tree before? We had hunted this area before. How could we have missed such a huge portion of the landscape?

The rest of the hunt was fair to awful. We probably had the least amount of birds of all our hunts on this land. It was getting close to noon, and we anticipated one of Mrs. White's fantastic meals in front of us, so we headed for the house.

In this part of the world dinner is the noon meal, and after dinner we were sitting around talking when I brought up the subject of the tree. "Mr. White, that is one fantastic magnolia tree you have on your property," I said.

He looked at me rather expressionlessly and stated that there were no magnolia trees on his property. Bill and I exchanged glances. He had to be kidding. As we looked at his expression, he didn't appear to be kidding. Bill said, "Come on, Leroy, that thing is a hundred feet tall if it's an inch."

Mr. White repeated that there were no magnolia trees on his property except the little one his wife had planted a couple of years ago. He was seventy-two years old and had lived on and farmed this land all of his life. Who were we to argue with him?

We had planned on just a morning hunt, but after dinner we decided the weather was so pleasant we would make a day of it. We hunted like we had never hunted before. We hunted for that hundred-foot tree and never did find it. We hunted the next day for birds and the tree. We found plenty of birds, but no tree. We continued to hunt on this same land until 1980, when we decided to retire from hunting for good. If the tree was there or is there, it eluded us.

This is the first time I have told this story. Because of his status as a respected minister, I see Bill as a more credible storyteller and have always allowed him to tell the story. One day when we were discussing the mystic magnolia, Bill said to me "We might as well face it. That tree was not of this world, and when we are no longer of this world we will find our tree."

"O.K., Bill," I replied, "I'll meet you there."

ᥬ · ᥬ

CRAZY WOMEN IN THE RAFTERS
by Paul Patterson
of Crane

During a land boom some years before, this sacred West Texas soil had felt the sting of nesters' plows, but those grangers soon starved out and drifted back down east, leaving Upton County on the Pecos one of the most thinly populated parts of the state. These departing squatters sold or leased their homesteads to ranchers who utilized the windmills and corrals but left the houses to wrack and ruin. These dilapidated shacks were to awake me to the horrible realization that God alone didn't ramrod this whole country. The devil also had a hand in it. This shattering bit of intelligence was passed down to me by my bigger brothers, Sog and Fush, while we were jostling along in the wagon on the road to JM ranch headquarters in 1915. They let me in on a secret that was to haunt me for years to come.

"Paul, see that old nester shack yonder?" Fush asked.

"Yeah," I said, neither impressed or depressed.

"Well, it's haunted. Full of ghosts and boogers."

Profoundly moved, I looked over at my bigger brother for a word of denial, rebuttal, or refutation, preferably all three.

"Sure enough, Sog?"

"Sure enough!" he said, solemn as a sick owl. "Either that or its rafters are chuck full of crazy women!" (We always confused rafters and joists in those days.)

"Awwww. Bawwww. Boo hoo. Ahhhh."

"Now, dry up that bawlin', Paul," Sog said, glancing uneasily toward Papa up on the spring seat. "They won't bother you less'n you stir'em up. Honest. Besides, they're just as skeered of you as you are of them."

"How you know?"

"It's what the cowboys say."

That settled it. Settled it, that is, as regards the mutual horror established between myself and ghosts, haunts, and boogers. Cowboys knew it all. This I knew because Papa was one. And how I wish he could have overheard this dialog taking place in the back of the wagon, so he could have verified it just for the record. But I didn't dare relay this bit of intelligence to him—at least not in the presence of Sog and Fush.

"Why all crazy women up in them rafters, and no crazy men?"

"Men like it out here. And don't go crazy. Exceptin' sheepherders. Women don't like it, and they go loco from pure lonesome."

"Then, Sog, why don't crazy sheepherders take to the rafters?"

"They are afraid of women, crazy or not. Druther be took to jail. Besides, they don't like women nohow."

"Don't like women?" Fush put in. "Then they ain't as crazy as I thought."

"Ain't they no crazy men at all besides sheepherders?"

"No. Only a couple of really real wild ones. But you won't never ketch them in no rafters."

"Where do they stay at then?" I asked, alarmed again to the verge of bawling.

"Long ways from here," Sog assured me, glancing uneasily toward Papa. "One runs down in Tippitt's on the Pecos. The other'n——one with his throat cut from ear to ear and head hangin' back 'tween his shoulders—he runs west of here way over in the Y beef pasture."

"Sog," Fush put in, "you forgot about the JM ghost. The one that allus rides in on a white horse."

Paul Patterson, who has seen
the very house where the crazy
women live in the rafters

"We apt-apt to run across him on this trip?" I asked, my blood clabbering
and my throat too constricted to bawl.

"Not 'less we stay till after dark," Sog reassured me—or thought he did.
Ordinarily I would have pressed for details, but now I was too pressed for
means by which to pry Papa loose from his augering the JM hands until
dark, as was his custom.

P. S.: Legend has it that they truly *did* find a crazy woman one time
crouching up in the joists of an old shack out in a greasewood flat.

8.
Feuding and Fighting

❧

A feud in a family, or between families, is like a civil war in a nation; it is cataclysmic during its eruption, and it is never really over. A feud is not just a fight or a shootout; it is a long-held grudge that explodes on provocation. It is a strange and sad thing in a family feud that a person can hate his kinfolks when he gets crosswise with them a lot more than he hates people outside of the family. Some of this intensity comes from his subconscious feeling of guilt that results from being at odds with his own blood.

Probably some of the intensity of feeling and hot blood comes from the nature of the settlers that moved across the South on their ways to Texas. Most were of Scottish, Irish, English, or Scotch-Irish ancestry, were contentious by nature, and had battling in their genes. Add to that several generations of marching through a lawless wilderness and making their own rules, and you come up with a society of people who are ready to solve a problem the quickest way possible, by elimination. The result was that in some cases whole communities, even counties, were involved in a feud. And families and neighbors clung together for survival. It became "us against them," and the winners lived and the losers died or moved on.

And then there were your casual, sometimes accidental fights and fits of violence that were consequential enough to become a mark in the family's history.

THE MITCHELL-COKER FEUD
by Dorothy Kennedy Lewis
of Ore City

Great-Grandpaw Mitchell was small of stature but large of mouth and high of temper. When he, his wife, and his sister came from Alabama to Texas, it was probably because he was run out of town—either as a welcher in a deal or because his life had been threatened because corn whiskey and high tempers don't mix. At any rate, soon after he, Grandmother, and Aunt Emma arrived he was able to marry Emma off to Uncle Bud Coker. Uncle Bud was as ornery as Great-Grandpaw Mitchell so a feud was inevitable.

Grandpaw was a very poor horse trader and continually made bad deals that Uncle Bud loved to tell about in the saloons they both visited on Saturday nights. The more Uncle Bud drank the sorrier Grandpaw became in his stories to the saloon visitors.

One night Uncle Bud was very drunk and Grandpaw had had enough of his insults for one night. So Grandpaw slapped him full in the mouth. But as you may have guessed Grandpaw had made another bad deal. Uncle Bud got Grandpaw's finger in his mouth and chewed it so badly that the finger had to be amputated at the second joint.

Grandpaw was drug bleeding from the saloon with the threat that he would "get even."

The following Saturday night Grandpaw Mitchell went to the saloon with his gun. He had full intentions of having it out with Uncle Bud. When Grandpaw walked in, Uncle Bud was already there at the far end of the bar. Grandpa drew a bead on Uncle Bud and fired. Just as he pulled the trigger, Uncle Bud turned his head and the shot removed his six front teeth—top and bottom. Strange as it may seem, that shot settled the score, and the men were fast friends for the remainder of their lives.

෨ · ෨

DUTCH JOE AND THE WOLF'S TAIL
by Gwendolyn Wingate
of Hamshire

Old man Perry McFaddin was having a lot of trouble with wolves killing calves on the ranch. He told Dutch Joe he would give him a bounty for every wolf he could kill, and just to bring in the wolf's tail as proof that he had killed it. Sure enough, every time Dutch Joe came to town he brought a wolf tail up to Old Man Perry's office, and Old Man Perry paid him. That went on for a long time, till Old Man Perry McFaddin began to believe that all the wolves in Jefferson County were congregating on his ranch. But then he noted that the tail looked mighty mangy and worn. Finally one day he caught Dutch Joe. Old Man Perry had been leaving the wolf tail on the desk for somebody in the office to dispose of. This time he caught Dutch Joe stuffing that old wolf tail in his coat pocket so he could collect on it again. That was when they fell out.

They were getting a little too old to fight it out, so when they met, this is what they'd do: Old Man Perry would rein his horse off to the side a little so as to pass Dutch Joe on his horse. Each man would pull out his pistol and shoot at something nearby, neither of them letting on that they saw the other. After proving to his own satisfaction that he could hit anything he shot at, each man would ride on by the other without saying a word.

ᴄᴏ • ᴏᴄ

JONES-SMITH FEUD
by Patsy Johnson Hallman
of Nacogdoches

Around 1900, the Jones-Smith feud in Cass County started after the Jones girl divorced the Smith boy. There was bitter argument between the families. It increased to hatred as the months passed. Finally the elder Mr. Smith challenged the elder Mr. Jones to a duel. The duel was scheduled for one morning at Oak Creek. The plan was for them to meet, turn back to back, walk fifty steps, then shoot it out. Mr. Jones, however, had a private plan, which he and his boys executed a few minutes before the encounter was to take place. As Smith approached the dueling ground, Jones shot him in the stomach with two rounds of buckshot. One of the boys emptied a .30-30 Winchester into him. And as Smith lay dying, Jones burst his head open with a hatchet and scooped out his brains, slinging them against a tree.

Jones was brought to trial and convicted on evidence gathered from the scene. The forefinger on his right hand had always been crooked, and the bloody mass of brains smeared on the tree clearly showed the shape of the crooked finger. He was given a fifty-year sentence.

After about ten years, he was released from prison. In a few days after he came home there was to be a meeting of the Farmer's Alliance at the community church, and Jones decided to attend. Now Little Bill Smith, son of the murdered man, heard that Jones was coming to the meeting. Grown up now, Little Bill met Jones at the door to the church, and with a loud oath, shot him three times. Jones' tongue was split, his arm, shoulder, and hip were broken, but he was not dead. In fact he lived to die a natural death years later.

Little Bill Smith was not brought to trial for the shooting. Said the foreman of the grand jury that considered the case, "Little Bill, we can't find a thing in the world to bill you for, but just remember, you can't go round every day shooting men!"

ها • ها

THE SULLIVAN FAMILY FEUD
by Mary Means Sullivan
of Brownsville

The Sullivan family feud is a story of a conflict between in-laws, mainly between Audie Christie and Doc Durham, both of whom had married Sullivan sisters, Laura and Ethel. The feud is set in Houston County in the early 1900s.

The seeds of the feud were sown early. Doc Durham is alone responsible for this first incident. Whenever he needed any timber for cross ties, he would select a tree that was on the Christie land. Doc was warned by several relatives that he was simply wading in and digging his own grave. The Sullivans did not hesitate to tell him he was making a mistake. Doc ignored all these warnings, and he continued to agitate the Christies.

One evening the Durham boys all went to a big dance. They enjoyed their whiskey and dancing until they overheard a comment made by Jewel Christie about the girlfriend of one of the Durham boys. Sollie and Little Doc immediately jumped on Jewel and nearly cut him to death. The Durhams hurriedly left the dance. Jim Sullivan picked Jewel up and carried the seriously wounded boy home. The doctor sewed Jewel up, and he lived.

After Jewel was cut up by the Durhams, the situation became more strained. More trouble developed. The Christie boys began shooting Durham animals without noticing the mark on the animals' ear, which was the identifying mark on an open range. They would shoot the Durham hogs and leave them to rot. Accusations were made and tempers flared.

The situation between the Durhams and the Christies was not only unwholesome but also dangerous. Doc attended the big dances, drank his whiskey, and ignored his wife's pleas to stay at home. A big dance was given one evening at a home rented by the Harris family. All the windows at the dance were closed and the shades drawn except for one. The host gave Doc a bottle of whiskey and pulled a rocker over in front of the only open window. Doc was laughing and enjoying himself; he was trying to pull the stopper out of the bottle when he was suddenly shot twice through the open window. Doc fell to the floor dead; blood was everywhere.

The lawmen at the dance hurried outside to search for the killer. Apparently someone had expected trouble; otherwise, the lawmen would not have been so handy. They were able to track the murderer across the fields to the Christie home. Uncle Henry Christie (Audie's father) and Laura had conveniently gone visiting over the weekend, as was usual whenever Henry had any dirty work for his boys to do. Audie refused to help the sheriff; the sheriff then forced his way in to search the house. Audie's shoes were found in a box under the bed. These shoes were compared to the tracks; they matched perfectfully. Audie's shoes even had a crack in one sole as was shown in the footprint near the window. Audie was charged with the murder of Doc Durham at the district court at Crockett. He was found guilty and sentenced to ninety-nine years in the state penitentiary at Huntsville. If he was paroled, Audie was not to live in Texas.

Animosity only continued to grow deeper between the Christie and Durham boys. Carr Durham seemed to harbor a deeper hate than the others. The Durham boys tantalized and threatened the Christie boys; they warned Dewitt and Jewel Christie that they would shoot them on sight. Both families carried guns wherever they went.

One afternoon Carr Durham was returning on horseback from a hunting trip with his Uncle Cruise Durham near Ratcliff. Carr had three guns on his horse; one was a pump shotgun and another was an eleven-shot .32 rifle. As he approached the lumber camp called the Diboll front, he spotted his Uncle Henry and the Christies riding up in a wagon. The Christies had been to the mill to grind some corn. Dewitt and Jewel were picking on a guitar in the back of the wagon.

When Uncle Henry saw Carr he yelled, "What in the hell are you doing with so many guns?" Henry then appeared to reach back in the wagon as if to get a gun. Carr quickly answered Henry's question with gunfire. Henry fell over dead. Dewitt and Jewel made a break for the woods. Carr shot Jewel down and finally stopped Dewitt. Dewitt begged on his knees "Carr, don't kill me; I'll be your servant for the rest of your life." Carr ignored Dewitt's plea and shot him.

Carr was tried for the murder of his uncle and cousins. He pleaded self-defense, even though he said, "I killed them because they killed my Dad." The jury cleared the murder charges. Later when Carr talked of the murders, his chin would quiver and his eyes fill with tears. He later confessed to his Aunt Pearl that the murders would always haunt him and that he would never understand why he killed them.

Carr was killed a few years later at Alazan in a gunfight. One of the Alazan boys wanted to see how tough Carr really was. Little Doc then drew his gun to kill his brother's killer, but the gun would not fire and he was shot. Nearly all the Durham boys met a tragic death.

Audie was pardoned in 1928 by Texas governor Ma Ferguson; he lived in Houston until his death.

৩ • ৩

A NEIGHBORLY DISPUTE
by Jo Wilkinson Lyday
of Houston

The central story in the canon of Great-grandfather Frank Wilkinson concerns his disagreement with a neighbor over livestock. This tale elevates Great-grandmother Emma to the role of a larger-than-life heroine worthy of such a man. As a teenager, I heard the old story about the neighbor's pig that regularly strayed over and kept rooting up Emma's kitchen garden. Twice Frank caught the pig and took it back to the neighbor, the second time warning the man that if it happened again, he would kill the pig. The neighbor responded that if Frank killed his animal, he would kill Frank. The pig invaded Frank's territory one more time and Frank killed it.

As Uncle Gorden tells it, Emma warned Frank not to go to work at the roundhouse that day because she feared the neighbor would carry out his threat. When Frank insisted that he must check out the engine before the next run, Emma insisted on going with him, even though she was pregnant at the time. She wore a cape, under which she concealed Frank's revolver. While Frank was under the engine, Emma saw the neighbor approaching; and she pulled the weapon from the folds of her cape and said, "Defend yourself, Frank!"

Frank defended himself, shot true, and the neighbor died. Frank was tried, convicted of manslaughter, and sent to prison. This harsh judgment was the result of a general movement at the time towards discouraging frontier justice, or the settlement of quarrels with firearms.

The faithful Emma had to wait until her baby was born, but then she went to each juror in turn to plead eloquently that they would sign a petition stating their belief that Frank was a good man who acted in self-defense and deserved a pardon. One juror asked for money to do so. Emma told this to one of Frank's friends, who rashly told Frank during a prison

Frank Wilkinson and his wife Emma, who saw to Frank's self-defense

visit. Frank sent word by this friend to the greedy juror to expect to see him when he got out of prison. Reportedly, this man sold his place and quickly left that part of the country. Eventually, Emma's efforts paid off, and Frank was released from prison after "less than a year," according to Uncle Gorden.

❧ • ❧

AUNT ELM AT THE COURTHOUSE
by Callie Coe Wilson
of Beaumont

One of the families at political odds with the Hooks family—over Prohibition, I believe—was the Dies family, a situation made somewhat awkward by the fact that my father's sister Elm was married to Tom Dies, who, at one time, was Hardin County attorney.

Aunt Elm is the central character in a stirring courtroom drama of the day in Kountze. As I have said, politically the Hookses were like a stand of pines, moved only by the prevailing wind, and those who prevailed didn't like the Dieses' politics.

The scene for the drama was set when Uncle Ben Hooks, duly elected spokesman for the Hooks clan, warned Tom Dies against using a certain piece of evidence in a case he had coming up in court. The action began

Aunt Elm Coe Dies, who outfaced Uncle Ben
Hooks in the Hardin County Courthouse

when, on the appointed day, Uncle Ben, being a cautious man, went to court "to see for himself" that Tom didn't use the information. One of Aunt Elm's younger brothers took her the news. She was in the middle of making mayhaw jelly.

"Uncle Ben has blood in his eye," the boy is said to have told her. The same blood stirred in the veins of my Aunt Elm.

She too went to court. She took her seat across the room from Uncle Ben and the clot of blood relations that had formed around him. When Tom Dies put his witness on the stand, the Hookses stood up—to be counted, I suppose. Across the aisle, Aunt Elm stood up also. People said that the courtroom was as still as the Thicket on a summer's day. For a second the Hooks aggregation didn't see Aunt Elm, but when they did see her, standing as firmly apart as a statute of the law, they all sat down—all, that is, except Uncle Ben. He continued to stand, and, across the silence of interrupted procedure, he alone met the unwavering stare of his older sister's daughter. Then, according to all accounts, he bowed to her, and taking up his hat, left the courtroom.

I never heard whether or not Tom Dies used the evidence. What Aunt Elm had to say was, "If anyone had hurt Tom that day, I was there to see for myself who did it."

"Of course, my jelly was ruined," she would usually add. "It sugared."

๛ • ๛

LEGENDS OF THE REGULATOR-MODERATOR WAR IN SHELBY COUNTY, TEXAS
by John F. Short
of Center

In the early 1840s a small war between two factions, or alliances of families, erupted in Shelby County, Texas, and to this day the families still tell legends of the war and the people in it. Of course, no one is still alive today (1966) who remembers the war, and not many children of the eyewitnesses are still here. A few oldtimers remember tales their parents told them of the war. In this paper I shall relate some of the families' legends that I have heard about the Regulator-Moderator War.

The Regulator-Moderator War was waged in this county from 1841 to 1844. During this time the warring factions fought several battles with loss of life and property. Troops of the Republic of Texas under General James Smith finally restored order, under the instructions of President Sam Houston. Peace was gradually restored, though the effects of the feud continued for some time, and families still remember whose side they were on.

The war owes its origin to the absence of law enforcement in East Texas. Although the war belonged primarily to Shelby County, its activities and influences extended into the neighboring counties of Panola, San Augustine, Harrison, and Sabine.

One account of the starting of the actual war has the following legend as its basis. In 1839 Alfred George, a man who was running for sheriff, had sold Joseph Goodbread a Negro slave and had been paid in land certificates.

A year later the Republic of Texas declared the land certificates fraudulent. George then demanded payment from Goodbread for the slave, and George enticed the slave to run away fearing that Goodbread might get rid of him. Goodbread then told everyone what George had done, hoping to ruin his campaign for sheriff. George then enlisted the services of Charles W. Jackson, telling him falsely that Goodbread threatened to kill Jackson. Jackson then rode up to Goodbread on the courthouse square in Shelbyville and shot and killed Goodbread, an unarmed man. He was arrested but not jailed.

After killing Goodbread, Jackson organized the Regulators mainly for his own protection. The Regulators soon took on another purpose, and that was to rid the county of people that they deemed undesirable. Their plan was to notify these people and tell them that their presence was not desired. With the threat of a gun, many innocent people were forced to leave the county. Thus the Regulators were able to acquire much property left by such people.

The Moderators came into being in order to oppose the Regulators and their lawless ways. They were supposed to have been organized in the Tenaha bottom near a great sycamore tree, with Ned Merchant elected as captain of the group. This information reached the Regulators, and one of their officers went to the place of meeting and climbed the tree. Secreted in a fork of the tree, he was able to learn the name of every person among the Moderators.

In the meantime Jackson had burned the homes of James Strickland and John McFadden, well-known friends of Goodbread. Jackson was arrested for burning the homes and was ordered to appear in the District Court of the Territory of Panola to stand trial, the main charge being the killing of Goodbread.

The Moderators armed themselves and attended the trial in a body. The Regulators also went with their leader Jackson to his trial. The sheriff of Shelby County brought Jackson into court without removing his firearms. For this Judge Hansford fined him. Jackson not only removed his gun and knife but his coat and shoes also. A jury was empaneled, and the court was dismissed until next day. In the meantime Jackson's followers sent threatening words to the judge that it would not be safe for him to bring Jackson to trial. The judge left town. The trial went on without the judge, and the defense council proved to the jury that Goodbread had threatened Jackson's life and that Jackson killed Goodbread in self-defense. The jury acquitted Jackson, and he went back to Shelbyville in triumph along with his band of Regulators.

Thus the feud began. The Moderators set about to avenge the murder of Goodbread, and to protect its members from the Regulators. The first thing they had to do was to kill Jackson. Soon the entire county was divided into two sections—those for the Regulators and those for the Moderators.

One day the Moderators heard that Jackson was on his way from Logansport to Shelbyville. Immediately a group of Moderators were appointed to ambush him at the fork of two roads. Soon Jackson and another man named Lour came along. Jackson and Lour were killed in a sheet of fire. The two dead men were left there in the road.

With Jackson dead, the Regulators met together in the Tenaha bottom and elected Watt Moorman as their new leader.

In the meantime Sheriff Alfred George had run away to Nacogdoches in fear of his life. His deputy, John W. Middleton, took over and got busy for the Regulators. He found out that the three McFadden brothers (William, John, and Bailey) were instrumental in killing Jackson. Middleton deputized some Regulators—Watt Moorman along with them—to capture the McFaddens. The Moderators heard of this and made plans to waylay the Regulators and kill all of them as they were traveling on the road between Shelbyville and the Attoyac River. Middleton found out their plans, however, and took a detour to avoid the ambush.

Middleton's men traveled to Crockett where they came upon the camp of the Moderators Henry and James Strickland, who were camping with a man named "One-Eyed Williams." They all escaped into the woods. Middleton went on further and stopped to eat at the home of a man named Albright. It was now dark. One-Eyed Williams and Henry and James Strickland came up, not realizing that the men were there. They saw each other at the same time and started firing. The Strickland brothers got away, but Williams was caught.

The Regulators forced Williams to tell them where the three McFadden brothers were. They set out and the next day they found the three McFadden brothers at the home of a man named Whitaker, near the town of Montgomery. The sheriff of the county was living in Whitaker's home then, and he was with John McFadden, not knowing he had killed a man in Shelbyville. A spy was sent to Whitaker's home by Middleton where he found out all of this. In some way the sheriff was brought to Middleton, who explained everything to him. The sheriff agreed to arrest the McFadden brothers.

That night the three McFadden brothers surrendered. They found that resistance was useless. Before giving up they forced Middleton into an agreement that they would be tried not by a jury but by the vote of the people in Shelbyville. It was agreed upon, and there was also an understanding that the Moderators would not try to rescue them.

The three McFadden brothers were tried at twelve o'clock on the day of their arrival in Shelbyville, before all of the citizens. After the evidence was submitted, the citizens voted unanimously (174 to 0) to hang John and William McFadden, and they were strung up at once on the public square. Bailey McFadden might have gone the same route, but a man made a plea for his life since he was so young. He was told to get out of town, but not until he had received twenty-five blows from a blackjack.

The war did not stop with the hanging, but went on.

Finally President Sam Houston of the Republic of Texas called out the militia and went in person to Shelbyville. He called on the leaders to leave their arms at home and come in for a consultation. He said that the war must end at once, if "he had to thresh the woods and hang every man engaged in it." All of the citizens accepted his declaration, and Houston then delivered an address deploring the awful situation. He asked every man to throw away his gun, go home and be a good citizen. The men on both sides took Houston at his word, quit fighting, and went to work.

Most of the families that remember hearing about the war and still tell stories about that feud favor the Regulators, even though the Regulators started the war, according to most reports. Not many people know about the war today, but it will go down in history and in the legends of some families as one of the bloodiest wars of the western frontier.

LEGEND OF A RANGER
by Mary Margaret Dougherty Campbell
of George West

One of our often-told family stories is about kinsman James Harrod, who was a Texas Ranger in South Texas around the turn of the twentieth century. After he married Josephine Reynolds, he retired from the Rangers to pursue a less dangerous line of work to support his growing family.

While he had been a Ranger, the Rangers had arrested a prominent South Texas rancher for cattle theft. After his retirement, James Harrod was called to testify at the rancher's trial, which had been moved to Floresville from Corpus Christi due to the possibility that the trial would not be fair if held in the home area of the defendant. At the trial, James Harrod testified against the defendant. His fellow Ranger—and best friend—had been bought, so to speak, and he testified in favor of the rancher. The rancher was acquitted.

Back in Corpus Christi shortly after the trial, Harrod and his Ranger friend were in a bar on Chaparral Street. Conversation turned to the trial and his friend's selling out for money when he knew the rancher had been

Texas Rangers Bach, McKinzie, James Harrod, and Ross in the early 1900s

James Harrod, Texas Ranger in the Bush Country, who was murdered in the line of duty

guilty. Harrod walked out of the bar into the sunshine, away from the argument. His friend followed him into the street and shot Harrod in the back, killing him instantly. He had killed his best friend and left Harrod's widow with four children under the age of seven.

According to the story, the man who shot Harrod felt such remorse for his deed that he went crazy. He ended his own suffering when he lay down on a railroad track and let a train run over him.

⁓ • ⁓

GRANDAD MCCALL AND THE OUTLAW
by John Artie McCall
of Crockett

Grandad Albert Pierce McCall was a law officer in Oakwood, Texas. Sometime in the late 1880s a noted outlaw from the Oklahoma Territory was in one of the saloons in town. Since Grandad McCall was the only peace officer in Oakwood, some of the citizens came and told him about it. Grandad told me that he was not much good with a pistol but was pretty good with his fists. He did not want to appear afraid so he hit on a plan. He walked into the saloon and up to the outlaw, extended his right hand, and pretended to be a long-lost acquaintance. When the outlaw shook hands, Grandad said, "I held his right hand in a vice grip and started hitting him with my left fist. We fought all the way outside and when I knocked him out, he fell into a coffee bin." In later years Aunt Gladys told how in his old age after too much to drink Grandad would come home with blood on his face after being in a fistfight. So, I guess he just enjoyed drinking and fighting.

Albert Pierce McCall and his wife
Nancy in Mississippi in 1873

❧ • ❧

THE BEDSPRINGS FEUD
by Martha Baxley
of Denison

In 1919, when Jack and Priscilla Baxley decided to leave Garvin, Oklahoma, in McCurtain County and move farther west, it was with mixed emotions. They both came from large families and had always remained close to both sides. But when Jack's brother, George, journeyed into the pretty valley near Red River in Love County, Oklahoma, he came back with tales of a land of milk and honey. This was their chance to buy good land of their own and no longer be sharecroppers or hired hands. George, Jack, their sister Donie, and her husband Mike Young, and two couples named Haynes, cousins to Jack and George, decided to make the move en masse. George and Betty had six kids, Jack and Priscilla had four (including Jack, Jr., a baby in arms), and Mike and Donie Young had eight. They were all farmers and planned to take along tools and livestock as well as household goods.

The five young couples had in common their destination, where a better life awaited them, as well as their families, their kinship, and their years of growing up together. Spirits were high as they worked together, all for one and one for all. The plan called for the men to load as many of their farming tools as possible into their wagons pulled by teams of mules. The young boys

181

old enough to help would go along, riding horseback, to drive their cattle. The trip took several days, with stops to camp at night along the way.

The men pooled their money to lease a boxcar, packed all the household furnishings into it, and made arrangements for the women and small children to follow by train to Wilson, the nearest town to their new home, which lay a good twenty-five miles farther away. The boxcar filled with their household goods would sit on a siding until they could locate their new farms, get their livestock settled, meet the families, and then go in a group to bring out the furniture.

When the men arrived at the station in Wilson, it was to find the boxcar open with all the Haynes' belongings gone. The Hayneses were gone, too. The only problem was, the Hayneses had taken all the good bedsprings, leaving the worn-out old flat ones for their relatives. This was especially galling to Priscilla Baxley, who had saved her egg money to buy new bedsprings that had been her pride and joy. Somehow she wound up with the most worn-out set in the bunch.

This started a feud that never ended until all parties involved were gone to their reward. The Baxleys never liked the Haynes after that, and refused to include them in family gatherings. Grandma Priscilla Baxley was a good and patient woman who never said anything bad about anybody, but she could not even repeat the name "Haynes" without a shudder and a twist to her mouth. She said that name reminded her of all the restless nights she spent on those old flat bedsprings.

⋘ • ⋙

FEUDING AUNTS
by Jean G. Schnitz
of Boerne

The most bitter antagonists I have ever witnessed were two of my aunts who carried on a bitter feud for more than thirty years.

There is evidence that the two ladies were friends during the 1930s, but something happened to set off this long lasting duel. What could have set off such a thing? I recently discovered that the cause was a hat. A hat! Two of the nicest people I have ever known fought thirty years over a hat!

The names of the participants have been changed to prevent a second–generation feud. The name of the small town is not mentioned for the same reason.

Sarah was the eldest of five sisters and the wife of the local undertaker. In this capacity she considered herself the authority over her siblings, second only to her parents and elder brother, Jack, the local postmaster. Martha was Jack's wife and Sarah's sister-in-law.

Jack and Martha lived two blocks away from Sarah in the West Texas town where both were popular in the town's society. Sarah played the organ at the Methodist Church. Martha was a popular leader in the Presbyterian Church. Both attended all the right teas and showers and generally felt they were members of the right social circles. Both Martha and Sarah dressed in the finest clothes that could be obtained in Lubbock. The two were the best of friends, confiding in one another regularly.

One day one of the ladies tried on an expensive hat she had bought. She decided that the hat did not look good on her. After duly considering the price she had paid for the hat, she decided to give it to her sister-in-law, who would surely appreciate such an expensive gift. Something in the way the hat was presented set off a physical screaming, shoving, clawing fight between the two women. The neighbors called their husbands, who arrived in time to prevent further bloodshed. Each screamed that they would never again speak to the other.

For thirty years they kept that vow. Sarah and Martha never again spoke a civil word to each other, but the verbal outbursts resulting from accidental encounters were the talk of the town. For those thirty years the two women proceeded to make their families and society circles in their town miserable. People giving parties dared not invite both, yet who should receive an invitation? If one was seen walking down the street, the street cleared as in the movie *High Noon* when the other was known to be in the area. I have heard stories of people dashing away from grocery stores if one entered while the other was known to be in the back at the meat market.

My mother always had a sick headache by the time we arrived for a visit with her family. She found herself caught between the two, with sister and sister-in-law exerting pressure on her to take sides in the matter. Visits were always short because they were so unpleasant.

When my grandmother died in 1970, all the family was in fear of what would happen when the two ladies came to the funeral, as they surely would. Much was made of the situation and there was fear and trembling about what would happen. As it turned out, when Martha and Sarah were in the same room for the first time in thirty years, there was no yelling match. Each managed to stay on the opposite side of the room from the other. I swear I saw them nod at each other once when they came close. But true to their vows, they never spoke to each other again.

9.

Hard Times

Bacon Beans and Gravy

I was born long ago, in 1894,
And I've seen lots of hard times, that is true.
I've been hungry, I've been cold,
And now I'm growing old.
But the worst I've seen is 1932.

Refrain:
Oh, those bacon, beans, and gravy.
They almost drive me crazy,
I eat 'em till I see 'em in my dreams–
In my dreams,
When I wake up in the morning,
A Depression day is dawning,
And I know I'll have another mess of beans.

We have Hooverized our butter,
And blued our milk with water,
And I haven't eaten meat in any way;
As for pies and cakes and jelly,
We substitute sow-belly,
For which we work the county roads each day.
[This song is sung to the tune of "Maggie's Drawers."]

The prosperity and boundless optimism of the Roaring Twenties *almost* made it through that decade. America had seen eight years of an expanding stock market and believed in continuing prosperity. Proving the investors' optimism, the stocks went up in what was called the Great Sleigh Ride of the summer of '29 to an all-time high on September 3. After that there was no way to go but down.

On October 24, Black Thursday, the Market tumbled. A group of bankers rushed in and bought stock and restored some of the trust, but confidence faltered over the weekend, and investors came back Monday morning ready to sell. Tuesday, October 29 was the Day of the Crash. The financial world of the Twenties and everything that was a part of it turned upside down on that Black Tuesday. Savings and investments were lost, and the financial dominoes began a tumble that soon would reach down to the least of persons in this bountiful land of ours. The Great Depression came to Texas, the U. S., and the world. It stayed until it was rescued by the World War II economy, and the effects were felt by everybody before it was over.

People of the Depression generation who are still alive are still telling stories of the 'Thirties. For them it was a time like no other time. Depression folk are still telling, "We were so pore that . . . " stories and trying to buy a coke and a moon pie for a nickel each.

But hard times had been here before. America had been through other depressions, and Americans had been through personal financial depressions that had fractured families from the beginnings of families. The stories of the Depression and hard times have always been important parts of family sagas because hard times are dramatic times of trial and trauma that always leave their marks. The triumph comes from living through them.

✂ • ✄

BLOWING AWAY IN THE PANHANDLE
by F. E. Abernethy
of Nacogdoches

During the good times of the 1920s, Grandad bought a large ranch on the Washita River in the Texas Panhandle. His dream was to have his four sons living near him and working on the ranch. Between the hard times of the Dust Bowl and the drouth, his dream for his family came apart in the process. Dad lost his car business in Shamrock in 1929, and we joined Grandad for a while.

The Jim Talbots—Pearl, Frances, and Jim—who dusted out during the Panhandle drouth

I do not know how long Dad and Mother stayed on the ranch. It was less than a year. The main story to come out of that time is Mother's time of departure. As a city girl, she had not wanted to move to the ranch in the first place, and the ranch was five miles from the mailbox and seventeen miles from Canadian, the nearest town. Mother told this story; Dad never mentioned it.

The bright time of her day, as she remembered, was early morning as she lay in bed and watched a mockingbird in its nest in a wild plum tree near her window. She watched the bird build its nest, lay the eggs, and eventually hatch them. She always stayed in bed through the baby birds' early morning feeding time. This was her only escape, she says, from the high lonesomes of the barren plains of the Panhandle.

Then, one morning as she watched and before she could do anything to save the biddies, a cat made a quick climb and a pounce and ended the mockingbird family. To hear Mother tell that story, before that day was over she was on her way to Childress to catch the Fort Worth and Denver back to Dallas.

Mother came back to the ranch to visit, but she never stayed very long. I spent much of my early life there and thought that it was the greatest place on earth. But drouth, Dust Bowl, grasshoppers, and the Depression were more than the old place could bear. We lost the ranch in 1935.

That last winter on the ranch a terrible blizzard snowed in Grandmother and Grandad and their invalid daughter for over a week. Grandad was sick and Grandmother was chopping up furniture and the flooring to keep a fire going. She used to tell of having to go out and dig down through the snow to get to the stable where the milk cow was kept. Those were hard times.

The story the family remembered and continued to speculate about was the moving of the Jim Talbots from the ranch. Jim was Grandad's cousin, and Grandad had built Jim a two-room house on the ranch. But by 1932 the drouth had hit, the bottom had dropped out of the cattle, grain, and cotton market, and there was no way that the ranch could support Grandad's family plus Jim Talbot and his wife and three kids. "Seven-cent cotton, forty-cent meat/How in the world can a poor man eat!"

Dad loaded everything those five people owned in the back of a bob-tailed truck, covered it with wagon bows and a wagon sheet and took the Talbots to South Texas. It was as close to *Grapes of Wrath* as you could get and not be in the movie. The exodus of the Jim Talbots was one of the most dramatic episodes of our family's life during those hard times of the Depression. Their story is still a part of the fabric of our family.

ᔕ • ᔐ

UNCLE LYNDON HARTMAN
from Uncle Carl Hartman
to Joyce Roach
of Keller

June 12, 1992

Dear Joyce,

I was thinking about Mama recently as I sometimes do—her hardships and struggles. I thought of an incident that greatly impressed me at the time it occurred. Well, I'm telling you this because you are the family historian.

The Hartman children in 1916: Lyndon, Carl, Glen, and Ann. Lyndon
was twelve when this picture was made. He was fourteen when he
made the journey from Billings, Montana, to Texas

This occurred in deep cold winter, perhaps January or February of 1919.
We, our family, had recently come back to Texas from Wyoming and we
were living in a house in Cleburne on Columbia Street. The house was across
the alley from Uncle Fred's home.

All of us had returned to Texas except Lyndon. He had a job in a sugar
beet factory in Billings, Montana, and he remained there earning his money.
I believe our old man was already in the Ranger oil field—not sure on this
point. Lyndon finished his job in Billings then headed for Texas.

He later told us he had bought his ticket to Trinidad, Colorado, where he would have to transfer to another train and so would have to buy another ticket. A severe blizzard was moving down the Rockies all the way into Texas. Lyndon said he was carrying all of his money in a billfold in his hip pocket. He went to sleep (on the train) and when he woke up his billfold and money were gone.

When Lyndon got to Trinidad he wired mama for money. She scraped up $50.00 and wired it to him but for some reason he didn't get it. Well days went by and we didn't hear from Lyndon. The blizzards got worse, the country was covered with snow and ice. Mama cried every day and every night. It seemed like this went on for at least two weeks.

One afternoon we went into the house, mama, sister, Freddie & me. A little bird had gotten into the house and was flying from room to room. When mama saw the bird she brightened up and became happy. She was smiling and said the bird was bringing good news—the old saying was that when a bird gets into a house there will be good news. Early the next morning Lyndon walked into the yard.

Lyndon had walked all night from Fort Worth to Cleburne. He stated he had gotten to ride at times on cattle and sheep trains moving south. I believe he got on one train that went in the wrong direction, to Western Colorado, so he had to double back. Eventually he rode a cattle train into Fort Worth. Fort Worth to Cleburne: 30 miles.

Lyndon was fourteen years old at the time.

Love—Carl

☙ • ❧

CLAUDE RUMAGE
by Lillian Ellisene Rumage Davis
of Angel Fire, New Mexico

My favorite picture is of Grandaddy rocking and talking. "I was foreman on the Carol Creek Ranch from 1914 to 1924," he said. "The Knox family sold to Worthington, so I decided to lease land for six years. I borrowed $20,000.00 from the bank, and lost everything when the stock market crashed in '29. We didn't want to declare bankruptcy. Lillie, the boys, and me worked, daylight until dark to pay back that debt. The kids like to tell about baling hay with the Wells family on the West Fork. One late afternoon Bunk saw the Wells boys heading home and said, 'Daddy, the Wells family is finished for the day. They'll beat us home.' I answered, 'That's all right. We'll beat them out here in the morning!' In the end it all paid off. I sold cows one year, went to make the final payment on the land, and Ed Sewell, the president of Jacksboro National Bank, gave me ten percent back."

As grandma reached for another skein of thread, she shook her head in dismay, "They were always hungry during those Depression years. I canned tomatoes in half-gallon jars and churned eight pounds of butter each week to sell at the grocery store. The butter brought five cents a pound. That helped some with the groceries. Still, we couldn't seem to fill those boys up. I stored cans of food by the case, kept them in the basement. Warren and J. T. would sneak down the steps and get pork and beans and salmon, hide them in the well house. When they were hungry, they would take the cans to the chicken house and sit on the roost to eat. Now wasn't that an appetizing place to be? We didn't catch them at that trick for a long time."

୧ • ୨

GETTING GOLD FOR THE HARD TIMES
by Lee Winniford
of Houston

When the Civil War broke out, most of the younger men on the paternal side of my family joined up. They were not slaveholders and had little interest in that issue, but they had come to Texas looking for independence and freedom from government "meddling," so they were ready to fight for "states rights." The womenfolk stayed on the farms, determined to hold onto the land, but it was their custom to "stand by their men" in any way necessary.

Great-Grandma Sarah had been an Alexander, one of the first families to settle that Hopkins County area of northeast Texas, and she was tough, hard-working, and fearless. She had not the intention of letting her soldier husband and brothers go without the basic necessities while they moved from skirmish to skirmish in Arkansas and Mississippi. The family raised horses and ample foodstuff, an elderly kinsman was a fair cobbler; and Great-Grandpa George Winniford's brother, Norvell, was a well-known gun-runner, reputedly associated with William Marsh Rice of Houston. Thus Great-Grandma had fairly easy access to much-needed supplies.

Under the direction of a couple of oldtimers, the younger boys in the family built a light weight wagon with a cleverly concealed false bottom, and Great-Grandma Sarah would haul guns and ammunition, salt pork,

Great-Grandma Sarah Alexander Winniford, who heroically looked out for the women in her family

Aunt Becky Alexander and Great-Grandma Sarah Alexander Winniford, who set aside some gold for the hard times

molasses, meal, flour, boots, and blankets to her menfolk, leading fresh mounts hitched to the rear of the wagon. It was said that Great-Grandma always had a pretty good idea where the Texas regiment was located though no one ever knew how she got her information. It was also said that she often took great uncles Norvell and Sam along with her because she figured that a lone woman with two small boys would look less suspicious if she were spotted by the enemy.

Great-Grandma Sarah soon discovered that she could sell any extra supplies she could carry to soldiers who could get their hands on gold but whose womenfolk were not so intrepid as she was. She insisted on being paid in gold coin, the story goes, but she did occasionally accept other gold pieces if she was certain of their quality. No one knew where she kept her stash of gold—considerable by war's end—and this was a secret she refused to share, even with her beloved husband who died of war wounds not long after returning to Texas. On rare occasions when the family was in dire straits, she would dip into her stash and bail them out of their stressful situation.

Robert L. Winniford and his wife Margaret (to whom Sarah willed the gold) with their son John H. Winniford, the author's father

Strong-willed and controlling, Great-Grandma Sarah reared her three sons with an iron hand and did not get along with the women they married. Certainly she locked horns with my grandmother, half Choctaw and wife of the youngest son, born several months after the death of his father. But when she knew her time had come, Great-Grandma sent everyone except my grandmother from the room. "I'm going to tell you where the gold is," she told my grandmother. "You've got a hard row to hoe in the first place, being part Indian, and you're married to a Winniford man, and one that's bad spoiled to boot. You're going to need all the help you can get. That gold of mine, that's woman's money," she went on, "woman's gold. I put my life on the line time and time again to make that money, so it's strictly for the woman of the house to use and nobody else. You don't tell anyone where it's kept. And it's not to be spent lightly. When you have to have it to hang onto the land, or to keep the family from falling apart, that's when you use a little of it. That's why I'm giving it to you, and you keep it a secret until the day when you're lying here dying like I am."

Grandma's gold was a family mystery—for she was, from all accounts, absolutely faithful to her commitment not to reveal its whereabouts. It was believed that the family survived and even prospered during the Great Depression because when a crisis arose, she retrieved some gold pieces and solved whatever financial problems her household faced. Had the gold all been spent by the time she took to her deathbed? No one is sure. If not, this may have been a secret she took with her to the Hereafter. Thus far, no one has confessed to having been given the privilege of knowing where her gold was hidden.

ᑫᐧ • ᑫᐧ

SHARECROPPIN'
interview with Annie Mae Stamey Rushing
in Houston, 29 December 1996
by Rhett Rushing, her grandson
of San Antonio

Annie Mae Stamey Rushing is speaking:

Luke (Luther Laden Rushing) and I met on my sixteenth birthday. He came to my house, and I played the organ for him. After that he started coming down to my house on the bus—we lived in Upshur County. He'd ride down there from Mt. Pleasant on Sunday afternoon at two o'clock and he'd stay till the eight o'clock bus. We'd walk out to the well and draw out a fresh bucket of water and come back and sit and talk in the living room. It

L. L. Rushing and Annie Mae, in 1930, when they were sharecropping in Upshur County

was a bedroom, but we called it a living room. Mother and my sisters were in another bedroom across the hall. On the return trip the bus driver would honk to let Luke know that he was turning the bus around and give Luke time to say goodbye.

We were engaged on Easter Sunday 1927 and married on October 16. I was seventeen. We were united in marriage while sitting in a buggy under the beautiful shade trees at the Methodist pastor's home about five pm on Sunday evening. There were about a dozen or more who watched. We drove on to Uncle Tommy Wells' home, where Aunt Carrie had cooked us a wonderful supper. We lived with them for three months until our home was available.

We rented a farm to sharecrop the land. Ma Rushing gave us a hen and baby chickens to get a start. Pa gave us a pig; I made a pet out of it.

Our well was down the hill where we drew the water. Had to go back up the hill with two buckets of water and the pet pig following, squealing and wanting food to eat. We had a wood cookstove to cook on—no dish cabinets, no nothing. Luke put up apple boxes on the wall to put our dishes in. We had a big garden with lots of fresh vegetables to eat. He planted watermelons and cantaloupes down on the side of the bank of the stream where it was rich.

We had no icebox, and we had no lights for many years. We had kerosene lamps, and we would get our five-gallon can filled with kerosene at a filling station in Midway (Upshur County). We went into Gilmer twice a year for big shopping. We had a big fireplace and when we had a fire going we would turn the kerosene lamps off and sit by the fire and watch the fire burn. We kept our bed in the room with the fireplace.

There was an old well in the yard and we used it when we dressed one of the chicks. We had to put it in a vessel and lower it in the well to keep it cool.

I would go in the fields sometimes whenever Luke needed me. I would chop cotton or hoe or dig potatoes. We grew cotton and corn and potatoes and watermelons and cantaloupes, and we had a vegetable garden. The cotton and corn we grew on shares with the man who was sponsoring us that first year. He didn't own the land, just rented it.

We had a pair of fine fat mules and later we got a milk cow. Luke could milk a cow before most people got settled under one. First he had to let the calf nurse to get the milk to come down. Then he would take the calf off and tie him to a post, leaving at least one side for the calf to have later. Then we would take the milk to the house and strain it and put it down in the well to keep it cool or it would sour.

We ate a lot of clabber. Take the cream off and make butter. Then take the clabber and stir it up and churn it and make buttermilk if you wanted it that way, or just eat the clabber. Clabber and cornbread made us many a meal and it was good.

At night we might sneak down to the creek and take a bath. If you didn't, then you had to take a bath in the washtub. When it was freezing cold, you didn't take many baths.

The first year we were married my mother and Luke's mother gave us covers and bedding, but after that we would piece together every scrap to make quilt tops. We'd invite the neighbors to come over and we'd get together and quilt out the tops and we'd have a lunch or something. We'd quilt it out in a day's time. We'd start in the morning and then have lunch and talk and talk and talk. The men would spend time cutting wood and then they'd take it to town and sell it for extra money.

When we were first married, we had some hard times. We had pinto beans and we had cream gravy. For breakfast I had biscuits and cream gravy—also had salmon patties fried—salmon was nine cents a can, but that was a Sunday morning dish. We worked on the farm, you know, and

Luke had to get out early in the morning and go plow and all that, and he'd come in for lunch. I gathered vegetables out of the garden—greens at first, mustard greens and turnip greens, then green beans came along and we made the best of it. We got along fine.

On special occasions we would have fried chicken, but not too often 'cause I didn't want to kill my chickens. I was trying to get 'em so I could raise some more and keep us in eggs.

We finally quit sharecropping in 1936, when Luke went to work for the railroad and got sent to Galveston. Then he got promoted and was sent to Houston with the Houston Belt and Terminal. Paul Rushing (Rhett's father) was born in 1937, and we finally settled down and bought a house so that we could stay there in Houston and send Paul to school.

৩৯ • ৩৯

THE SHARECROPPER'S COW
by Barbara Pybas
of Gainesville, TX

Kinzie Bonner worked for the Gunter outfit, which owned several thousand acres of river bottomland in Sivell's Bend and Warrens Bend in Cooke County, Texas, in the 1920s. The landowner sometimes let the family sharecropping the bottomland have the use of a cow while she was fresh, until she was put out to pasture to breed again. Usually, the family was also given space for a garden and could raise a hog or two.

Kinzie said he made the rounds to sharecroppers to pick up the cows. He arrived at one family's house at dinner time. Several ragged children were running about, and the men were coming in from the field, tired and dusty. The mother opened the door and asked Kinzie to come in and eat. All there was on the table was some field corn they had just gathered and milk. He didn't have the heart to tell them why he was there, and he didn't take their cow.

The sharecropper usually furnished his team and equipment. If the landowner had a house, he furnished it. If he didn't, he let them put up a lean-to or a tent. The landowner would get a third of the crop, after the farmer had gathered it, picked the cotton and pulled the corn. The number of acres a sharecropper could farm depended on how many kids he had and how many teams he had. A family with only one helper and one team could only farm about forty acres or less.

In the early days in Warrens Bend, cotton was the only cash crop they had, their little bit of spending money. A gin was established in 1884 and continued in operation until 1927. Cotton and corn would produce much more in the river bottoms than on the upland. Wheat and grains produced about the same. But the wheat had to be hauled to Gainesville or to a railroad line to be sold and would not bring nearly as much cash as a load of cotton, ginned or otherwise. Sometimes, they were able to pick up enough pecans to sell, but those were split with the owner, probably picked up on the halves.

The sharecroppers raised all the food for their animals and their families, with the exception of flour and sugar and coffee. Most of the 'croppers were good hunters. Some of them had good dogs and would hunt raccoons, opossums, rabbits, quail, dove, and an occasional deer. Wild game would help with the food supply and also provide some extra cash through their fur pelts and skins.

The dogs were not pets. They had to earn their keep. The standard food for the dogs was corn bread. The farm wife made a big pan, maybe twice a day. What the family didn't eat went to the dogs or sometimes was made especially for them.

These were hard times, but families drew together and not having any money were happy with any success with a day's fishing at the river or a new litter of pigs or a pair of new shoes.

ﰀ • ﰀ

STOLEN CORN
by Jean G. Schnitz
of Boerne

One year when there had been a bad drought in Comanche County, my great-grandfather Addison Lee found that he had used all the corn to feed the family and had none left to plant. He tried to buy and to barter some cattle for corn in nearby towns, but no one would sell to him because of his Yankee affiliation during the Civil War. He tried to buy corn from his neighbors, but no one would sell him any corn. In desperation, C. A. Lee crept into a neighbors' barn and stole a large sack of corn. He planted his purloined corn and raised a good crop. After the harvest, he returned that sack of corn, *plus* another sack to his neighbor and confessed what he had done. His reputation was not enhanced by this incident.

A DOLLAR A DAY
by Henry Wolff, Jr.
of Victoria

My dad told of one year during the Depression when he was down to his last dollar. There had been some rains and the weeds and the Johnson grass was getting ahead of his cotton, which needed chopping badly, and he needed someone to help him get it done before another rain. He had heard that a Negro neighbor might be willing to help him, but that he charged a dollar a day. Dad had one dollar.

Dad was walking toward the lane that led to the man's house when he found a little clutch purse beside the road that ran in front of our place. He opened it and there was a dollar inside. "What luck!" he thought to himself. "I can pay the man and still have a dollar left."

Sure enough, the man said he would help him, but he would only work if his wife could work with him and that she also got a dollar a day for chopping cotton. Dad hired them both.

While it didn't work out exactly the way that he had figured it, Dad always thought of that as being one of his lucky days.

ↄ৶ • ৶ↄ

HARD TIMES AND LOW PAY
by Carl Halsell
for his daughter,
Lou Rodenberger
of Baird

I went horseback to a little one-teacher school known as Friendship, four miles west of Cisco. It was a big district with three trustees and three one-teacher schools. Each trustee run, I mean *run*, his school. The trustee for Friendship was a big, hard-looking, black dutchman by the name of Will Parmer. He owned about half the land in the district and had about $100,000 in a Cisco bank.

When I found Mr. Parmer, he was plowing barefooted with one mule and a Georgia Stock in some new sandy land. I asked him if he needed a teacher. He implied he could use one. Not knowing any better, I asked him how much he paid, and he said $65 a month. I could leave it or take it. He asked me how much I thought I was worth. I had done a little hoss tradin' so I told him that I had been making $10 a day. He told me I had better go back to my job. I said "Mr. Parmer, I'll take the job for $75 a month." He

Carl Halsell, who spent forty-three years in the school business

said, "No!" I offered to split the difference. He said, "No!" Then I told him I would take the job at $65 a month, and he said, "To tell you the truth, young man, I think that's all you're worth."

I didn't ask him if I was hired. I just pulled out a contract and started filling it out. He said, "You hold on a minute. If I hire you, you will have to board with me, and that will be $15 a month." Afraid he would back out, I told him that was O.K. by me. I handed him the contract, he scribbled his name on it, and I mailed it in to the County Superintendent's office the next morning.

That was the beginning of forty-three years as a teacher in Texas' rural schools.

❧ • ❧

POSSUM AND SWEET 'TATERS
by "Wildwood" Dean Price
of Bonham

I learned early on how to prepare and cook coon and possum, delicacies in their own right. Late one evening, while running the trap line, Dad spotted a huge fat possum in a fence row persimmon tree. I can still hear Dad making his case to Mom: "Possum's nature is that whatever he's eaten on is what he's gonna eat on until it's all gone. See how fat this possum is. He ain't been eaten on no dead cow." Dad proceeded to dress out Mr. Possum, being careful to trim off all the excess fat.

My mother made her case to all of us: "Well—my word, I ain't never! I will neither cook, nor eat any possum—period!"

Joe Leslie Price, "Wildwood" Dean Price's father, who caught the 'possum, and Wildwood's mother Sybil, who reluctantly ate it and enjoyed every bite! The shadow in the background is the ghost of Uncle Lewis Barnett, who formerly lived in this house.

Dad finally got the possum ready for the baking dish, in which it was placed with lots of sweet 'taters, and was promptly put into the oven. Soon the smell of a hardwood fire and roasting sweet smelling meat and sweet 'taters browning began filling the house with a mouth-watering aroma. By supper everyone was starving and Mother ate almost all of Mr. Possum up from us.

Mother claims until this day, "The only reason that possum was so good was because we hadn't had any meat in so long."

10.
A Brush with History

❦

A family that has been around a long time and has kept some family memories intact, has had—by the law of averages—some brushes with famous
people or some notable event in history. Most people in my part of East
Texas have encountered or know people who have encountered Bonnie
Parker and Clyde Barrow and can tell stories about them. In my
grandfather's part of West Texas, most of the old cowboys told stories about
seeing the Comanche chief Quanah Parker. Some ancestor of yours or mine
has shaken hands with a president or fought at the Battle of New Orleans or
was in the crowd at Kennedy's assassination.

I was a proud youngster of twelve years when Governor James Allred
spoke on the courthouse steps at Palestine, and I was bold or pushy enough
to shake his hand. In our part of West Texas and western Oklahoma those
Sooners who went in to claim and prove their claims are part of frontier
history, as my grandparents were, and the core of the families' stories is that
big adventure. Those ancestors who were close to some memorable, textbook part of history added a little stature to their lives—and vicariously to
their descendants' lives—and to their family's legends.

The brush with fame can be fatal. Jerry Lincecum's father likes to tell
the tale of his relative, Joe S. Blackmon, who was resolutely non-political
until W. Lee "Pappy" O'Daniel launched his campaign for governor of Texas
in 1938. When O'Daniel was elected, Mr. Blackmon decided to go to Austin
and witness the inauguration of his hero. Unfortunately, he stood outside

in a cold rain during the festivities and came home with a chill, which led to complications that resulted in his death on January 29, 1939, twelve days after O'Daniel's inauguration.

🖜 • 🖘

SANTA ANNA'S "SUICIDE"
by Tom Davison
of Nacogdoches and Austin

[Tom Davison wrote this paper in 1940, when he was a journalism student at UT.—Abernethy]

The general lay gasping for his life's breath as a hot August sun bore down upon his face. His hands tore out clumps of grass from the ground beside him. His body quivered with the agony of approaching death. Santa Anna, the Napoleon of the West, had taken poison.

Quickly he was taken into a nearby house and seated in a large mahogany chair. The doctor was summoned, and he made quick use of his stomach pump on the patient. The effects were favorable. Soon the victim was breathing easier.

And Santa Anna was saved, saved to torture himself all over again with thoughts of his failure at San Jacinto four months before, of his routed army, and of a free Texas which held him prisoner.

In 1940, when this article was written, this incident of Santa Anna's attempt at suicide was one of the favorite family stories of seventy-eight-year-old Mrs. Almira Phelps Garrison, who lived in Nacogdoches. She remembered being told as a child how her grandfather, Dr. James Aeneas Phelps, saved Santa Anna's life with a stomach pump.

It was on Dr. Phelps' plantation, Orizimbo, on the banks of the Brazos River in Brazoria County that the leader of the vanquished Mexican armies was held prisoner from August 1 until November 26, 1836. There Santa Anna was given the hospitality of a favored guest, and almost as much freedom. He slept on the finest feather bed and ate the best food that the Phelps family could offer. There Santa Anna had used his influence to have a prized family Bible, which had been taken by Mexican soldiers, returned to the Phelpses. It was there that Stephen F. Austin came to visit Santa Anna, and they sat and talked under the great elm tree.

And it was under that same elm tree that he was found writhing in agony one afternoon shortly after dinner. Expecting to be shot as a prisoner of war, the despondent, defeated general had bribed a sympathetic Mexican servant in the Phelps household to slip him poison with his food.

Even though Santa Anna had made several attempts to escape and take his life, Mrs. Garrison remembers being told that he was never kept in chains. Several years later, after Santa Anna had been slipped back into Mexico by U.S. government agents, the general sent a long letter of gratitude to Dr. Phelps in appreciation of his kind treatment, and with the letter was an expensive Spanish blanket. But that was not all the most hated man in Texas history was to do in return for the kindness received from the Phelps family.

In 1842 a ragged, half-starved band of Texas raiders was captured in the desolate mountains of northern Mexico. The men were the remnants of the ill-fated Mier Expedition. Among the captives was Orlando Phelps, the eighteen-year-old son of Dr. Phelps. The boy had been in school in Mississippi, but he had returned to his home in Orizimbo in time to join the Mier expedition.

The prisoners were jailed, and Mexico's famed tribunal of justice—the bean jar—was called upon to determine the fate of these captives. For a prisoner to draw a black bean meant death, and Orlando Phelps drew a black bean.

Santa Anna, seeing the familiar name of Phelps on the list of those sentenced to be shot, called the boy in and found young Orlando Phelps to be the son of his old host, Dr. James Phelps. Orlando Phelps was offered his freedom if he swore allegiance to the Mexican government, but he refused, apparently sealing his fate all over again.

Santa Anna's mind must have gone back to those days at Orizimbo and the many kindnesses of the Phelps family, for young Phelps was released despite his defiance of the Mexican government, which had the right to end his life.

Orlando Phelps was given a military escort to the Texas border and $500 in gold, according to Phelps family history.

"So you see Santa Anna was an important factor in my life," said Mrs. Garrison. "First, my grandfather saved his life; then Santa Anna responded by saving the life of the man who became my father."

Still standing at Orizimbo is the elm under which Santa Anna talked with Stephen F. Austin and under which he lay dying from poison that August afternoon over 150 years ago. The big mahogany chair in which Santa Anna sat while being administered the stomach pump is now in the Capitol visitors center in Austin.

Times have changed since those days in the mid-1800s when Orizimbo's mansion stood by the banks of the big, muddy Brazos. Dr. Phelps' plantation went the way of most plantations after the Civil War, and the shell of the old house, a ghost-like reminder of the days of the Texas Republic and the Old South, was destroyed by a storm in 1932. Today on the site of Orizimbo's mansion and built of its wood, is a tenant farmer's ramshackle dwelling.

Mrs. Garrison likes to think about Orizimbo as it was in the days of its prime. That's why she doesn't care to go back and see it today. "I'll just think of it as it was long ago, when I was a little girl and before I was born. Those days will never come again," she mused. "I like to talk about those days, but not many people today stop their rushing about long enough to listen."

૭ · ૭

GALVESTON STORM
by Nancy Carr
of Longview

In 1910, my grandfather William Carr and his family lived in a two-story house at Caplen on the Gulf Coast of Texas. For a living, he and his boys operated two sailboats carrying produce from Caplen to Galveston and Houston. The Carr family was involved in two of the Gulf Coast's famous but deadly hurricanes.

In the summer of 1910 a large hurricane began approaching the Caplen area. The first indications of the storm appeared in the form of storm birds three to five days ahead of the storm. These black birds have a straight-line sailing type of flight. Approximately two days before the storm, all marine life in the area disappeared. Preparations were made. Valuables were carried to the upper rooms of the house. The sailboats were stripped, sunk, and anchored securely to be raised again after the storm.

When the storm came, water filled the first floor of the house. Debris that would have destroyed the house was stopped by a line of salt cedar trees twelve feet high that grew in front of the house. After the storm, the family had to start over, but the sailboats and other equipment were saved.

Again in 1915 a storm threatened the area and the family decided to leave. Some went to Galveston; the rest drove inland. A make-shift house had been made in Fannette to receive the family. My grandfather, Neil Carr, was responsible for driving a loaded wagon to Fannette. On the way he pulled up a small sapling for use in hurrying the mule. When he reached Fannette, he jumped from the wagon, stuck the sapling in the ground and said, "Well, we made it." By some quirk of nature, the sapling took root and grew into what is now a large cypress tree. Nowhere between Caplen and Fannette on the route he traveled have there ever been any cypress trees.

෴ • ෴

HANGING BILL LONGLEY
by Jane Barnhart Burrows
of San Antonio

The legend told most often in my family is the one about my great-great-grandaddy, who helped in capturing the outlaw Bill Longley. My great-great-grandaddy, Frank Johnson, rode all the way up to the Kansas Territory with a posse, where they captured Bill Longley, and then brought him back to Texas for trial. At the trial they found him guilty and decided to hang him. The first time they tried to hang Bill Longley, they found that he was too tall to hang from a branch because his feet would touch the ground. To solve the problem they tied the end of the rope to a bridge rail and threw him over.

෴ • ෴

GIDEON LINCECUM AND CHOCTAW CHIEF PUSHMATAHA
by Jerry Lincecum
of Sherman

As a result of his living in the Choctaw Nation in Mississippi and learning to speak and write their language, my ancestor Gideon Lincecum became a close friend of Chief Pushmataha, one of the heroes of the Choctaws in the early nineteenth century. In addition to being held in high regard by his own tribe, Pushmataha chose to join U.S. forces against the Creeks during the War of 1812, and he fought so well that General Andrew Jackson conferred upon him the appointment of brigadier general.

Pushmataha was also a shrewd negotiator and a great orator, and Gideon witnessed and wrote about his performance at the treaty negotiations at Doak's Stand, Mississippi, in 1820. On this occasion Andrew Jackson found his friend to be a formidable antagonist, as he and General Hinds represented the U.S. government in negotiations with the Choctaw chieftains in Mississippi.

This treaty was the first of a series that ultimately led to the forced removal of the Choctaws (and several other tribes) to present-day Oklahoma. In his opening day speech Jackson made a personal appeal to Chief Pushmataha, calling him "Brother Push."

The Choctaw Chief Pushmataha, who fought with Andrew Jackson against the Creeks during the War of 1812. Jackson awarded him the rank of brigadier general as a result of his bravery in battle.

But the next day, when Pushmataha spoke for the Choctaws, he had a surprise for Jackson, whose description of the new territory offered to the Choctaws was based on inaccurate maps. Gideon took careful notes and recorded the exchange as follows:

"In the first place, General Jackson speaks of the country he wishes to obtain from us as 'a little strip of land,' whereas it is a very considerable tract of country. In the second place, he represents the country he wishes to exchange for the 'little strip' as being a very extensive country 'of tall trees, many water courses, rich lands and high grass, abounding in game of all kinds.'

"I am well acquainted with that country, having hunted there often. I have had my feet sorely bruised there by the roughness of its surfaces. It is indeed a very extensive land, but a vast amount of it is exceedingly poor and sterile, nude of vegetation of any kind. There is no timber anywhere except on the bottom lands, and it is low even there. The grass is everywhere very short. The game is not plentiful, except buffalo and deer in the western sections. The account of this land given by my friend General Jackson has proven to me that he is entirely ignorant of the geography of that country, and therefore I acquit him of any intention to defraud."

At this point Jackson interrupted, "See here, Brother Push, you must be mistaken. Look at this map; it will prove to you that you are in error."

But Pushmataha examined the map carefully and said, "The paper is not true." He then proceeded to mark out with a pipestem a more accurate orientation of the Red and Canadian Rivers and said:

"There is another matter which you do not seem to be apprised of. The lower portion of the land you propose to swap is pretty good country, but what of the American settlers already in that region? There are a great many of them, some of them substantial, well-to-do settlers with good houses and productive farms, and they will not be ordered off. Are they to be considered Indians or white people when this exchange of countries is completed?"

Jackson interrupted again, "If that is true, I will send my warriors, and by the eternal I'll drive them into the Mississippi or make them leave."

Eventually a settlement was reached, and the Choctaws gave up five million acres in Mississippi in exchange for 13 million acres of what is now Arkansas and Oklahoma, plus a package of educational and other benefits. But almost immediately a clamor arose in the Arkansas Territory, as Chief Pushmataha's prophecy about the resistance of numerous American settlers already present proved accurate. The Choctaw chieftains were called to Washington in November, 1824, to renegotiate the treaty. After being wined and dined extravagantly for ninety days, they were persuaded to give back a large portion of the Arkansas land.

But not before Pushmataha contracted croup from overexposure and died on December 24, 1824. He was in his sixtieth year. His last request to his old friend, Andrew Jackson was: "When I am gone, let the big guns be fired over me." It was granted, and this great American leader was buried in the nation's capital with the full military honors befitting a major general.

Several years later, while Gideon was touring in several Southeastern states with an exhibition team of Choctaw ballplayers, he made the trek to Washington to see the grave of his friend, Choctaw Chief Pushmataha.

൙ • ൕ

DAVY CROCKETT
by Jeanne Blackstone Almany
of Nacogdoches

My grandmother tells a story about her maternal great-grandfather and Davy Crockett that she swears is the truth. Her great-grandfather, George

Mathews, was a close friend of Davy's, since they both had lived for a number of years in the same area in western Tennessee. When Davy decided to come to Texas in late 1835, he asked Mr. Mathews to come with him, and Mr. Mathews enthusiastically agreed. However, all this occurred before his sons found out about the proposed trip. The Mathews boys told their father that they would not go to Texas with him at that time and that they did not want him to go alone. Mr. Mathews, not wanting to split up his family, reluctantly told Davy that he wouldn't be able to make the trip. George and his family did come to Texas later, but they always believed they were very fortunate not to have come with Davy Crockett since, as my grandmother says, her great-grandfather Mathews would probably have been killed with Davy at the Alamo.

◌ ・ ◌

THE MAYOR AND PRESIDENT ROOSEVELT
by Jean G. Schnitz
of Boerne

My grandfather, Ira Scudder, was always interested in politics. Once while the Scudder family lived in Seymour, the word got out that Theodore Roosevelt was scheduled to make a speech in Wichita Falls. This was probably in early 1912 when Roosevelt was running for a third term as president of the United States under the Bull Moose Party banner.

Ira rode his horse to Wichita Falls to hear President Roosevelt. It was a trip of nearly fifty miles. He got there early so he was able to get a front-row seat.

Ira reported that when it came time for the meeting to begin, the mayor of Wichita Falls got up to introduce the president. As small town politicians are prone to do when they get a crowd assembled, the mayor talked on and on and on—mostly about himself. Ira and the rest of the crowd were getting restless because they had come to hear Mr. Roosevelt—not the mayor.

Finally, Roosevelt reached up and grabbed the mayor by the long tail of his coat and pulled him down into the chair, then quickly stood up and began his speech, much to the delight of the crowd. Ira came home and told his family that seeing Roosevelt handle the mayor like that was worth the trouble of the horseback ride to and from Wichita Falls. Ira told everybody, "He gets my vote."

FOREVER FORD
by Laurette Davis McCommas
of Whitewright

Before World War I, my Grandpa Ginsky worked for the Wayne County Sheriff's Department in Michigan. One day he was told to deliver a subpoena to Henry Ford.

He drove to Mr. Ford's house, and saw him and another man working in a field. Grandpa parked the car and walked to the men. "Are you Henry Ford?" he asked.

"Yes, sir. I am, and this is my friend Harry Bennett. What can I do for you?"

Grandpa shook hands with both men and reached into his pocket and handed Henry Ford the document. Grandpa said he was the only person ever to serve a subpoena to Henry Ford, but Mr. Ford wasn't upset about it. In fact, they had a friendly chat. Grandpa told him that he would like to work for Ford Motor Company.

Mr. Ford said, "Go see Harry Bennett tomorrow, and he'll give you a job."

Grandpa worked for Ford all through World War I, the Depression, and World War II. His son, who became my daddy, graduated from Henry Ford Trade School and became the chief powerhouse engineer for Lincoln Mercury. Uncle Glen worked on the Ford railroad tracks when he was sober. Uncle George and his wife both worked for the parts division of Ford. Uncle Al Martin fixed sewing machines used for upholstering Ford cars.

Uncle Miles Bennett, who married Grandpa's daughter Norma during the Depression, was a Canadian. They had a baby named Carol, but he couldn't come to the U.S. until he was assured of a job. Grandpa wrote a letter to Harry Bennett, and a job on the line was his. Whenever there was a layoff, all Grandpa had to do was write or call Harry Bennett, and none of the family members ever lost their jobs.

When I learned about this part of my family history ten years ago, I acquired a new appreciation for Henry Ford. All of my older family members still drive only Fords or Lincolns today, and some of them were quite upset to learn that I drive a Toyota.

GRANDMA WALKER AND JOHN WESLEY HARDIN
by Frances B. Vick
of Dallas

The Brannen and Dial relatives have all known for years that Grandma Walker, nee Azalene Dial, helped John Wesley Hardin after the shootout at Gates' Saloon in Trinity. It has always been told as the gospel truth, so I suppose it is.

Grandma Walker was a Dial who came to Texas with her father Lewis Dial after the Rawhide Fight. She married A. J. Walker and they had one daughter, Charlotte, who married William Jefferson Brannen. They had six children—five who survived to adulthood—and when these children and their children got together it was quite a reunion, with the Dial relatives also joining in. One of the stories told at these reunions would be about Grandma Walker and John Wesley Hardin.

John Wesley's father was the circuit-riding Methodist preacher who lived about twenty-five miles from the Dial home in Trinity County and became a good friend of the family as he rode about preaching. John Wesley had become quite a gunman and had already killed several men before he got in a gunfight with Phil Sublett at Trinity. They were playing against each other at Gates' saloon and ten-pin alley when an argument ensued over the wagers and the shootout resulted.

In the fight John Wesley was severely wounded. The wounded gunman made it to the Dial place on his way toward home. His Dial friends took care of him. He hid in the woods near the house after his wound was dressed and waited several days for it to heal. Azalene, the eighteen-year-old Dial girl, took food to him each day at his place of safety from his enemies and the law.

In the biographies that have been written about the event in later years, John Wesley, after seeing a doctor and being told that he was going to be arrested for assaulting Sublett with intent to murder, was carried by friends two miles east of Sulphur Springs, an area about four miles outside of Trinity on Sulphur Creek. He was hiding about six miles from downtown Trinity, which would place him about two or three miles from the Dial home, so it would have been possible for Azalene to have helped out this outlaw son of the Methodist circuit-riding preacher.

Azalene Dial Walker—Grandma
Walker—around 1888, when she
was around thirty-four years old, after her adventure with the outlaw
John Wesley Hardin

❧ • ❧
DOR!
by Kenneth W. Davis
of Lubbock

No one in the Davis family had the status or the money to join such
prestigious organizations as the Daughters of the Republic or the United
Daughters of the Confederacy, but we had our own "initial" group, the
DOR—"the damned old Republicans!"

My grandfather was a lifelong Democrat, who in his last twenty years
worked in the state capitol building at a beefeater's job. His contempt for
the Republican Party was full, complete, pristine, whole, and total—as he
gladly proclaimed from time to time, especially when he had had a shot of
good Tennessee sour mash. He had a neighbor who in the Twenties and
Thirties—when Texas was still almost totally a Democratic Party strong-
hold—voted faithfully the Republican ticket. When a rural peddler asked
Granddad for directions to the Republican's house, my grandfather replied,
"Hell, why do you want to go see that damned old Republican?"

The younger males in the family had long been cautioned against using
swear words, but could get by with the initials DOR. An expression my

grandfather used aptly characterizes his political beliefs: He was a Democrat born, and when he died, he was a Democrat dead.

In his final illness, the then governor of Texas, Allan Shivers—who had abandoned the Democratic Party to become a Republican—came to the hospital to show respect for Granddad, who from the late Thirties until his death in the early Fifties had sat at the information desk in the rotunda of the capitol building. My uncles who were present later said they all prayed that Granddad would not be caustic. Their prayers were answered; Granddad treated the Governor of Texas with civility and correctness, if not with warmth. But just as soon as Governor Shivers left the room, Granddad painfully reached for the call button to summon a nurse.

My uncles thought that the moment of death was imminent, but when the nurse arrived, Granddad in a surprisingly strong voice for a man moribund said, "I don't want to see that turncoat Republican ever again. If you let him back in here, I'll brain him with a bedpan." To my knowledge, the governor never heard of Granddad's near-death venom.

✍ • ✌

SOUSA AND MR. SAM
by Silva Boze Brown
of Commerce

My little sister Billie wrote to me every week after I married, telling me about kindergarten in her hometown of Commerce. She told how Miss Boren had taken the class to see the sheep shearing at the college barn. She said that the little sheep said, "Baa, baa," when the mothers were returned to them, and that the mothers could not tell which lamb was theirs. She felt sorry for them because they could not find their own mamas.

Another thing she wrote about was riding on the lap of John Philip Sousa. They sat on the spring seat, behind the mules hitched to the little wagon my father drove around the East Texas State College campus. Papa was the first farmer for the college's Agriculture Department. Mr. Sousa would trust no one to unload his own band instruments without his personal supervision. He chose Papa to do just that, and they made four trips back and forth to the train station to get all the instruments. It took four boxcars to haul the rest of the band's equipment. Big day in Commerce!

As Billie chatted with Mr. Sousa, he asked her if she was coming to the concert. She said, "No," that she did not have a ticket. He replied, "We will see about that." Guess who was sitting in the reserved seats for the first performance for the very first concert. You guessed it, all the little Bozes, sitting proudly between Mama and Papa.

On another occasion, Billie was visiting her sister Vera at Bomar's grocery store in downtown Savoy. It had the usual spit-and-whittle bench out front. From this vantage point one could get all the good and the bad news. The talk was going at full speed that day for Mr. Sam was coming to town—Sam Rayburn himself, Speaker of the House!

Billie, who was only six years old at the time, was playing with the beans in the bean bin, which was near the door, listening to all the hullabaloo inside the store, where Mr. Sam had taken temporary headquarters. When Mr. Sam would see a man coming into the store, he would ask Sister Vera who he was. Vera would tell him his name and tell him a little something about the person. Mr. Sam would then greet the caller with something like, "Good old Joe. Why, I would know your hide in a tan yard. How are all the kids? Heard that your oldest, Sadie, got married. Too bad about your father's death." On and on he would go with each person. Mr. Sam was a politician.

After awhile there was a lull in the conversation and the Speaker turned to Billie and said, "How do you like me, Billie?"

"I do not like you at all," she replied, looking him straight in the face. To this, he gave a big laugh and wanted to know why. She continued emptying the shovel of beans and filling it again. "Because you tell stories and Mama says it is wrong to tell stories."

Sam Rayburn remembered that episode when Billie was in college, and he would come and sit on our front porch in Commerce. He would recall the occasion in the grocery store and he would say, "Even a politician can be seen right through, all the way, by a child."

Mr. Sam was our neighbor in Fannin County and always said that my daddy was the best friend he ever had who never voted for him. Papa was Republican.

❧ • ❧

PASSING UP A BRUSH WITH FAME
by Florena Williams
of Sherman

My uncle Lee Williams had the opportunity to become famous for capturing Clyde Barrow, but he decided to pass it up.

During the 1930s he was employed for a number of years as a night watchman for a small North Texas town. Walking up and down the dark streets, he checked the doors and windows of the stores and offices. One night, while on his rounds, he stopped off at an all-night diner for a cup of coffee. As he sat there sipping, a young man came in and ordered food to go. The man looked familiar, but it took Lee a few minutes to recognize him as Clyde Barrow.

Immediately, visions of heroic proportions filled his head. What a coup it would be for him to become the one who captured Clyde Barrow. He carefully surveyed the entire scene, and as he did, he saw her. Outside the diner, slowly walking back and forth, was Bonnie Parker, with a machine gun under her arm.

Lee settled back and sipped some more coffee. He wasn't a coward, but neither was he suicidal.

ꙅ • ꙅ

BONNIE AND CLYDE
by Faye Leeper
of Irving

One spring day when I was of preschool age, my father was working in his fields; and my older brothers and sisters were in school. My mother, perennially pregnant and with two little children on hand, had put out the family wash. When she used up her clothesline space, she hung the rest on the barbed-wire fence that bordered our yard. About three in the afternoon, a storm appeared imminent. When the wind became stronger, she ran to fetch in the family clothing and linens, still wet, but too precious to lose in a bad wind.

In her fury to retrieve the loose garments, she looked up to see a Model A Ford with a man and a woman in it. They asked directions to the Standfield Ranch. My mother told them it was just three miles on down the road but that they'd better come with us to the storm cellar until the wind dissipated. They declined but thanked her generously and quickly departed.

By the time she had collected the family wash, a slow rain had started. That was generally her signal that the storm had abated. She came in and watched out the window until it had stopped.

She had sat down at her pedal sewing machine to mend a garment when two policemen on motorcycles pulled up into the yard. When they left, she took the double-barreled shotgun off its rack and loaded it. After she put it back on the rack, she sat in her rocker where she could see out the window toward Standfield Ranch. My brothers and sisters soon got off the school bus. She told them to stay indoors until my father came home.

I learned later that the policemen had told her that it was Bonnie Parker and Clyde Barrow who had asked the way to Standfield Ranch. The big

Jessie Pirtle, who generously invited Bonnie and Clyde to join her family in the storm cellar, with son W. A.

gun stayed within easy reach for several days. To the day she died, I doubt that my mother had as much as shot a rabbit, but I do not think her record would have been that good if the Model A had come back.

I remember the day Mama asked Bonnie and Clyde to join us in the storm cellar, and I remember taking the gun from its rack. My younger brother, who was almost four years old at the time, recalls the day that he was "down at the mailbox" about a hundred yards from the house when Bonnie and Clyde stopped and asked if they could get them some buttermilk. He ran up to the house to tell Mama. She, not knowing who they were, sent him with a syrup bucket full of buttermilk. Bonnie reached out of her window to take it and then put a quarter in his hand.

My mother would have offered a handout to anyone who asked, and a body would have to have been mighty scared to turn down a shiny quarter in those days. Mother remembered those happenings well, but as Mark Twain says: "She remembers everything that ever happened—and a lot of things that didn't."

VILLA RAID
by Jesse Thompson
of Boerne
as told to Austin T. King
of Pittsburg

In the fall of 2000, strictly by chance, I was talking to a party by phone, who after learning I was interested in the Villa raid on Columbus, New Mexico, in 1916, suggested that I should contact Mrs. Jesse Thompson in Boerne, Texas, who was the last survivor of the Villa raid and who had profuse documentation of the raid and the events surrounding it. I found a gold mine of information in her family tale of that time.

Mrs. Thompson said that her grandfather, Mr. Ritchey, owned a hotel in Columbus, New Mexico, and was killed by the Villistas, and his hotel was burned to the ground. The Villistas came to the hotel looking for the hardware merchant who lived there and who had taken Villa's money, promising guns in return. The merchant's name, she told me, was Raebel, but he was not at the hotel the night of the raid. He was in El Paso. Whether he had information that Villa was on his way for an accounting that night is not known, but there was advance information that Villa was on his way.

Pancho Villa, Mexican revolutionary who made a disastrous raid on Columbus, New Mexico, and killed Mrs. Thompson's grandfather

Mr. Ritchey himself had been warned to leave or take up arms, neither of which he would do because he was a Quaker. Also he would not leave his womenfolk, although there was hard information that the Villistas would not harm American women. The Villistas killed Mr. Ritchey and two of his guests, a surveyor and a medical doctor. According to Jesse's family remembrances, Villa gave orders from the sidewalk and was seen by the woman telephone operator.

"The Villistas killed my grandfather," she related, "but the raid was a disaster for the Mexicans. One hundred and fifty were killed after an American lieutenant ran barefooted to his machine gun and swept the main street. There were nine Americans killed. There is a report which says thirteen, but it was only nine," she said.

"The next day I was taken by my mother to view the burning, now smoldering, hotel and the dead Americans. Everyone was crying but since I was only three I was not able to comprehend it all, but I remember it well."

⮞ • ⮜

MEETING PRINCE CHARLES
by Laurette Davis McCommas
of Whitewright

Laurette and her son, Mark, always touched base by phone each week while he was going to the University of Texas at Austin. It was 1987 and Prince Charles had come to visit the campus.

After they had their usual talk about the mundane things in life, Mark said, "Oh! I almost forgot to tell you that Prince Charles visited our campus the other day."

"Yes, I saw that on the news," Laurette said.

Mark continued, "I went to a class, and there are usually about forty students in it, but the instructor wasn't there, and there were only three of us. One guy said, 'I just remembered this is the day Prince Charles is to walk across the center of the campus.'"

"I hurried out, and there were almost no students lined along the parade walk, but I stood there, and guess what? The cameras were rolling, and Prince Charles reached over and shook hands with me. He wasn't very tall, and he wasn't very good looking. His handshake was weak. I felt sorry for him. I thought he was trapped by birth into his position in life."

"Did you buy a newspaper?" Laurette asked. "Your picture was probably in it."

"No, I didn't think it was very important," he responded.

11.

The Wars

Most families have members who have fought in and lived through a series of wars in this and the last century. In our own time we have heard first-hand tales from our kinfolks about World War I and II, Korea, and Vietnam, not to mention Desert Storm, Afghanistan, and other military excursions in which our nation has been involved.

When my own grandchildren ask me if I saw much action in the Pacific, I tell them about the second disaster at Pearl Harbor, long after December 7, 1941. The day started badly as the minesweeper U.S.S. *Harkness* pulled up to moor alongside other minesweepers, and in the process I threw the heaving line through a clothesline of skivvies on the outboard ship. Then that noon on guard duty, I leaned across between ships, accidentally unbuckled my guard belt, and watched helplessly as my .45 pistol and all the ship's keys sank to the bottom of Pearl Harbor. That afternoon I was sent to clean up a pile of trash on the fantail and later heard somebody ask, "What happened to the .50 caliber gun covers?" I spent the rest of that day going through a garbage dump to retrieve the gun covers that I in my diligence had thrown there. I smelled like garbage for a week. —And we still won the war.

We won the war when we did because we finally got the Japanese' attention at Hiroshima and Nagasaki. I have told my own story of the A-bombs to my family with utmost seriousness, and I presume they will pass the story on to their children. The U.S.S. *Harkness* was sailing some-

The editor in 1943, when the war was still fun

where around Okinawa on V-J Day. We were in convoy with a half-a-dozen other ships heading to God-knows-where. They never told us anything. We sailed blacked out and at battle stations, wearing helmets and life jackets, both of which we hated. We also had been listening to the radio and knew about the big bombs dropped on Hiroshima and Nagasaki, so we were sweating it out, hoping the war would end before we had to invade Japan.

Then, about ten o'clock that morning the destroyer leading the convoy blew its whistle and ran up the flags spelling "Victory!" We screamed and hollered and jumped around like a bunch of crazies, and some idiot yelled "Unload through the barrels!" Well, we fired everything we had, the big gun—a three-inch fifty—twenty millimeters, fifty calibers. Crewmen broke out carbines, .30-06s, and .45 automatics from the gun shack and shot at anything that floated or flew. They did the same thing on the other ships, and it's a wonder we didn't kill and sink each other and every ship in the East China Sea.

Our whole convoy headed toward Buckner Bay. We made port that evening, and the main thing I remember is the Japanese mourning dirge that played continually on all of their radio stations. Now that we were the victors we could allow ourselves—dimly—to recognize that a nation of human beings was bowed down in sorrow.

I don't remember much shipboard philosophizing about the morality of the A-bombs. Considering the bloodshed involved in taking Iwo Jima and Okinawa, admirals and deck apes alike agreed that if we had to march up the mainland of Japan and take it by force of arms, our dead would number in the tens of thousands. We were awed, even frightened by the power unleashed at those holocausts, but we *never* questioned the necessity *nor* the morality. We would have been fools to have had it and not used it, and gold-star mothers would have hanged Harry Truman from a sour apple tree if he had let the war go on and not stopped it as totally as he did.

Many of the war stories that follow, like those above, are not yet folklore. They have not yet matured, as folklore must, into family legends, although they are personal legends. They have not been passed down from one generation to the next, with each generation telling the story with its generation's attitudes. I imagine that some of my descendants will delete my atom-bomb story from our family's canon. But the stories of recent wars that veterans and their families tell now will be passed on by later generations. If the stories are good enough to last, they will become legends after a multitude of tellings and after years of listenings.

These opening legends about wars long past, however, have maturity.

ဆ • ဆ

SON OF THE AMERICAN REVOLUTION
by Gideon Lincecum (1793–1874)
edited by Jerry Lincecum of Sherman

[Jerry Lincecum is the great-great-great-grandson of Gideon Lincecum, who recorded this story in his autobiography, published as *Adventures of a Frontier Naturalist: The Life and Times of Dr. Gideon Lincecum* (College Station, TX, 1994).]

According to family tradition, the Lincecum males were almost wiped out during the American Revolution. Gideon Lincecum I (?–1779), residing in Georgia, was Captain of a company of Rangers, one hundred strong, under pay of the local government. They had been organized for protection against the incursions of the Muskogee Indians, who were very trouble-some on the border settlements of Georgia, being hired by the British to kill and scalp the people of Georgia. From the British government, the Indians received for each scalp (of man, woman or child) a bottle of Rum and $8.00 in money. Captain Lincecum and his Rangers made frequent excursions along the Oconee River, the boundary line between the Indians and the white people.

Shortly after Augusta, Georgia, fell into the hands of the English forces (1779), Colonel Nace Few sent an order to Captain Lincecum, directing him to collect his Rangers and meet his forces, one thousand men, at a certain place on the following Monday. Captain Lincecum notified his company, ordering them to assemble. When the appointed day came Captain Lincecum and eight of his Rangers set out for the rendezvous together. They had pro-gressed about half the day, when at a point a few miles outside of where Sparta, the county seat of Hancock County, Georgia, now stands, they came to a bunch of rawhide ropes that had been dropped in the path. Here they made a halt and one of the men dismounted to get the ropes. At that instant the Indians, who had been concealed in the switch-cane that covered the ground in that new country, rose up and fired into the crowd. Except Cap-tain Lincecum (who received a shot in the thigh), and Jonathan Hagerthy and Wm. Higginbotham, all fell dead on the spot. The Captain and his two surviving companions beat a hasty retreat, the Indians pursuing with aw-ful yelling and firing. They had not proceeded exceeding half a mile, when the Captain, who was bleeding and who seemed to be greatly excited, turned and faced the approaching savages.

His two men begged him not to stop any more and rode on a few hun-dred yards further, during which time the Captain had again charged his rifle and stopped a second time. His men kept urging him not to stop, for there were at least thirty Indians in sight. He seemed not to heed their ear-nest admonitions but dismounted from his horse and made ready to fire as the Indians came running and yelling towards him. He fired on them, as did also his two men, who pleaded with him to mount his horse. There was yet time to escape but he seemed busied reloading his rifle, paying no at-tention to their pleadings. The Indians had now approached sufficiently near, and having opened fire on the little party, the bullets were rattling thickly all around them. The Captain fell mortally wounded, and seeing that there was no possible chance to do anything more, his companions reluctantly left the field.

Higginbotham raised a company of men and went the next day to bury the dead. They came to the Captain first. He was pretty badly mutilated, having had five scalps taken from his head. The signs were that he fought to the last, having fallen with his hand full of powder, showing that he was loading his gun when he received the death wound. He had two very large, well-trained dogs that fell with him; and the positions in which they lay, as well as the torn-up ground, bent-down grass and bushes around the blood-stained place, all goes to show that there had been a dire conflict with the dogs before the Indians obtained their scalps from the Captain's head. Thus my grandpa (and namesake) met his death.

Grandfather Gideon had three sons: Edward, John, and Hezekiah, as well as three daughters. Hezekiah was only nine years old when his father died, but his brothers were old enough to fight and both were taken prisoner and shot soon after the Battle of Cowpens. Thus reduced to a single male, the Lincecum line was in danger of dying out. Fortunately, Hezekiah, who was my father, turned out to be prolific, fathering seven sons and two daughters.

ꙮ • ꙮ

ISOM PARMER, SARACEN, AND THE BATTLE OF SAN JACINTO
by Frances B. Vick
of Saron and Dallas

Martin Zuber, who was married to Martin Parmer's granddaughter, Louisa Liles, wrote in a letter to Parmer's grandson, A. W. Morris, about this incident with Isom Parmer, Martin Parmer's son. Zuber wrote that he had learned about this "from Isom Parmer himself."

Isom accompanied Martin to Washington–on–the–Brazos and was elected doorkeeper to the Convention. He was apparently as feisty as his father when it came to fighting because he had served under his father in the Fredonian rebellion, and in 1835 he served in the siege of Bexar in Captain John M. Bradley's company and participated in the Grass Fight. In 1836 before accompanying his father to the Convention, he bought a very fine-looking large, gray horse, paying four hundred silver dollars for it. The horse was named Saracen. Zuber wrote in the letter that he often saw the horse, who was a "handsome animal, but not very nimble."

At the conclusion of the Convention, when Sam Houston was organizing his army, he was sorrily mounted and wanted a better horse. He told Isom that the commander in chief of the army ought to have a horse that looked like he was the commander in chief, so he talked Isom into selling him the horse for the same amount Isom had paid for him. Isom hated to part with the horse but he wanted to do this favor for the general, so Houston rode off on Saracen, ending up at San Jacinto. It was this horse that was shot out from under Houston at the battle on April 21, 1836. Isom was also in the battle but on another horse he had purchased for the four hundred dollars he got from Sam Houston.

ன • ஓ

C. A. LEE: WHAT SIDE WAS HE ON?
by Jean G. Schnitz
of Boerne

The Civil War stories from my mother's Lee family who lived near Cassville, in Barry County, Missouri, would make a good novel. Some of these stories also explain why my Great-grandfather Columbus Addison Lee came to Texas. C. A. Lee (who bought a dulcimer just before the Civil War in Sedalia, Missouri—the one I still play) was not the first or last person to come to Texas to escape his past. He did a good job of escaping his past. In Texas he became a leader in his church and community and enjoyed a good reputation throughout the latter part of his life.

My grandmother's stories always portrayed her father, Columbus Addison Lee (C. A. Lee), as being a staunch Confederate soldier. She told her children and grandchildren (including me) that he had stayed close to home during the war. In 1990, my research and a report from the archives in Washington, D. C., revealed that C. A. Lee had joined the Union Army on January 3, 1864, and served until the end of the war. Elder members of my mother's family refused to believe C. A. Lee had served in the Union Army, yet I held in my hands copies of his service records. Not only that, but I have in my possession records to show that both he and his widow, P. C. Lee, collected pensions from the U. S. Government for his army service.

Other Lee family stories reported that he was a bushwhacker and didn't support either army. There is considerable evidence that these stories are also true.

Then, in late August 2001, another Lee family researcher provided copies of C. A. Lee's Confederate service record, showing that on October 6, 1862, which was fairly early in the Civil War, C. A. had enlisted as a Private in Co. I, Mitchell's Regiment of the Confederate Missouri Infantry. Therefore, my grandmother's stories had been correct. She certainly must have known that he also served in the Union Army, but she didn't tell that part of the story.

Here is how it happened, based on records and family stories.

Brother against brother was a reality during the Civil War in southern Missouri, officially a "Union" state, where feelings ran high. According to his Confederate service record, on October 6, 1862, Columbus Addison Lee, my great-grandfather, joined the Confederate army as a private in the Missouri Infantry, though he had no real interest in being a Confederate soldier except that he considered himself a Southerner. My grandmother told me stories about his staying near home, hiding in the fields during the day and coming to the house at night.

Before long, C. A. Lee apparently left the Confederate Army and "took to the woods" with many of the other young men in Barry County, Missouri, along the border with Arkansas, including several of his brothers who didn't want to fight for either side. From family stories told by Edgar E. Weston and others, I have good reason to believe that C. A. Lee was involved in bushwhacker activities. Lawlessness was rampant, and there was nobody to stop anybody from doing whatever they wanted to.

The eldest Lee brother, William Wheeler Lee, joined the Union Army early in the Civil War and became a captain. He was angry that his brothers had not joined the Union Army. He ordered his younger brother, Newton Lee, to join the Union Army immediately. When Newton did not join, W. W. Lee sent a squad to ambush him. Newton Lee was shot while swimming across the White River near where Roaring River State Park is now located. His widow was summoned to bury his body, and she spread the word about the ambush.

A few weeks later William Wheeler Lee ordered another of his brothers, John S. Lee, to join the Union Army. When John did not, he was shouted from the house where he was shot from his horse by a squad of soldiers sent by his brother William. He was buried where he fell near the front porch of his home in Lee Valley, near Cassville, Missouri. After the Civil War, his descendants put a Confederate flag over his grave, which flies there to this day.

Soon after John S. Lee was killed, a messenger sent by W. W. Lee arrived to tell Columbus Addison Lee and his two younger brothers to go immediately to Springfield, Missouri, to join the Union Army or they would be next! C. A. Lee, having lost two brothers, was a believer by that time, so he enlisted in the Missouri Cavalry of the U.S. Army on January 3, 1864. He drove a supply wagon until he was mustered out at the end of the war. In the mid-1890s he received a pension for his service as a Union Army soldier.

SOLDIER BOY
by Laurette Davis McCommas
of Whitewright

["My dad told me this story. He and I used to wash our dog in the laundry tub in the basement, and this is where he told me many of his stories." Laurette Davis McCommas]

The newsboy on the corner shouted, "Extra, extra, read all about it. To hell with Spain, remember the *Maine*." It was 1897 and Frederick William Ginsky was almost fourteen years old. He rushed forward to buy a newspaper along with throngs of others.

Cuba wanted its independence from Spain, and many of Cuba's citizens had been put in concentration camps. Thousands had died of disease, starvation, and exposure. The United States was not yet a world power, but Cuba was in its backyard. President McKinley was forced by Congress to send the battleship *Maine* to the Havana Harbor, at least to show moral support, but something had gone horribly wrong. No one really knows to this day if the explosion that caused the *Maine* to go down was an accident or a planned deed, but Spain was blamed. This caused the cry, "To hell with Spain, remember the *Maine*." The U.S. Congress forced the President to declare war with Spain in 1898.

Although Fred was now fourteen years old, he was six feet tall and weighed 190 pounds. He overheard two guys talking to each other: "They didn't even ask me to prove my age. I'm only seventeen, but I told them I was eighteen. They didn't ask to see any proof, and they told me to report to the depot tomorrow at noon. I'm in the army. Why don't you see if you can get in too?"

Exciting ideas flashed through Fred's mind. If they could do it, maybe I could too. He went home, polished his shoes, combed his hair and used a piece of coal from the fireplace to darken his chin. Then he walked into the recruiting station, and using an air of importance, went straight to the desk. "I'd like to join the army," he said.

The soldier behind the desk asked, "Can you ride a horse? Are you healthy? How old are you?"

Fred replied, "Yes," to the first two, and "f-f-eighteen," to the last question.

"O.K. You're now in the Coast Artillery Corps of the United States Army. Be at the depot tomorrow at noon. The new troops will be inducted and sent for training to Arizona."

Frederick William Ginsky in 1899, when he was sixteen years old and serving in the Philippines. This was his second hitch, having already served during the Spanish-American War.

Fred couldn't believe it himself when he came bursting into the kitchen to tell the news. His stepmother and his five-year-old brother, Ernie, were the only two home. After Fred told the news, Ernie said, "I hope you die," and Fred never forgave him for it.

The train ride from Detroit to Wilcox, Arizona, was terrible. It was hot and dirty. Fred thought this must be the only place in the world with so many mountains, so much desert and so little water. He hated the crawlies that found their way to the dirt floors of the barracks, but he was a soldier, and that's what he wanted.

Teddy Roosevelt had now taken his Roughriders, minus their horses, to Cuba. The war was over in eight months, and Cuba was independent, but Fred was still in Arizona. The U.S. never wanted to make Cuba a possession, but the power of the U.S. military was now evident. Spain had other possessions too, such as the Philippines, Puerto Rico, and the Virgin Islands. Spain could see that its world power was gone because other European nations would have fought against them if Spain didn't treat their possessions fairly.

Still in Arizona at this time, the young soldier Fred Ginsky was told to report to base headquarters immediately, which he did. Fred had been in the service for the entire eight months, but he hadn't been sent to Cuba. "At ease soldier," the officer said. "I understand that you had a birthday recently."

"Yes sir," Fred answered with the military clip that he had learned.

"How old are you?" the commander asked.

"Nineteen, sir," Fred answered.

"Don't you mean fifteen?" The commander asked, as he glared into Fred's eyes.

"Yes sir," Fred answered still using his military clip.

"Well, Fred, I have here on my desk a train ticket from Wilcox, Arizona, to Detroit, Michigan. You be on that train. You're dismissed. You're too young for a dishonorable discharge. Other than lying about your age, you have been a good soldier."

A few months later he again walked into a recruiting station. Again he told them he was eighteen, and again they believed him. The war between Cuba and Spain was over, but the United States sent naval vessels to guard Manila Harbor in the Philippines. The United States had become a world power. It had bought the buildings in Manila through a payment to Spain, but chose not to annex the island nation as a U.S. possession.

After basic training, Fred's outfit was sent to the Philippines. He found the heat in Manila worse than in Arizona. It was wet heat. Hardly a day went by without rain. The uniform that he was so proud of stuck to his skin. An infected anopheles mosquito bit him, and he suffered from malaria for the rest of his life. Worse than that, he was nauseated most of the time. At first he thought it was the food at the mess hall, but finally he had to go to sick bay. A doctor poked and prodded.

"Hmm," he said. "Son, I think you might have a ruptured appendix. I think in order for you to live, we'll need to remove it." By then, Fred was so miserable that he didn't care what they did to him.

"O.K.," he said. "Go ahead. Get it over with." However, it wasn't a ruptured appendix, but a gallbladder gone bad. In 1899, in the Philippine Islands, that was no small surgery, but he did recover.

He spent months as a hospital patient, and during this time the Philippine tribal girls would entertain the troops. There was one who really caught Fred's eye. He fell madly in love with this beautiful girl and wanted to marry her. Her father was a tribal king, and she was a lovely princess. Fred was told that he had to make a deal with her father, and through an interpreter Fred was told "no."

The old king said, "She is my youngest and most beautiful daughter, and I can't let her move so far away. I would never see her again." It was Fred who never saw her again.

Trouble in China had been brewing for many years. Cannon fodder was needed in Peking, now known as Beijing, during the Boxer Uprising. The Coast Artillery Corps of the United States Army was sent there, and Fred was present on August 14, 1900, as they marched triumphantly into the Forbidden City. He was not seventeen until August 26, 1900.

After more than two years in China, Fred was finally sent back to the United States, where he married Annie Bredlow. They had six children. He received a medical disability discharge with excellent character. His military age of 71 is engraved on his tombstone, but actually he was only 68 when he died at the Dearborn, Michigan, Veterans Hospital.

The only person Fred ever told about the beautiful Filipino princess whom he wanted to marry was his son, who passed this story only to *his* daughter, Laurette. The fact that Fred may have been the youngest soldier in the Spanish-American War and the Boxer Uprising, as well as the story of the beautiful princess, lies buried forever in a soldier boy's heart.

෴ • ෴

DADDY'S WORLD WAR I STORY
by Frances B. Vick
of Dallas

This is one of the few stories my father told me about his World War I experiences. When my father, Andrew Brannen, was a Marine in World War I, he was wounded at Mont Blanc when German machine gun bullets hit the bandolier across his chest, exploding the bandolier bullets. He told us that he was wounded not by bullets but by the debris flying off the bullets and the bandolier that hit him in the mouth, causing him to bleed. His uniform was torn to shreds and bloody and he must have looked frightful. The officer in charge sent him back to the aide station, sending with him some German prisoners for him to guard along the way. He got a kick out of talking about how his buddies' eyes bugged out when they saw him going by because they thought he had been hit by bullets and was so tough he could still guard the German prisoners on his way back to the aide station.

The doctor at the aide station put him on an ambulance bound for the hospital. At the hospital the doctors x-rayed him and thought they saw a

Carl Andrew Brannen, a Marine wounded on the front line in World War I. Doctors found the WWI bullet in him sixty years later.

bullet, which concerned him, but he was relieved when they decided the bullet was a button on the back of his pants.

He enjoyed telling that story for years and we enjoyed hearing it. He would always get tickled about the bullet that turned out to be a button. It wasn't until he was dying from his last illness, some sixty years after the Mont Blanc wounding, that during x-rays doctors indeed found a bullet in him—the one from World War I. This, of course, has started another legend in the family.

๛ • ๑

A HEROIC VETERAN OF FOREIGN WARS
by Marlene Rushing
of Houston

My father, John McKinley Washington Brown, was born March 4, 1897, in Dabney, Arkansas. He was fourth of six children born to John R. and Mida Hope Asbury Brown. My father carried the proud names of two American presidents to whom the family was related. John R. Brown died and left Mida with six young children. She had been trained as a schoolteacher, so she taught her own children around a kerosene lamp after a hard day's work picking the agricultural crops of the season.

My father had never traveled beyond the borders of Arkansas and Oklahoma, and he hadn't seen a very bright future for himself there—so as a young man he enlisted in the army during World War I. The army was totally confused by his having four names and the perplexed sergeant enlisted him as McKinley Washington Brown. (Since my father used John M. Brown as his legal name, it took much paper work to get this straightened out later.) When he completed his basic training he was assigned to the 109th Engineer Battalion, Company D and sent overseas.

While on board the troopship he immediately became violently seasick and spent the entire voyage in sick bay where he also contracted pneumonia. Upon landing in Liverpool, England, he was hospitalized. During the ensuing months in England he caught measles and influenza. The first day he was allowed to leave his hospital bed was November 11, 1918, the day the Armistice was signed. Germany surrendered and Armistice Day was declared.

Since the sick and wounded were the first to be sent home, Daddy was loaded back onto a ship and sent to New York City. Though he had bravely signed up to fight the enemy, his entire tour of duty consisted of sick bay and hospitalization.

Hailed among the conquering heroes, Daddy toured New York where locals wouldn't allow a man in uniform to pay for his own meals or walk a block without someone shaking his hand or thanking him for his service.

After a very enjoyable time in New York, Daddy traveled to Camp Logan, Texas, to receive his honorable discharge on February 13, 1919. He was mustered out and paid in full the amount of $15.17.

Daddy spent the next few months riding freight trains around that part of the country—often working at sawmills—and eventually getting into the oilfield business where he drove supply trucks from rig to rig in oilfields across Louisiana and East Texas.

Daddy always said he was a "hero" because he took all those shots and medicines so other soldiers didn't have to.

ৼ৹ · ৯৵

WHEN THE TELEGRAM CAME
by Frances B. Vick
of Dallas

Everything changed in our family forever the day the telegram came. We lived in Lake Jackson where my parents were teaching. My father had a supervisory position in the Brazosport Independent School District and because of gas shortages carpooled to Freeport with Pop Blair, who taught history at the high school. They were old, old friends from Trinity County, before the war threw our worlds into upheaval.

My oldest brother, Andy, was out in the Pacific stationed on Tinian Island with Patrol Bombing Squadron 102. They flew a PB4YI, the navy version of a B-24. My other brother, Joe Pat, was a student at A&M. I was in the fourth grade at Lake Jackson Elementary School. Andy was nineteen, Joe Pat was seventeen and I was nine.

On this day, I was out in the front yard playing with friends when I saw my father arrive in Pop Blair's car, get out, and lean back in the car window to respond to something his friend was saying. My mother arrived at the house from her school about that time and seeing an envelope sticking out of my father's back pocket, playfully pulled it out, which was typical of her. Dad grabbed for it but it was too late. She had already seen what it was and her playful demeanor was gone. It was a telegram from the War Department that had come to my father at the administration offices and he had carried it around all day.

Andy was missing in action, shot down over Marcus Island. Mother knew immediately that he was gone and never held any hope. My father, though, felt that Andy could have made it to an island and that he might be a prisoner held by the Japanese, or in hiding on one of the islands, particularly since he was such a strong swimmer.

Andy Brannen, whose plane was shot down over Marcus Island, May 9, 1945

The plane went down May 9, 1945, just three months before the end of the war. When the war was over my father sat for hours by the radio listening to the names of released prisoners being read over the radio, but Andy's name was never read. My mother later told me that my father came in one evening and told her that he knew Andy was gone and that he had reconciled to it. He told her that Andy had ridden with him all day long as he made his rounds to the different schools and had let him know that he was okay, thus his reconciliation.

During my mother's lifetime she placed flowers on the altar at church on the Sunday closest to May 9. After her death, I placed flowers on the altar at my church on the Sunday closest to May 9 and have all these years. I am sure one of my children will take up this tradition when I am gone. He has never been forgotten.

෮ • ෭

MY LONGEST DAY
by J. Willis Hastings
of Sherman

August 22, 1944, was the longest day of my life. I was a pilot returning from a bombing mission deep into Europe, and we were shot down by enemy fighters over Hungary. As I went down I had visions of what would follow. Would I be lucky enough to fall into the hands of a member of the underground? When I got close enough to see the earth, it was obvious my impending arrival had not gone unnoticed. Several men and women were rushing toward my destination, carrying hoes, scythes, and pitchforks from their work in the fields.

Only by last-minute maneuvering of the chute did I avoid impaling myself on some stakes in a vineyard. But this increased my rate of fall and I struck the ground so hard that my right ankle was severely sprained. So painful was it that I expected to see a fractured bone. My next jolt was the sight of a very young boy pointing a shotgun at me. Soon I was surrounded by fifteen to twenty hostile peasants. I raised my arms in surrender and was quickly relieved of the .45-caliber automatic in my shoulder holster.

One large fellow struck me behind the ear, knocking me down, and others came close and spat in my face. Worse yet, another cut a shroud line from the parachute and began making a noose. My left ear was bleeding from a blow struck by the most vocal of my captors. As I struggled to stand upright on my injured ankle, blood poured from my ear.

The South Carolina state seal

But the most embarrassing experience came when they held me by my arms and legs while one of their companions tore open the fly of my trousers, ripped open my undershorts, and carefully examined my penis. Apparently satisfied, they then allowed me to button up. This was a mystery until my examiner used the word "Jud," and shook his head, "no." I knew then that they were checking to see if I bore the Jewish mark of circumcision.

In an instant I recalled the briefing at which we were told that half of the Hungarian people were pro-Allied. Why did I have to land among the other fifty percent? Then fate intervened, and perhaps my life was saved by a tiny medallion of St. Christopher, patron saint of travelers. On a whim, I had placed it on a chain with my dog tags, in spite of my Calvinistic Presbyterian background. I guess I believed it best to cover all bases.

When the medallion was revealed, apparently one of the women said, in effect, "This man is a Roman Catholic Christian or he would not be wearing this St. Christopher medal." Anyway, there was a great deal of discussion, and enough time delay to permit the arrival of a man in a black uniform with a rifle strapped to his shoulder, who took charge. I later learned he was a member of the Hungarian National Police, and he took me into his custody. And believe me, I was grateful.

When he delivered me to a very small village nearby, named Goldap, I was placed in jail with four or five other Americans who had been shot down. None were from my crew. The next nine months as a POW were an ordeal, but one thing that sustained me was my recollection of the Latin phrase on the seal of my beloved home state of South Carolina: Dum Spiro Spero, which translates, "While I live, I hope." I was alive, I was breathing, and I knew some of my fellow airmen were not.

ରେ • ରଚ

MY WWII BRIDE
by Elmer Kelton
of San Angelo

When I went to Europe in the last weeks of World War II, I never had any thought of finding a bride. My main interest, joining an infantry company just in time for the Rhine River crossing, was in staying alive and someday getting home. Fortunately the war was winding down, and our main problem was in staying up with the German retreat.

In May 1945, the war in Europe was over. The army started preparing us for transfer to the Pacific for the invasion of Japan. To everyone's great relief, two atomic bombs eliminated that necessity. Lacking enough points to go home on the army's rotation system, I wound up in the army of occupation, assigned to a unit in Ebensee, Austria. We guarded German prisoners of war while they cut trees in the forest to help fire up stalled European industries.

Austria is a magnificent country, and Ebensee is in one of the most beautiful parts, the Salzkammergut, a land of spectacular mountains and deep glacial lakes below Salzburg. Perhaps those helped set the mood for me when one evening I encountered a nice young lady down at the boat landing. She had come to check the schedule for her parents, who planned to take a side-wheeler steamboat across the lake the next day to the market in Gmunden. Her name was Anni Lipp (pronounced Leep). I had picked up some fractured German from talking to former Wehrmacht soldiers. Despite the language barrier—she spoke no English—we managed to carry on a conversation of sorts, and I walked her home. Just before her mother looked out the window and brusquely ordered her to come into the house immediately, I asked if I might come over and visit her again.

I was there the very next day and found her cooking an apple strudel. She claims it was the strudel that did it. In any case, I was hooked for life, though it was a while before I realized it. I kept going back to her house, whether she fixed strudel or not.

Elmer Kelton and Anni Lipp, his Austrian war bride in 1946

Here's a "fifty-years-later" photo of Elmer and Anni.

It was an unlikely romance. We had nothing in common but youth, she an Austrian working girl who spoke no English, me a kid from a ranch in the Crane County sand hills. But with a lot of sign language and my bad German, we got by.

Early in 1946 I was transferred to Linz, the provincial capital, as a "gofer" in a military government unit. I was still just a Pfc., the rankest I ever got. Every weekend I rode the train or hitch–hiked on military vehicles the fifty or so miles back to Ebensee. On one occasion I rode a couple of miles on a hay wagon. By this time I knew it was serious.

Protocol demanded that I ask her father for her hand, and I practiced up on the right way to say so in German. He had evidently read my mind and was prepared. He said simply, "Take her."

That was much easier said than done. The military discouraged G.I.s from marrying in Europe. I had hardly made a dent in the red tape before I got orders in June to return home for discharge. My slow train trip to Linz after our last tearful goodbye was one of the bleakest times in my life. Back in Ebensee, people were telling Anni that she had seen and heard the last of me.

She hadn't, though. As soon as I became a civilian I started the process of getting her to this country. Even with help from Senator Tom Connolly's office, the legalities consumed about a year. I did not know until later that she was having more trouble than I was, including several long train trips to Vienna to sign papers and undergo examinations. Finally we had all the T's crossed and the I's dotted, we thought.

Her trip across Europe to the embarkation point at Le Havre, France, turned out to be a nightmare of border crossings and missed connections, compounded by a French railroad strike which forced her to talk her way onto a bus and land in Paris at the wrong place, without French currency and hampered by a language barrier. But as I have found during some fifty-five years since, when she sets her mind to something, she gets it done in spite of hell or high water.

We were married in my grandmother's house in Midland, Texas, July 3, 1947, almost two years after we first met. Despite some people's misgivings, we think it is going to work. And by the way, everybody calls her Ann now.

ৎৎ • ৯৶

MY SISTER JOINS THE MARINES
by Martha Baxley
of Denison

Though my early childhood was spent in the era of the Great Depression, my teens coincided with World War II. That infamous Sunday afternoon in December, my parents went for a long walk after our Sunday dinner. I was sewing and listening to the radio when the announcer broke in with the news about the attack on Pearl Harbor. The Japanese ambassadors were staying in the White House, and we had been told that peace was a sure thing. I was so excited that I walked out to meet my parents and to inform them of the situation.

Our lives changed overnight. Men were drafted in large numbers and many volunteered, saying that gave them the choice of branch of service. There were signs all over showing Uncle Sam pointing a finger at you with a slogan, "Uncle Sam wants YOU!" The first time I saw a soldier in uniform I stared unabashedly, but before long the streets were filled with servicemen, and one of my hobbies was identifying each branch and the insignia of each man.

Along with this came a custom of placing a little flag in your window if you had a family member in service. When my brother-in-law enlisted, my mother hung up a flag with one star. After Glenn and I married and he was in uniform, our family got a flag with two stars. When my sister enlisted in the Marine Corps, we were one of the few families who had a flag with three stars.

She had always wished she were a boy, so when she was in high school she changed her name from Emogene to Gene, saying that at least she could have a boy's name. When manpower became a problem with men leaving to fight, it was decided to allow women to enter the armed services. The theory was that women could do office work, run errands, work in mess halls, drive jeeps, and release men for active duty.

Thinking it a great adventure to be included in a traditionally male activity, Gene had enlisted and was on her way to boot camp before she told anyone. The green Marine uniform was becoming to her red hair and hazel eyes, and she served until the end of the war. She even got a trip to Hawaii and all G.I. benefits for the rest of her life.

Private Margaret (Gene) Ryan, U.S. Marine Corps in 1944

THE RAIN IN KOREA IS AWFUL COLD AND WET
by James Ward Lee
of Fort Worth

Up to now, I have tried to keep it quiet that I was involved in the Korean War. A WWII vet friend of mine always called it "the war we tied." He was a member of the Greatest Generation, and he had been written up by Tom Brokaw. My father served in the First Division in the Argonne Forest in the Great War, or the War to End all Wars. My great-granddaddy Wyatt was in the 30th Alabama and died following Vicksburg. Another ancestor of mine was at Cerro Gordo in the Mexican War.

And I was mixed up in a war that wasn't a war. It was a police action— only 54,000 Americans died and another 164,000 got wounded. Vietnam and Desert Storm were fought on television and got all the publicity, but we pretty much conducted our police action in secret and way off camera. Only a few of us remember the song lines: "The rain in Korea is awful cold and wet/And them rotation papers is mighty hard to get." Those 54,000 escaped the rain finally. And are now forgotten. We don't even have a wall in D. C. that everybody who goes to Washington has to see.

Well, fifty and more winters have passed since Korea, and I have decided how I'm going to tell my stories.

Oh, my yes, we had our narrow escapes. We could have all died. One night an ensign who had come fresh from the U.S. Naval Academy was on watch when a Chinese junk was discovered on radar. Ensign Pulver—I think that was his name—woke up the two Korean liaison officers, broke out the guns, and readied the searchlight. The Chinese junk crew was told to surrender peacefully or be killed by American fire. The Korean officers warned them that we were going to turn on the searchlight and we had better see hands in the air Gene Autry style.

No Reply.

"All right," Mr. Pulver said, "Tell them to get ready."

The Korean officers said something incomprehensible and we turned on the light.

The buoy we illuminated bobbed gently in the water, and a good time was had by all. All except the ensign, who proved what we common sailors had known about him all along.

Two nights later, same ensign, same Korean officers, same rifles, same searchlight, same threats, same buoy. We all knew we had lost that round to the enemy buoy and went on our way to fight at a later day.

The very next night I had an early watch and slept through until morning. When I went on deck, I found five or six North Korean youths standing around a crude wooden boat and two battered oars.

"Omigod," I said, "We have been captured, and they didn't wake me up."

Wrong again. The Koreans had slipped up on our ship in the night and had banged on the fantail with the oars begging to surrender. Somebody finally told Mr. Pulver that we had company, and he slowed down enough to take the enemy and their rowboat aboard. We then dressed them in navy dungarees and blue shirts and let them wander around the ship for several days until we came up on a South Korean frigate. We transferred the prisoners and drifted on to future glory. I always suspected that the South Koreans slit the throats of these bold pirates and took the new uniforms.

But, hey, war is hell.

It was really hell for some old North Korean guy up near Yangyang Harbor. He was trying to make a crop up on a hillside while we were bombarding the town about half a mile below him. He seemed to be plowing a mule, but it could have been a water buffalo. (They didn't teach animal husbandry in boot camp.) Anyway, he seemed to be a little unconcerned about the firing aimed in his general direction. He thought better of our marksmen than I did. I knew we couldn't hit anything on purpose, but the old farmer might be out a mule just from one of our strays. Our objective was a tall smokestack rising up out of the town of Yangyang. Why we wanted to hit it was never clear—gunnery practice, I suppose. So every morning at about 0800 we lay off Yangyang and fired our allotted five-inch rounds. Probably twenty or so. Every morning we missed the smokestack, though I am sure we killed lots of women and children and dogs and cats. But we had not hit the smokestack when we were sent off to the Yellow Sea on the other side of Korea to lay waste to more Korean countryside. If we could hit it.

Once we rounded the bend of Korea and headed north up the Yellow Sea side, we lowered the U.S. Flag and raised the tasteful blue and white of the United Nations. Now we were policing for the whole civilized world. And we ran with Colombian destroyers, New Zealand frigates, Australian carriers, Canadian vessels of one sort or another and the occasional Thai gunboat.

Our job up there was purely shore bombardment, for we had done so well on the other edge of Korea that we were a natural for the more serious

James Ward Lee, who performed valiantly in the China seas during the Korean "police action" and was never without his trusty comb should shore leave be granted

Yellow Sea side. So we steamed slowly up and down the west coast of Korea firing off occasional shots at farmers and ranchers and rice paddy workers. Once, in a dense fog, our radar picked up the ever-present Chinese junk. Even though nobody in the Navy ever saw a Chinese junk, we all knew that the waters were crammed with them. "Thick on the ground," one old country boy from North Carolina said.

Very quietly, without all that bonging that usually signals General Quarters, we were whispered to our battle stations. We were ready to kill some commies. Blow them out of the water with our five-inch guns and then wipe out the survivors with our twenty-millimeter machine guns.

I was on the bridge manning some headphones between the captain and the gunnery officer. The fire control radar began to twist and turn and someone whispered, "Lock On!"

"Stand by to fire," the captain said.

I told the gunnery officer on the headphone, "Stand by to fire." Nervously.

"Standing by," the gunnery officer said back to me on the headphone.

Suddenly from up on the fire control radar atop the bridge, a reserve officer who had a full-time job at Sears Roebuck, said, "Wait! Wait! Wait!"

The fog had lifted enough to reveal the Chinese junk as a Canadian cruiser with nine or so six-inch guns. All trained on us.

We stood down. And so did the Canadians. I was relieved, but in later years I wondered if the Canadians could shoot any better than we could. But then in 1989, I bought a Canadian-made Ford Crown Victoria that ran like a Singer sewing machine, so maybe they did have some technical know-how. And I could be lying at the bottom of the Yellow Sea right now.

I wasn't much scared back in those halcyon days, but now I am terrified when I think how much of a mess our war was and how we had hundreds of young officers whose competence could have got all of us killed. Maybe there is a reason nobody remembers Korea. We were inept, but I am sure all our present-day warriors know exactly what they are doing. So Bin Laden had better watch it.

Later in the war—the Police Action—I was sent down to the South Pacific to help out with the H-bomb tests, and I am proud to say that only one H-bomb got away from us. No Americans were killed outright, but several Japanese fishermen on *The Fortunate Dragon* went to join their ancestors.

❧ • ❧

A LIGHT IN THE DARKNESS
by Robert Flynn
of San Antonio

"It's Christmas Eve," a Marine said. "Tomorrow is Christmas."

Another Marine shrugged. This was the 'Nam in 1970. Every day was the same until the day you rotated back to "The World."

I was a reporter at a platoon command post in the heart of "Indian Country," with Sgt. Burris assigned as my bodyguard. The Army called them "escorts," but the Marines insisted they were bodyguards. Lt. Smith, platoon leader, and four Marines manned a double-decker bunker, dug four feet deep into the top of a small hill and sandbagged on the first level. Around the bunker was barbed wire laced with trip flares to let everyone know Charlie was coming, and mined to make him wish he hadn't.

A few miles away was Baldy, a combat base on a barren hilltop with a battery of 105 howitzers, a mortar platoon, and a reaction force. If our command post came under heavy attack on this night, we could expect artillery support from Baldy in one minute and helicopter gunships in ten minutes. A reaction force from Baldy was not likely to come down the road after dark. Too easy to ambush.

Robert L. Flynn during his first tour of duty as a Marine in Korea and during his second tour as a war correspondent in Vietnam

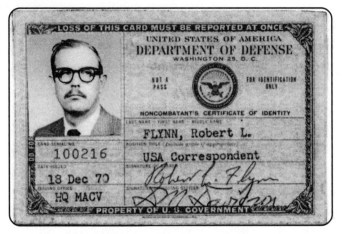

No one was eager to go into the hot, cramped bunker. We stood outside and watched flares that bloomed over the scrub-covered hills, the lush paddies, and impenetrable tree lines.

Rifle fire punctuated by grenades broke out at a command post a couple of hills away. Ricocheting white tracers spun lazily into the night. Two Viet Cong units had stumbled together and opened fire on each other. Then the night went quiet again except for the thump of mortars followed by the pop of sizzling flares.

"Time to open the presents. It's Christmas eve," Lt. Smith explained to the puzzled Marines. They nodded without cheer.

Except for the radio watch, everyone crowded into the upper level of the bunker where a small Christmas tree stood atop an ammo can. Under the tree were packages sent by friends back home. Smith lighted a candle to see by and distributed the presents. Books, games, playing cards and edibles were pooled for everyone. Pens and stationery were equally divided, with an extra box of stationery for the Marine who would write "thank you" notes to school children and other friends of Nam soldiers.

Lt. Smith broke out a near-empty bottle of Jack Daniels and passed it around, each man deciding his share and Smith taking the last drink. He blew out the candle. "If we're attacked, drop into the lower level," he said. "The top won't take a direct hit."

The Marines pulled off their boots and lay down fully clothed, including the hot flak jackets. No one wanted to search for essentials in an attack. I dozed, aware of the hum of mosquitoes, the rustle of rats, the soft murmur of the man on radio watch below, the mortars firing flares.

Twenty years earlier, while I was in the Marines in Korea, I had spent Christmas apart from family, but this was the first time I had missed Christmas since I had married. But Christmas can be whenever you celebrate it, and my family had celebrated before I left for Vietnam. On our private Christmas morning, my daughters Deirdre and Brigid were awake way earlier than on a school day, before the arrival of the appaloosa foal that we had selected for Deirdre's special Christmas gift. Brigid spotted her new bicycle immediately, but we had to tell Deirdre that we had ordered a present that hadn't come but would surely be there by the time we finished breakfast. It wasn't.

It was no longer possible to keep Brigid off her bicycle, but she promised not to go far and to come back frequently. Soon after Brigid cycled off, a horse trailer appeared with an appaloosa filly, weaned a little early, big-eyed after its first trailer ride, and standing frightened in a strange place with strange people. It was love at first sight as the filly and Deirdre got acquainted with each other. Brigid soon returned to admire the filly briefly and to be released to go even farther on her bike and to stay even longer.

It was the last Christmas the four of us would celebrate together. I dozed lightly, half hearing the murmur of the radio watch below, not dreaming that Brigid would die two months later.

That wound was still in the future, and the four of us were laughing at the Christmas table when Lt. Smith shouted, "Merry Christmas." I sat up to see the mortars on Baldy paint a Christmas tree of red and green flares dangling under a sizzling white star at the top. Slowly the flares drifted to the ground, taking peace on earth and goodwill with them. The night returned to the thump of mortars and the pop of flares that sizzled in the darkness.

12.
The Cycle of Life

The Cycle of Life includes stories of birthing, meeting and marrying, and dying. A dear old Baptist lady of Nacogdoches told me and other assembled club members about the start of her marriage. She was double dating with her best friend, and her friend and her sweetie decided to cross the Sabine to Many, Louisiana, and get married. The lady and her date would be the bride's maid and best man. The elopement was so exciting that she and her date decided to get married too. They did, and she took this new husband home with her, but like a coward he got up and left before dawn, leaving her to tell the family. The only thing wrong was that she didn't want to leave home and go live with her husband. Her mother spent a tearful morning explaining that after a girl married a man, she had to live with him, something she hadn't thought about the night before. She finally did though, and they were still living together fifty-plus years later. She probably hadn't gotten used to it yet.

And when Grandad's mother was dying, she called in all her children one by one—except Grandad, and because of his wayward ways, she called him in twice.

BIRTHING AND NAMING

HERSCHEL AND LEO
by Frances B. Vick
of Dallas

At family reunions, sooner or later the "Old Folks," as my cousin Herschel Brannen, Jr., called our parents, would get to *their* stories, having gone through the stories of the ancestors. Uncle Herschel's story of his birth was a favorite. He was born in November 1905 at Saron in Trinity County, during a cold snap. He told us that when he was born he was put inside the oven of the wood-burning stove so he could be kept warm. The best part, though, was that he swore that he could remember being inside the oven.

When Lottie Brannen—Charlotte Walker Brannen, my grandmother—was pregnant with her third child, she went to Groveton, the county seat, for shopping. In those days of 1900, it was the habit of the court during a trial for the bailiff to call out of the courthouse window the name of the next witness who was to appear on the stand. On this occasion, Lottie heard the bailiff call out, "Leo Bergman, Leo Bergman." She was so taken with the name she heard that when the baby came he was named Leo Bergman Brannen, or at least that is the story Uncle Leo told at the reunions.

ൟ • ൠ

VOODOO CHILD
by Marlene Rushing
of Houston

My mother, Myrtie Lea Starling Brown, was born October 12, 1904, in Munday, Texas. Mother went through two marriages that ended in divorce, when at age thirty she married my father, John M. Brown. Mother desperately wanted to have children, but this dream always seemed to elude her.

For four years she followed my daddy from oil patch to oil patch and was living in Algiers, Louisiana, when on New Year's Day 1938, she and some of the other oilfield wives went to see the newborn baby of a Creole woman who did laundry for all of them. Mother took this tiny baby in her arms and sat down on the floor to play with it. As she sang and rocked to and fro, the old Creole midwife asked her if she had any children of her own. Mother responded that she did not and would give her right arm to have a baby. The midwife asked if Mother wanted her to "say the words over her" so she could get pregnant? Mother and her friends laughed as she gave her permission. The midwife mumbled a chant as she shuffled around Mother (still sitting on the floor holding the new baby). She sprinkled something over Mother and upon completion, told Mother that she would have a baby "before the year was out!"

Mother and her friends laughed about this all the way back to their homes where Mother related all this to my Daddy. Together they had a good laugh as she described what had happened.

I was born December 1, 1938. Mother always said I was "conjured." I was Mother's only child.

ഹ • ൏

ALMOST A BASTARD
by Barbara Pybas
of Gainesville

Kenneth Monroe Pybas of Bedford County, Tennessee, served in General Nathan Bedford Forrest's escort. As a junior officer, Forrest raised several companies during that conflict, but as they were mustered, the companies were removed from his command and placed under West Point-trained officers. Not having attended West Point, Forrest was appointed a general only after distinguishing himself in battle. After the units were removed from his command, Forrest demanded that his escort of thirty to forty men be left intact. K. M. Pybas served in that escort capacity as a scout in several battles.

On one scouting trip behind the Union lines, Pybas crept back to his farm and family in Bedford County to find that his wife and five children were faring somewhat miserably. While the homestead was still in Confederate hands, the army needed whatever foodstuffs they could provide, leaving the family only subsistence supply. With the Union soldiers sweeping the area they cleaned out the corncribs, drove off the hogs, and left the family surviving on roots and wild game.

Pybas slipped in under cover of darkness. His wife, Eleanor, was elated to see him and have him in her warm bed that night. They did not wake the children, as he would leave before daylight to return to his unit to give his scout information. Wisely, Pybas woke the Negro mammy, who still was on the farm, to tell her that he had been there.

If he had not been fortuitous in giving that information to his faithful servant, his son, Kenneth Monroe Pybas, Jr., born March 9, 1864, would have been a bastard child. As everyone knew, Pybas was away serving in the Confederate Army, nine months before his youngest son was born.

JANE HOLDER
by Artiemesia Lucille Brison Spencer
of Pittsburg

Mrs. Ray Jordan of Newsome (nee Dovie Lee Loftis) told me that a grandmother of hers was born on a caravan of wagons coming from Alabama to Texas. It was a common occurrence for babies to be born on these caravans, which took several months to get to Texas. Mrs. Jordan said that the entire caravan pulled up and camped until the baby was born. The women of the wagon train all gathered around and assisted in the birth, and all went well.

Later, these women came by and each gave the baby one of their own given names. Thus, she was Luiza Matilda Eliza Jane Joan Laura Belle Holder. The parents chose to call her "Jane." And to make this child extra special, the ladies bought six sterling silver spoons to give to her. Jane cherished the names and the spoons, and years later, when she had babies of her own, she gave each of them one of the gift spoons.

COURTSHIP AND MARRIAGE

SUSANNAH AND ALEX AULD
by Lora B. Garrison
of Utopia

In 1875 my grandmother, Susannah Lowrance, married William Gibbens, and they had two children, "Dolly" (Mary Ida) and James, but William died, and so did little James. Already seasoned to hard work, Susannah set about caring for the needs of little Dolly and herself. She had long been accustomed to the rugged frontier life and its many hardships. She knew how to manage livestock as well as farming. Like her mother before her, she knew how to round up wild cattle and milk them, collecting wash tubs full of milk to make clabber cheese. She took in laundry and did anything necessary to make ends meet.

In 1878 Alex Auld came from Glasgow, Scotland, settling first on Turtle Creek, a few miles below Kerrville. He was first in the sheep business with Casper Real, and then he started surveying for the railroad, taking only a small portion of his pay in cash and the rest in railroad land. In a short time he had accumulated extensive land holdings on the Edwards Plateau.

One day Alex went to see Captain Schreiner and told him that he had 2000 mother cows and calves, and it was lonely out there on the ranch. He needed a helpmate! Someone who could help him run the ranch and knew about livestock. Captain Schreiner didn't hesitate to recommend the widow Susannah Gibbens. He said she was doing a better job of paying the mortgage on her farm than when her husband was living. He thought she would be a good match for him.

That very day Alex went to call on Susannah. It was not ever told what was said during the next two days. They evidently struck an agreement, a liking or bargain, no one knows. But three days later they came into Kerrville and were married. Susannah packed everything she owned in her wagon, tied her milk cow to the back and moved to Alex's ranch.

Alex built Susannah a log cabin of pinion pine. It is said to be the largest pinion pine cabin in Texas. This cabin is now at the Botanical Gardens in San Antonio, Texas. Alex and Susannah had two more daughters, then five sons.

Alexander Auld built this pinion pine log house for his wife Susannah. Alex was a rancher and hog drover of Uvalde County and grandfather of Lora B. Garrison.

AUNT ROSA'S "SWEETHEART STORY"
by Gwen Choate
of Nacogdoches

Romance was alive and well at the turn of the nineteenth century. In the memoirs of my Aunt Rosa Hancock there is a sweet story about how she met D. L. Hancock, the man who was to claim her heart forever. The meeting occurred at Briley Town School, near Garrison, Texas, in 1907, when Rosa was five years old.

Here is how she told the story in her memoirs:

"One cold morning at school, my arithmetic class was having our lesson and I was at the blackboard working. There was a heater near us, and a grown boy named Edgar Curry happened to be in our room, sitting by the heater. He was holding a small boy, seven years old.

"He said to the boy, 'Which one of them girls is your sweetheart?'"

"I was closest to him, writing on the blackboard, and the young boy laughed and said, 'That one right there.'

"I heard him and turned around and saw them looking at me.

"That seven-year-old boy was my D. L., my husband."

ᕽ • ᕽ

THE OUTHOUSE LETTERS
by Sandra Brownlow
of Timpson

A young bride was making her first visit to the home of her new parents-in-law. She made her first visit to the family's outhouse. There she found that the toilet paper consisted of a box containing old letters. With a little time and nothing to do, she started reading the letters. She quickly discovered that many of the letters were from her new husband's old sweethearts. The couple lived through this embarrassment, and speculation was that the letters were deposited by the mother-in-law.

ᕽ • ᕽ

HOW MY GRANDPARENTS MET
by Carol Hanson
of Cedar Hill

Richard Baldwin (my Grandmother Nettie's father) and Johnny Ross (Nettie's Uncle) had the same birthday—May 5. So one year, in the spring of 1915, the wives decided they would have a joint birthday party for their husbands with all the kinfolks. Many of the Ross aunts and uncles lived within fifty miles or less. And, Uncle Johnny also wanted the local "young folks" invited. Maybe he had the idea of getting certain "young folks" together. So, as Grandmother said, "We went to the party and that's where I met Ed, your Grandpa, and I thought he was the best looking boy I'd ever seen! And he was!"

Then, later that year after a box supper, Grandmother remembered: "We had to get up enough money for a Christmas tree. To get a tree we had to go out five or six miles to buy a cedar, because there weren't hardly any trees around Scullin. And at that party, Ed asked if he could see me home. I never went with anyone else after that."

Ed and Nettie Worthy married in September 1917.

Nettie and Ed Worthy got together at a birthday party.

MASCULINE MODESTY
by Lee Winniford
of Houston

My Grandfather Ward in Hopkins County had nine sisters. Whether all nine of these girls preceded their brother in birth is not clear since there are disparities in census and birth records.

Perhaps because he was so overwhelmingly outnumbered by females in his household, Great-Grandpa Ira Ward was painstakingly modest with regard to his personal habits; and my grandfather, being if not the youngest at least one of the younger children, was likewise trained to bathe and dress himself and attend to other personal matters in privacy and to refrain from doing or saying anything that might draw attention to life's grosser processes. Of course, men generally, in that time and place, tried to be chivalrous and protective of their womenfolk.

One of the older of the nine sisters was engaged to marry a young man whose family owned the farm that lay next to the land that belonged to the Ward family. The wedding was imminent, and one hot summer day the bride-to-be walked across the fields to call on the woman who would be her mother-in-law. As she made her way quietly through tall rows of corn, she suddenly came to a startled halt. Some distance away, with his bare backside turned to her, the young man she expected to marry had squatted down among the cornstalks to relieve himself.

The girl was horrified because she had never even given a thought to how men attended to the calls of nature. Crimson-faced, she backed away unseen and silently departed. The unexpected sight was so disgusting to her that she could not think of the young man romantically after that, and ultimately the wedding was called off. Unlike her sisters, she insisted on being sent away to normal school and trained to be a teacher—and not until many years later did she marry a man that she insisted was "just like Papa."

ⰘⰘ • ⰘⰘ

THE LOCKET
by Mary Margaret Dougherty Campbell
of George West

In December 1989, my great-aunt Catherine gave me a special wedding gift, a beautiful gold locket, a family heirloom which was being passed on to a fifth generation. Aunt Catherine told me that the locket had belonged to her grandmother, Josephine Gussett Reynolds. Expecting to find a pic-

Josephine Gussett Reynolds, the Lady with the Locket

ture of an ancestor, what I found inside surprised me—it had *hair* in it! Under the tiny oval glass was a lock of light brown hair. Aunt Catherine explained to me that in her grandmother's day, people kept locks of hair of loved ones. But whose lock was this? Not knowing for certain, Aunt Catherine had a theory.

In the 1800s, when Josephine was a teenager, many parents customarily sent their daughters away to boarding school for lack of reputable girls' schools in Texas. Norwick Gussett sent his oldest daughter to school in Lebanon, Tennessee.

The headmaster of the school had a son, apparently living in Lebanon, who was enamored by the lovely Josephine and began courting her. As soon as Gussett learned of his daughter's suitor, he immediately set out for Lebanon, Tennessee. Upon his arrival, he checked Josephine out of school and brought her home, a closure to the romance and to her formal education.

Aunt Catherine's theory is that the suitor snipped a lock of his hair and gave it to Josephine just before her father escorted her home to Texas. Josephine placed the treasured lock of hair in her gold locket and kept it all those years, passing it on to her granddaughter who, in turn, passed it on to me, her great-niece.

THANKS TO A PSYCHIC IN SHANGHAI
by Lucy Fischer West
of El Paso

When a psychic in Shanghai told Frank Fischer, my fifty-five-year-old Merchant Marine father, in 1946 that the widow he'd met there in Shanghai and wanted to marry was not right for him, he believed her. And when Madame Hahn announced that he'd have to go to a Latin American country to find his soul mate, he came to Texas, took the streetcar across the Rio Grande into Mexico and found her on his first stop. My father went to Juárez on a Sunday outing to see a bullfight. Instead, he found a *fiesta* complete with *bailes folclóricos* sponsored by the Lion's Club. The *Plaza Alberto Balderas*, normally teeming with avid bullfight fans in the era of the great Manolete, was the setting for a gala evening to raise funds for children's projects.

The music was varied, everything from *boleros, tangos,* and *valses tradicionales* to Big Band Swing. The crowd was varied as well, everyone from socialites to schoolteachers. My mother, Lucina Lara Rey, was one of the schoolteachers who had been invited to chaperone the young people attending the event. She was a raven-haired beauty with wild wavy tresses and sparkling black eyes, which immediately caught my father's attention.

In a custom of the day, with the music setting the rhythm for their movements, the men walked counter-clockwise around in an outer circle and the women walked in an inner circle going in the opposite direction. On the first sweep, my mother spotted my father's seaman's uniform and thought to herself that a sailor seemed out of place in the desert. On the second round, she was struck by his pale blue eyes. By the third sweep their eyes met and they were in each other's arms, dancing to Cole Porter's *Begin the Beguine.* And so the courtship began, with a night long on dancing but short on conversation, since neither could speak the other's language.

My thirty-six-year-old mother went home and announced to my grandmother that she had found the man she was going to marry. The comment was met with ridicule. According to my grandmother, my mother was an old maid, way past her prime, incapable of attracting a man. And when my mother told her that he was a Merchant Marine, my grandmother laughed out loud, cautioning her about sailors' reputed practice of having a girl in every port. But my mother knew he was the one.

Their first date was for dinner, but she only had a banana split at El Paso's Downtown Oasis because she wasn't sure what the implications were of accepting a full dinner from this American sailor. On the third date, he gave her a diamond engagement ring and asked her to marry him. She accepted, but for propriety's sake thought it best not to jump into a hasty marriage. He courted her for two weeks while he stayed in the El Paso Armed Services YMCA and then proceeded by train to New York, where he reenlisted for another stint in the service.

For the next two years he wrote letters, sometimes in the Spanish he'd taught himself at sea, and he lavished her with gifts from all over the world. He sent her flowers or candy anytime he docked in the United States. My father proposed once again in writing, using a round-cornered light cardboard sheet used in packaging nylon stockings. My mother used to ask him who got the stockings.

Frank Fischer came back to Juárez in the spring of 1948 and married Lucina Lara Rey in June, in the *Primera Iglesia Bautista* in a setting overflowing with friends and students spanning my mother's twenty-four-year teaching career.

One of Madame Hahn's prophecies had come true. Others were yet to materialize. She had told my father that my mother would become pregnant in the first year of marriage, suffer a miscarriage, recover, get pregnant again, and bear a healthy baby girl. These things happened, and the baby

Thanks to a psychic in Shanghai, German sailor Martin Frank Fischer met and married schoolteacher Lucina Lara Rey in June 1948

girl was me, born in Catskill, New York, in August 1949. The rest of the predictions spoke of my mother's further childbearing difficulties and near death experiences. Those also came to pass. In the space of six years, everything that the psychic in Shanghai had predicted occurred in the sequence foretold. My parents settled in El Paso and enjoyed a thirty-one-year marriage, which lasted until my father died at the age of eighty-eight. I lost my mother twelve years later when she was eighty-one.

Thanks to Madame Hahn, a sailor from Hamburg, Germany, and a schoolteacher born in Camargo, Chihuahua, found each other, fell in love, and settled in the desert Southwest. What are the odds?

᭒ • ᭒

ALWAYS HOPEFUL
by Sheila J. Spiess
of Helotes

Grandma married George W. Terry in December 1906. He was forty years old; she was nineteen. Their courtship was short but determined. George wooed Grandma for a few minutes each day as he passed her house on his daily walk up the nearby mountain. She admired his dedication to his health regime and to his business and civic activities. She also admired the gold watch he consulted to keep himself on schedule. (Grandma's father had only recently moved his wife and unmarried daughters from their home in East Texas to Indian Territory, where he abandoned them to the care of his only son.) Grandma yearned and hoped for security and love. George promised to love her so completely that she would soon return his love. He called her "Sunshine." She called him "George." He died eleven years later, leaving her with six small children and his promises of love only partially fulfilled.

Years of hardship passed. Finally, after losing the home George had provided for them, Grandma and her children left Oklahoma and went home to Texas and settled in San Antonio. When all six children were beginning to establish their own lives, Grandma decided to test the winds for romance.

Grandma was a faithful member of San Antonio's Taylor Tabernacle, where she met her next husband, "the soldier, Mitchell." We know nothing about the courtship, and very little about the marriage. Daddy would only say, "It didn't amount to anything." We did hear whispers that Grandma's sons "ran Mitchell off" because he was so unsuitable. A recent family exchange of photographs produced a picture, the only known picture, of a smiling Grandma leaning on the arm of a handsome, young husband. The photograph is signed by Grandma, "Mr. and Mrs. J. Mitchell."

Grandma Christi, "always hopeful," with her first husband, George Terry

Not to be discouraged, and still yearning and hoping, Grandma married another man she met at Taylor Tabernacle. This third husband has been identified to us as the "broken-down preacher, Carmichael." Carmichael and his two grown sons moved in with Grandma and her grown children. The "broken–down preacher" and his sons were lazy. Uncle Robert, the youngest of Grandma's brood, took great delight in reporting the transgressions of all the Carmichaels: "I told Mama about Carmichael's habit of smoking behind the barn. I fixed him." The situation was doomed and lasted about a year. Again, Daddy always observed, "It didn't amount to anything."

By 1940 Grandma was living alone. A neighbor asked Grandma to accompany her on a visit to see her brother, an old bachelor who lived in the country. Grandma liked what she saw. Mr. Nance raised chickens on a tiny farm that was located in the Medina Irrigation District. Grandma said, "He seemed nice. The ground was sandy and easy to cultivate. The ditch, with all that water, ran right by the place. I knew that I could raise anything we needed to eat. And flowers, I could raise flowers."

Grandma's pursuit and yearning for love and security had entered a more pragmatic phase. Grandma and Mr. Nance were soon married. She called him "Sweetie." We only heard him call her "your mother" or "your grandmother." Sweetie was her last husband. Mr. Nance passed away and Grandma had seventeen years of widowhood, during which time she never became immune to the idea of marriage and was still always hopeful.

DEATH AND BURIAL

PAP PASCHALL AND BURIAL BY SEWING MACHINE
by Patsy Johnson Hallman
of Nacogdoches

Patman Paschall and his fourth wife spent several years together on the farm south of Miller Grove in Hopkins County. Then one winter that was particularly long and cold, Aunt Lou took pneumonia and soon joined the other wives. Pap paid her burial expenses with her sewing machine. A receipt among his papers read:

"One coffin requiring 40 feet of lumber, 6 yards of coffin lining, and 2 pounds of coffin nails. Paid in full by Pap Paschall by receipt of a sewing machine. 1889"

‹ð · ð›

SHROUDS FROM SHEETS
told by Mary Ann Long Ferguson
transcribed by Odessa Hicks Dial
and Alice Dial Boney
of Forest

I gave birth to another son, Thomas Peter, February 5, 1858, and about two years later on June 17, 1860, Emma Elizabeth was born. Two years later, June of 1862, these two children were stricken with measles and whooping cough and died within the same week. I sent my oldest son on horseback to tell the nearest neighbor, and they helped me lay them to rest in the Old Eutaw Cemetery. I used my last linen sheet to make their shrouds (the others had been traded for supplies long ago). There was not even a minister to hold a service. This happened after Mr. Ferguson had gone to fight the War Between the States.

‹ð · ð›

RUSHED BURIAL
by Lee Winniford
of Houston

My grandfather had nine sisters. One of these sisters had a little boy who was given to cataleptic seizures. On several occasions his parents thought that he had died, but after a few hours, he revived. A doctor (a specialist of sorts) in one of the larger neighboring towns warned the couple never to bury the boy without first contacting him and letting him check the child.

During one bad winter, the boy came down with the flu. He was very ill for several days, running a high fever. The father drove the wagon into Cumby and brought out the local doctor as well as another of the nine sisters, an opinionated and tyrannical old maid who came to help tend the house and the sick child.

The boy did not improve after the doctor's visit; in fact, his condition worsened until finally he apparently died. The sorrowful couple did not prepare the body for burial, however. The father went to fetch the specialist, and the mother continued to sit at the boy's bedside. As misfortune would have it, the father's quest was fruitless. The specialist had gone on a trip and was not expected to return for another two or three weeks.

In the interval, a couple of days had passed. The old maid sister began to insist that preparations be made for burial. It was uncivilized, she said, to leave the boy where he was. She argued that the body was already beginning to "stink." (Close, overly warm sickrooms often had a foul odor, especially when the patient was feverish.)

At last the father relented and drove back into town to purchase new pine lumber for the casket. He lined the pine box with black velvet, even padding and lining the lid. The mother, still unable to believe her child was actually dead, demanded that the boy be buried at the back of the orchard instead of miles away in the cemetery.

Satisfied, the old maid sister helped clean out the sickroom and left. The mother remained inconsolable. Day by day her doubts and anguish increased. She was certain they had buried the child alive. Finally, seeing no other way to relieve her mind, the father and two neighbor men opened the grave. When they lifted the lid to the casket, the child's body came up with it. Suffocating, and trying to claw his way out, the boy had tangled his fingers in the torn velvet of the casket's lid.

Some years later, the family had to sell the farm and move. Fearing that she might be denied access to her child's grave behind the orchard, the mother insisted that her husband take up the body and move it, at last, to the cemetery. The man did so privately.

ALLEN'S LAST ROUNDUP
as told by Sloan Matthews
of San Antonio
to Mrs. Tom Matthews
of Houston

When I was ten years old my father died, and one September morning one year later my brother Allen took three of us south and commenced driving cattle up spring creek. He had the drive stopped three miles from the corral and was busy cutting some out. An unbranded yearling heifer tried to come out near me, and I was circling it around the roundup, holding my own by riding full speed, when I heard Allen say, "Turn it in, Sloan."

His tones were kindly and I knew he realized I would need help. They were his last words. Looking back, I saw him following me. The yearling went behind my horse, and the knees of Allen's horse hit it in the side. I saw it all. His horse tried to jump it, but it caught him with all four of his feet off the ground. I have never seen such a fall, except when a horse jumps a strong fence and falls. The horse's head never touched the ground. Allen stayed in the saddle.

I remember it as well as though it were yesterday; in fact there has never been a day since then when I have not thought of it. I saw them both off the ground, Allen in the saddle and the horse's legs sticking straight up in the air. They came to the ground and rolled over once. The horse got one-halfway up before Allen left the saddle on the right side. His neck was broken and his back crushed.

This frightful tragedy made me the youngest ranch foreman in the State of Texas at only eleven years old. The shock to my widowed mother was pitiful, and while I was sitting beside her grieving for our loved Allen, I wondered what had become of that happy carefree life I had been living a short time before.

♠ • ♠

ARTHUR SCUDDER AND THE GREEN PECANS
by Jean G. Schnitz
of Boerne

This is a deathbed story, with a twist. I heard it many times from my grandmother, my mother, and my Aunt Esther.

In their new home near Seymour, my grandparents, Ira and Dora Scudder, and their young family were trying to get settled before the birth of their fifth child when tragedy struck them. Their beautiful blond-haired son, Arthur Scudder, died October 7, 1899, as a result of eating too many green pecans. He was not yet two years old.

It happened this way: several cousins of the family came to visit and the family sought the shade of nearby pecan trees as they spent the afternoon laughing and talking. One of the cousins sat there all afternoon peeling pecans for little Arthur, who ate pecans as fast as they were handed to him. By evening, his stomach had swelled up and his intestines were apparently blocked, resulting in his death.

The death vigil for the child, Ira's "beautiful angel," was a terrible experience for all the family. When it became apparent that the child would not survive, Ira Scudder was so grief-stricken that he cursed God and swore that he would never again believe in God. As the time of death drew nearer, Ira went outside to grieve, leaving Dora, the doctor, and the women to tend to the dying child.

Ira walked a short distance from the house and sat down with his head in his hands. As Ira looked toward the house, he saw a ray of light approach the house. In a few minutes he saw a larger ray of light leaving the house, moving toward the heavens. Then someone came to tell him that his son had died—but he already knew.

William Ira and Dora Lee Scudder, whose lost child returned with a sign from God

JOHN DOE
by JoEllen Ham Miller
(stories told by my paternal grandmother)

an other story I heard my mother tell she said one time a stranger came by her fathers house and asked to stay all nite (like people did them day) of chorse they taken him in, her father happened to be gone from home that nite but her mother taken him in, gave him his supper. He coplained of being sick. She gave him some medecin, and taken him another dose of the medecin and a glass of watter in his room, and put it on the table by his bed, to be taken latter on. So as they ware scrce of beds my uncle was made to sleep with the man, who my Uncle said rolled and moaned all nite. but like a child he wasent alarmed, but when they awoke and got up next morning the man was dead. No one knew what to do, when my Grandady come home he got out and tried to find out something about the man—but no one knew him, so they buried him as best as they could. and advertised in all the papers a discreption of the man but never did know who he was. Mama said he was a smart man, but never had any papers or any thing to identify him. and no one will ever know who he was or where he come from. this happened when my mother was 9 years old.

᭡ • ᭢

JOHN AND LIZZIE ROSS
by Carol Hanson
of Cedar Hill

My great-great-grandparents were John and Lizzie Ross. They lived in Cooke County, Texas, and for at least ten years in Hood, Texas. Their oldest daughter was Elvie Florence Ross, who married Richard Alexander Baldwin there in 1891. They were my great-grandparents. My grandmother, Nettie Baldwin, was born to Elvie and Richard in 1895 around Era and Rosston. When Elvie's parents moved in the late 1890s to Indian Territory, just across the Red River from Cooke County, Richard and Elvie followed with their young family. John and Lizzie settled near the communities of Holder and Lebanon, just east of Marietta.

One fall, Lizzie decided to knit a pair of red and yellow mittens for Nettie's fifth birthday, which was on December 24, 1900. Sadly, Lizzie died on that day, from an unknown cause. Nettie treasured those mittens the rest of her ninety-five years. Now I have them.

All the family grieved for the loss, of course. John still had three sons, who had not reached their twentieth birthday—Marion, was almost eighteen; Johnny, not yet fifteen; and Abe was about twelve years old.

No doubt their older sisters, all now married, had to help their father and brothers with many household chores, including the cooking. John may have tried to be a strong father about the situation.

But on the night of April 13, 1901, it seems the stress of grief was too much—he got up and walked out of the house, making a stop in the barn. He never returned.

The next morning a search party was formed by some of the neighboring men. They had discovered a rope missing from the barn. Since they were only a mile or two from the Red River, they soon began looking about the river. Finally they discovered a rope tied to a tree, the rope extending into the river. When they pulled on it, they finally discovered John Ross' body—it was bound to a large rock, said to be one hundred pounds in weight.

John Ross, who could not live without his wife Lizzie—with Johnny, Marion, Etta, and Abe, four of their six children

THE LAST POKER GAME
by Thomas P. Carolan
of Sherman

It was early spring in 1926, April 7, to be more precise. My great-grand-father John Carolan, then in his eighty-eighth year, was gravely ill with the grippe. He had moved into the town of Decorah, seat of Winneshiek County, Iowa, from his farm in Bluffton four years earlier, a farm that he had worked for fifty-seven years. He was born in Ballyjamesduff, County Cavan, Ireland, in 1838 and emigrated to America in his late teens or early twenties. He now lived with his daughter, Mary Carolan, my great aunt, known to all as Mayme.

Due to the gravity of John's illness, his first illness in a long life, Mayme had summoned Father Hogan to administer Extreme Unction, the Sacrament for the dying. It was the custom to make a small offering to the priest on such an occasion, and Mayme had given the good father a gift of ten dollars.

After administering the last sacrament, Father Hogan was making his farewells downstairs when he was invited by a group of John's relatives to join a poker game in progress in the diningroom. During the game, John arose from his deathbed and came down from his bedroom to investigate the commotion. He joined the card players, gravely ill though he was, and with his skill, shrewdness, good humor, and some luck, managed to separate the other players from their money.

During the last hand of a game of five-card draw, John drew into a straight. Father Hogan had three aces and John's brother Tom held three sixes. Needless to say, Tom and Father Hogan raised with the rest of their money, including the ten-dollar offering, and called John's hand. A victorious and satisfied but deathly ill John returned to his bed and expired shortly thereafter.

The *Decorah Journal* recorded that "The funeral was attended by a large concourse of people . . . who came to perform the last act of respect and esteem for the aged gentleman. Rev. M. Hogan officiated . . . Mr. Carolan's death has removed a family and a beloved character and many mourn his passing." Predictably, word spread about John Carolan's last card game where John had won back Mayme's offering to Father Hogan. Although the story may never have been memorialized in stone or upon paper, it truly became a part of the oral tradition and spread throughout the diocese.

John Carolan, who drew into a straight and won the Last Hand, and his wife Johanna

13.
Family Matters

Beyond the stories about the family essentials—birth, courtship and marriage, and death—are the stories that families pass along about the happenings in everyday life. Most of these stories illustrate some family characteristic, such as wisdom or bravery, but some stories are remembered because they are funny or sad or indicative of the character of some favorite ancestor. Most are remembered because they reflect a family quality that still makes the descendants proud of its ancestry, or at least satisfied that they ended up in a family with its own particular character.

On Sunday after church and dinner, the family goes driving.

AUNT MARY
by Lou Rodenberger
of Baird

When Aunt Mary Garner watched eleven of her twelve children drive off with Uncle Sam for a Fourth of July celebration in Lockhart, she already knew how she would spend the day. She pushed her rocking chair into a shady spot on the front porch, took up her mending, and started rocking. At the other end of the porch sat one of her sons, glumly cleaning his pistol. His pa had ordered him to stay home to keep his ma company. Suddenly, he stuck the pistol in his belt and declared, "Life ain't worth living. I'm gonna go shoot myself." He trudged off toward the barn. Aunt Mary gave him a steady look and rocked on without comment. She heard a shot. She rocked on. Still enjoying her peaceful time alone late that afternoon, Aunt Mary looked up to see her young rebel peer sheepishly around the corner of the house. "Well," she said, "I thought you shot yourself."

꿈 • ꩜

A CALF FOR A CANDY STICK
by Lora B. Garrison
of Utopia

On Christmas day of 1867 the children of my great-grandparents Daniel Boone and Leah Ann Lowrance of Kerr County got peppermint candy sticks, the first store-bought candy they had ever had. The boys ate theirs the first day; and when they found out that their sister Susannah hadn't eaten hers, they began to badger her for it. They tried to trade for it or trick her out of it. Finally one of the boys offered her a little crippled calf. Susannah made the swap and took the calf and raised it. It was a heifer and every year she would get a calf from it. She sold the bull calves for meat and kept the heifers. By the time Susannah was grown and ready to be married, she had a herd of cattle and enough money saved to help her husband make a fine down payment on a farm. All that from a stick of peppermint candy!

꿈 • ꩜

ALMOST A CATASTROPHE
by Frances B. Vick
of Dallas

When my brothers, Andy and Joe Pat, were young—before I was born—they were playing with a doll on the porch of the house at New Willard where our father, Andrew Brannen, was principal and a school teacher. The boys were changing the clothes on the doll, whose fasteners consisted of safety pins. Joe Pat put one of the safety pins in his mouth and swallowed it. Andy ran to Mother to announce the catastrophe. She took Joe Pat to the hospital for x-rays and sure enough, there was the pin, open with the point sticking up. The doctor tried to retrieve it, to no avail. They finally pushed it down into his stomach and operated to remove it. The surgery was a success and from then on the story was told when the family got together. The kids' entertainment was looking at Joe Pat's scar.

Joe Pat Brannen and his brother Andy, soon after "the swallowing"

❧ • ❧

THE HANGED COUSIN IN GREER COUNTY
by Martha Cavness
of Hollis, Oklahoma

In 1889, my husband's grandfather and wife and four children travelled thirty days in a covered wagon from central Texas to Old Greer County, Texas. They were taking part in a land rush. They staked a claim and homesteaded on a quarter section of land. Later, other Cavnesses came to Oklahoma to live, also.

There was a distant cousin who lived with Jim Cavness's grandfather for a time to help with their farm and then he left. One day he came back, saying that there was a posse after him for horse-stealing. Grandfather Cavness decided to hide him. When the posse came, Grandfather Cavness even volunteered to show them some places to look for the cousin. Naturally, they didn't find him.

The cousin left soon after and they expected—and wanted!—never to hear from him again. A week or so later, Grandfather Cavness and family decided to make the sixty-mile trip to Quanah for supplies. Imagine their surprise when, somewhere between their farm and Quanah, they found the cousin strung up beside the road. The posse, or somebody, had caught up with him. Grandfather Cavness just felt lucky that the posse hadn't come back for him.

⟳ • ⟳

THE BEST CHRISTMAS EVER
by Al Lowman
of Stringtown

In 1935 President Franklin Roosevelt signed an executive order creating the Rural Electrification Administration, and the next year Congress allowed the REA to make self–liquidating loans to cooperatives established by the farmers themselves. Having spent much of 1937 in futile negotiation with the Central Power and Light Company, Mama, Daddy and the neighbors decided to form a rural electric cooperative and to try for an REA loan. To guide them through this uncharted territory, they hired Cecil Burney, a twenty-three-year-old attorney freshly graduated from the University of Texas Law School. Burney's perseverance resulted in a $400,000 loan to the newly formed co-op, and electricity seemed on the way.

So, all that summer and fall of 1938, hole diggers, pole setters, spikemen, and stringers constructed power lines while farmhouses were wired for electricity and farm wives cautiously bought washing machines, refrigerators, and newfangled irons. By mid-December everything was ready, waiting only for the lines to be energized.

Our Christmas tree stood framed in a livingroom window to the right of the front door. Mama had decorated it with something I had never seen on any tree of ours—colored lights.

And so it came to pass that on an unusually mild December morning it was suggested, somewhat pointedly, that I go sit on the front steps and watch for the co-op service vehicle that would soon appear on the horizon. The men in that truck, I was told, would turn a switch that would give us electricity.

I'd been seated on the steps only moments when I saw a pickup moving west on the Corpus Christi road. It turned north at Uncle Joe Merritt's house and headed our way, stopping near the entrance to our driveway. There, by the mailbox, stood a utility pole with a transformer at the top. From the transformer two electrical wires connected to the house. It was obvious to my not-quite-four-year-old mind that whatever was about to happen was going to take place out front. When I saw Daddy walking down the driveway toward the parked vehicle, I ran to join him. With his long arms, a child had no problem reaching to hold his hand, and this I proceeded to do.

As we reached the mailbox a lineman had finished putting on spikes and was ready to climb the pole to the transformer. With my right arm around Daddy's left leg, I watched the lineman's ascent. When he reached the transformer, Daddy said, "Son, look back at the house. You see the Christmas tree in the window?" Of course I saw the Christmas tree in the window. "Well, keep your eye on it." Suddenly the lineman flipped a switch in the transformer. The lights on the tree came to life.

It was a moment of sheer magic. Nothing else in my experience has even come close. Nothing.

I stood for a few brief seconds totally mesmerized by the sight, then suddenly let go of Daddy's leg. At this point my memory fades like the features of an old photograph.

The last thing I can remember is running toward the house as fast as I could go.

⸙ • ⸘

A TOUGH OLD WOMAN AND HER COLT
by Elaine Scherer Snider
of Conroe

My husband's stepfather, Henry Jouette, tells this story about his grandmother. It is another "gone to Texas" tale, and it explains the Jouette family's move from Louisiana to Beaumont, Texas.

After the death of her husband, Rhea Daniels Jouette kept a boardinghouse in Lecompt, Louisiana (near Alexandria), for the sawmill owned by her brother-in-law. Having several children (three girls and a boy) to raise by herself, Rhea Jouette turned for assistance to her brother-in-law, a man who thought only of himself. In her own words, "He thought he was just a notch below God." My father-in-law describes him as "a ruthless cutthroat. His employees were paid so little that they were soon forced by necessity to use credit at the company store. Being in their boss' debt, they were completely under his control. My grandmother became just another employee, to be used as a laborer at any job he dictated."

It was hard work, running the boardinghouse for her brother-in-law and raising her children, but the physical labor was not as grueling as being under the thumb of her brother-in-law. Rhea Jouette intensely disliked being unable to make her own decisions for her life and the lives of her children. Without telling anyone, Mrs. Jouette made a deal with the railroad, which ran right up to the boardinghouse so that food and supplies could be easily unloaded. When the next delivery was made, the railroad agreed that she and her children and belongings could be loaded and taken to Beaumont. When the day arrived, Mrs. Jouette supervised the loading of all her furniture and possessions, without the knowledge or permission of her brother-in-law.

The live-in tattletale ran to tell his boss what was going on at the boardinghouse. Arriving as fast as he could, he simply said, "You're not going anywhere." Pulling a Colt .45 on him, Rhea Jouette said, "You watch. I'll blow your head off if you try to stop me." She supervised the loading of the last of her belongings with the Colt leveled at this head, boarded the train with her children and rode to Beaumont. (Her threat was no idle one. My husband's grandfather remembers his mother sitting on the porch in Louisiana with the Colt at her side. If she spied a snake or other varmint, she reached for her Colt and finished it with one shot.)

The year was about 1912 when Rhea Jouette and her brood reached Beaumont, a town that had outlasted its boom days and was fast developing into an oil center. Again, she opened a boardinghouse on Van Buren Street, but this time she was her own boss. She ran the boardinghouse until she married Knox Miller, a man "who hardly ever drew a sober breath" according to my father-in-law. This marriage gave her several more opportunities to use her Colt.

One occasion is vividly recalled by my husband's grandfather. He and Mr. Miller were in the yard when his stepfather became angry at something and struck his stepson on the head with a hoe, knocking him unconscious. A neighbor ran across the street and thrashed Mr. Miller before carrying my husband's grandfather into the house. Mrs. Miller walked outside and laid the Colt against her husband's head and threatened him in much the same way she had threatened her brother-in-law: "You touch one of my kids again and I'll use this on you." My husband's grandfather can remember at least one other time when she pulled the Colt on her husband in order to keep him in line.

My father-in-law delights in telling this story, for to him Mrs. Miller was the tough, strong-willed kind of woman he admires. He enjoys telling how he used to go to her house to crank her lawn mower so she could mow her lawn when she was in her 90s. My husband's great aunts do not recall the story in quite the same way, however. To them, the brother-in-law was a successful businessman. Their mother left Louisiana simply to make a better life for her children, and they are vague about the reasons and details. Knox Miller was a fine man who had a great deal of responsibility thrust upon his shoulders. The aunts cringe when someone mentions the way their mother spoke to the son of the brother-in-law (an undertaker) during her last illness. "If you're sitting' there waitin' for me to die, you're goin' t'be mighty long in sittin'."

The toughness of the old woman is symbolized by her Colt .45, which is now owned by my father-in-law. It is still in excellent operating conditions but is no longer made. The mold for this particular model was destroyed over fifty years ago.

୶ • ଚ

THE DAY GRANDPA PETERSON JUMPED INTO THE WELL
by Gwen Choate
of Nacogdoches

The story I heard most often when I was growing up was a joke about the time, around 1910, when my grandfather, Tom Peterson, jumped into the well. He had killed a yearling and stored the beef in the spring house, a little structure built over a spring where meat was kept in a barrel sitting in the cool water.

On that day, Granny Alice Peterson sent two of her daughters to the spring house for beef, then told Herman, a fairly small boy, to draw some water at a well just off the back porch. There was a bucket at each end of the well rope, and unfortunately the one Herman filled and set on the curb had a bad hole in it. Soon, all the water leaked out, causing that bucket to shoot up toward the pulley while the second bucket plummeted into the water.

Granny, concerned about her young son, heard the noise and ran from the kitchen yelling, "Herman's fell in the water!"

Grandpa, hearing the commotion, came tearing after her and without blinking an eye vaulted over the curb and into the well. Once there and barely able to stay afloat, he felt about with his feet and soon realized there was no child down there.

Now confusion mounted, with Granny above ground, calling children until she accounted for all ten, including Herman and the two girls at the spring house. All this time Grandpa was desperately dog paddling below and trying to figure out how to get out of the well. It wasn't an easy thing to

Grandpa Tom and Granny Alice Peterson and their family (and dogs) near Garrison in 1910. Herman is the middle-sized boy standing between Tom and Alice.

do. The well pulley was damaged, and he couldn't safely climb the rope, so they had to send to Garrison, two miles away, for help.

Soon half of the men in the little town knew about Grandpa's dilemma and had come to the rescue. Now, even after all these years, we still laugh about the story while at the same time marveling at the fatherly love that motivated my grandfather to risk his life for his child.

◡ • ◠

CURED WITH A HOT IRON
by Ernest B. Speck
of Alpine

If the winter spent trapping cured Grandpa George Washington Templeton of one ailment, once he had another illness more serious in character. He developed a sore on his back between his shoulder blades. Grandpa said that the sore would not heal and began to enlarge. The next time he was in a settlement large enough to have a doctor, he had his sore examined. The doctor said that it was a cancer and the only way to get rid of it was to burn it off. Grandpa agreed to the operation.

They went to a blacksmith shop, and Grandpa took off his shirt and underwear top and stretched out face down on a workbench. The doctor put a flat iron in the forge and let it get white hot. Then he went to work on the cancer.

After he told the story, Grandpa had only one comment on the whole procedure: "It taken four men to hold me." When I used to help him get his baths, either in a number three wash tub or in the creek just below the spring, I ran a washcloth over that four-by-five inch, roughly heart-shaped scar between his shoulder blades. We buried him with it.

❧ • ❧

DAD'S NEW PICKUP
by Mildred Boren Sentell
of Snyder

Daddy will look out over the ranch that he has spent most of his life on or close to and will say he likes Christmas colors: red cows on a green pasture. When it has rained and he has had a good year, he will exult, "I've got money in the bank and cattle in the breaks!"

Recently as he neared his eighty-ninth birthday, he said, "I'm not done yet. Uncle John was ninety-five when he died and Aunt Martha was ninety-three, and I'm eighty-eight and I ain't sick." The next week, though he no

Walter Boren, who had money in the bank and cattle in the breaks

longer drives, he bought a new pickup with a stereo. When he went to in-sure the new pickup, he told Bryan J. Williams to drop the insurance on the old one. Bryan asked where the old one was, and Daddy answered: "Up at the house under a tree." Bryan asked: "What kind is it?" And Daddy an-swered, "Hackberry."

৩ • ৫

LEV AND HY AINSWORTH
by Jim H. Ainsworth
of Campbell

My great-grandfather Lev Ainsworth (1840–1918) inspired many tales. We were told that he died on the ground in his bedroll under a chuck wagon during a cattle roundup. He and his brother Hy were inseparable as boys and remained close throughout their lives. When twins were born to Lev and his wife, they named the boy after Hy and the girl for Hy's wife. The boy twin was my grandfather. When time and circumstances separated the brothers, they took turns making annual trips by horseback to visit.

During one trip, Hy stopped at a saloon near Lev's home. He intro-duced himself to the bartender and ordered a drink. A couple of fellows

Lev Ainsworth (on the left, with beard) and friend. He laid down part of his life for his brother and died in his bedroll under the chuck wagon.

joined him at his table and ordered a bottle. Hy had his drink and one from the bottle before stepping outside to answer nature's call. When he returned, his new friends had departed. The bottle was gone. When the bartender demanded payment for the bottle, Hy offered to pay for the two drinks he had consumed. The bartender disagreed and laid a shotgun on the bar to make his point. Hy was narrow-minded about such things and refused to pay a bill he did not owe. When the bartender picked up the shotgun, Hy pulled his sidearm and shot him. The bartender lived long enough to whisper "Ainsworth!" before he died. Not wishing to involve his brother, Hy rode away fast. With the bartender's dying utterance fresh on his mind, the sheriff rode to arrest Lev, the only Ainsworth he knew, for the killing.

Hearing the charge against him and unaware of what his brother had done, Lev reacted angrily and violently. He pistol-whipped the sheriff and rode off. He stayed gone for three years. It was a year before the brothers learned what had brought about their plight. Lev sent word to his brother that it was too late to change anything.

My grandfather says that Lev camped every night of that three years within sight of the house's lamplight. The children and Lev's wife took turns meeting him at prearranged locations. Angry about the pistol-whipping, the sheriff never gave up the hunt.

One moonless night, my grandfather was the messenger to Lev. He felt himself pulled up and thrown across a horse running full speed. Struggling to free himself, he heard his father's voice. "It's me, son." They did not escape the posse that had followed my grandfather. Stories differ as to Lev's punishment. Some say he spent five years in prison for Hy's offense. Others say the shooting was declared self-defense because the bartender was known to have pulled the scam before. Lev's punishment never came between the brothers.

✍ • ✎

PATCH
by Jim Vause
of The Woodlands

An interesting story was told in my family about my great-grandfather, Leroy Allen, a farmer born in South Carolina in 1825, who subsequently moved to and farmed in West Florida. He was reported to be a kindly gentleman with a hobby of whittling. He enjoyed making whistles and toys for children and gifts for family and friends. He liked to sit and whittle, and neighbors and friends would stop by and chat as he was engaged in that activity. One afternoon, he noticed one of the men among his visitors had a patch on the back of his pants that in no way matched his pants. My great-grandfather could not imagine why this man's wife would have patched his pants with such a mismatched piece of cloth.

But that patch became more significant in a following episode.

For some time, great-grandfather Allen had been noticing meat missing from the smokehouse, and he vowed to discover what was happening. For many nights he had been attempting to sleep lightly with the window open and his dog beside his bed.

One night the dog woke him up and alerted him that something was wrong. They hurried toward the smokehouse and found a man running away. The dog gave chase and overtook the man as he climbed over the fence. Great-grandfather Allen called the dog back, and the dog returned with a patch in his mouth, undoubtedly the same mismatched piece of cloth he had noticed on the neighbor's pants the day before. He told the story to the family, all except the name of the neighbor. He never would reveal the name of the neighbor throughout the rest of his life, not even to his wife. He always said had he known the man was so hard up, he would have been glad to have given him some meat.

I like to think of that as the way a gentleman should act to protect his neighbor's name. And, after all, the case had been settled out of court, so to speak.

∽ • ∽

BLUE EYES
by Tom Chesnut
of Austin

My grandparents, Mr. and Mrs. T. J. Jefferies, left Fort Worth, Texas, in the late 1800s to homestead a section of land on Tee Pee Creek in Motley County near the Matador Ranch. Their first year was spent in a dugout while a house was built.

The Matador cowboys became friends with the Jefferies and would often come to the house to trade a side of beef for some chickens, which were hard to come by in that part of the country.

One Matador visit brought an unexpected surprise:

Rap, rap, rap . . . Grandma Jefferies leaned her head toward the front door as she mixed the cornmeal for the night's dinner of cornbread, rice, and beans. Rap, rap, thump, thump . . . Grandma called for Grandpa as she ran to the door to discover three Matador cowboys at her doorstep. The

Grandpa and Grandma Jeffries who homesteaded in a dugout in Motley County and nursed the Matador cowboy "Blue Eyes" back to health

middle cowhand was braced by the others. His long, lanky arms draped over their shoulders and his cobalt eyes seemed weary as he twisted his torso in pain.

"Blue Eyes took a fall ma'am," said one of the Matadors. "Think he broke some ribs. Sure could use your help gettin' better."

Grandma graciously accepted the task of healing Blue Eyes. She cleaned his cuts and assessed his bruises, making him comfortable in a quilt-draped cot in the kitchen. Within a few weeks the healing was well underway, and Blue Eyes was healthy enough to help around the house gathering wood, making repairs and doing chores to earn his keep. Growing close with the family, he stayed until spring that year.

"Thank you kindly for helpin' me and keepin' a roof over my head," said Blue Eyes as he prepared to leave on the horse Grandpa Jefferies gave him. "This won't be the last you'll hear from me."

For many years later, Blue Eyes continued to correspond with the Jefferies family, sending letters and postcards. He always signed his name "Blue Eyes," the only name the Jefferies ever knew him by.

In West Texas, it did not matter who you were, just what you were.

౭౯ • ౬ఌ

UNCLE HENRY
by Edward R. Raasch
of Sherman

Uncle Henry was born in 1882. He lived a rollicking life until 1945, but he looked old at thirty-five. This was because of his hard living. Although he was a brick mason, and one of the best, that varmint in the whiskey bottle took over his life.

His work bounced him between Galveston, Houston, Corpus Christi, and San Antonio. During the 1920s and 1930s, his kind of reckless frivolity gained him a reputation in each of these locations. Most of his friends were in the high name category, such as: judges, prosecutors and sheriffs. He played poker on a regular basis with some of them. They all thought a lot of Uncle Henry, and they banded together to try to wean him from the bottle. Since he was getting his booze illegally during Prohibition, they threatened him with jail time. Uncle Henry was afraid of jail, and he slowed down on his drinking habit.

One time he offered to take my six-year-old brother out on his birthday. He promised my mom that he would take brother Ray to the movies and a soda. This was in 1934. Somehow because of missed streetcar stops, they wound up in several taverns. There was even one stop at a house of prostitution. Finally, they made it to the movie. Ray tried to explain to his mom what a good time he had with Uncle Henry. He innocently didn't leave anything out. Naturally, Uncle Henry's name turned to mud in our household.

Uncle Henry felt sorry for my two sisters because he thought they were over-worked doing house chores. So he went to a pet shop and bought them a monkey that he said was trained to help. I can still hear the screams of terror from my sisters. The monkey was returned.

I liked Uncle Henry. He was very kind. I still remember his advice to me: "Don't grow up and live the style of life I enjoyed."

৵ • ৶

CAROL
by Patrick Mullen
of Beaumont and Columbus, Ohio

I like to tell a story about my older sister Carol; we all called her "Sissy" when I was growing up. She was almost six feet tall and quite an outgoing person. She married a cowboy, Bob Smith, and after living in Texas for years, they settled on a ranch near Ovando, Montana, a tiny town whose social life was centered on Trixie's Antler Saloon.

Carol and Bob were good friends of Miss Trixie's, and there was a family atmosphere among the regulars at the saloon. One day a stranger was sitting at the bar when Carol walked in and stood next to him. He looked her up and down and said, "You're the biggest woman I've ever seen!" Carol came back, "And you're the ugliest son of a bitch I've ever seen."

Carol Smith ("Sissy") of Baytown, who was not to be intimidated

৵ • ৶

DADDY WAS OUR BLACK SHEEP
by Martha Baxley
of Denison

It is always funny to talk about other families' black sheep. Every family has at least one. If that one happens to be your very own father, it is not a laughing matter. Daddy was handsome, a teetotaler, never smoked, and bathed regularly. The man was educated, had good grammar, and excellent table manners. He was a leader whose followers never stopped liking him. He had one big problem. He could not leave women alone.

John Ryan had always been a cheat, and as he grew older he grew bolder. By the time I came along, and I was the youngest, he was flagrant with his womanizing. If we went in for hamburgers, he was flirting with the waitress by the time she brought the menus. If Mother were along, he would be so hateful and insulting with her that she would flush dark red. When we got to the car, he would say he dropped something and go back to make a date. It boggles my mind how the women responded to a man obviously married with a family. He left home when I was seven, and I had very little contact with him for many years.

After it was too late, he said he was sorry that his addiction to sex had cost him his family. When he was old, he came back, and in leading him into paths of the past, I elicited the information that over the years he had (and kept score on) nearly five hundred women. Beside the four of us, he had fathered one son by his second wife and about a dozen others that he knew about, including a set of twins.

I already knew about the twins. The girls were born to a couple who once lived on the farm next to my parents. These people had several children, all with mousy brown hair, when, as an afterthought, they had twins with flaming red hair. That man not only accepted the girls as his, he was very proud of his beautiful red-haired daughters, and he put them through college and gave them both nice weddings. One of them held a responsible job at our county courthouse. Once when we went to the courthouse to put a deed on record, my husband came back to the car and asked, "Did your parents once live at Pooleville?" My answer was, "Yes, why?"

"No reason." He replied. "I want you to go into the courthouse and look at the woman in the deeds office." It was like looking into a mirror. And I knew in my heart she was my sister. Once, after he was old, Daddy came face to face with the woman involved. After giving him a long, piercing look, she said, "Johnny, I have known you for a lot of years, and in all that time, you have not improved one bit."

Another time as I walked along Main Street in our town, a strange woman raced across the street to strangle me with an embrace and kisses. She insisted that I was her daughter-in-law. "I never saw you in my life," I gasped. After a long moment she agreed with me though not at all sure about it. When I saw the girl I was mistaken for, again it was like looking into a mirror, the same red hair and brown eyes, the same fair skin, arch of eyebrow and curve of mouth. I knew her parents had lived with just a fence between their land and ours, and a mere fence would never stop my daddy when he was on the prowl.

ა • ๑

"OH, MOLLY HAIR!"
by Margaret A. Cox
of Austin

Annie Hall Dail Murray Baden Happy, twice a widow and twice a divorcee, was a genuine "stem-winder" who greeted each day in Eden, Texas, during the first part of the twentieth century with an abundance of verve and drama. By the time I, her first grandchild, was two years old, my grandfather, Zack, had taught me to sing along with him his favorite teasing song to Annie: "Oh, Molly Hair, What you doin' there, a-kicking up your heels, as hard as you can tear?" And she seldom ever slowed down.

In all matters, Annie took decisive action. She reminded her husband several times about the loose boards on the back porch. After tripping one time too many, she marched out to the woodpile and brought the axe back to the house. Her three children stood by in awe and wonder as their mother gave the porch two or three good whacks. Then she said: " Now, Zack, fix that porch!"

Annie was the family healer, using home remedies for every ache and pain. Once when her youngest son was hurt, she reached in the cabinet for the iodine (or monkey blood), grabbed the red cake coloring by mistake, and gave the wound a good dousing. It healed all the same.

Annie didn't have any vices to speak of, except snuff dipping. When she was twelve or thirteen, she and her cousin Jenny Wren took up the habit of their elders at home in Comal County. They called their Garrett's or Honest snuff, "gal-baccor." Later, Annie attempted to hide her habit from her husband Zack, but he told her he already knew about it, and it was all right with him. Zack's mother was a snuff-dipper, too. So Annie continued dipping, to the amusement of all her family and friends, all her days.

Annie hated to be old-fashioned, so she kept up with all the latest styles. She tossed the Tiffany lamps when they became outdated; she trimmed the Victorian mantel chime-clock to make it look Art Deco; she gutted the player piano and made it into a conventional piano. And she was the first woman in Eden to discard her rub-board and wash tub and to embrace the new washing machine with the wringers on top. But she never, ever gave up making lye soap. As a girl she learned to make lye soap in the big black pot in the backyard, then continued the practice in later years by saving her bacon grease, adding lye powder, and whipping up some fine batches on the top of her cookstove, whether gas or electric. I saved a sample of her last soap, made in the 1960s.

Speaking of stoves, Annie thought wood cookstoves were a trial and a tribulation. She was only too happy to replace her old wood stove with one of the new light-weight kerosene models. Now the family no longer had to bother with chopping so much extra wood, but they were presented with a fresh challenge. The glass containers of fuel attached to the sides of the stove frequently caught fire, and everyone knew that when they heard mama's frantic yell—"Everyone, come quick!"—that it was imperative to make haste to the kitchen and help carry the burning stove out to the backyard until the fire subsided. This stove was soon replaced with a safer, heavier kerosene model.

Annie Murray, a "stem winder" with a niece and nephew in the mid-1920s

Annie and Zack Murray, Sr., in the late 1920s

Annie had firm views of what was safe and what was unsafe. Any dark thunderhead that threatened hail or windstorm was a clear signal to her that the whole family should run to the storm cellar. And sometimes the things lying in wait in the storm cellar—such as cobwebs, black widow spiders, or rattlesnakes—could be almost as hazardous as the threatening weather. But nothing could be worse than cyclones, Annie thought.

Model T automobiles and hills were other bones of contention. Annie had experienced several rollbacks during her lifetime, and she seriously doubted that the family auto could make it over even the slightest hill in the area. Therefore, anytime the family set out for San Angelo, and reached Frog Pond Hill, Annie had Zack stop the car so she and the children could get out. They all walked over, while Zack drove, and once over the top and on level ground, they all re-boarded and continued on their way.

When the Great Depression of the 1930s hit and a kidney ailment slowed Zack down, Annie became the chief bread-winner. A super saleslady, she drove her little black Chevy coupe all over the Concho County area selling burial insurance and tombstones. In the backseat of her car she carried catalogues filled with pictures of granite and marble monuments, which she showed to her friends, hoping to entice them into buying memorials for their late loved ones. She sold a lot of monuments, and often took produce as payment. Nearly every evening she came home with sacks of corn, a side of bacon, or whatever crop or garden was in season. The family was well fed, and any surplus food was shared with neighbors in severe financial straits during those tough times.

Old "Molly Hair" never slowed down. Annie made a great impression on all the people whose lives she touched. If she had her way, she would still be kicking up her heels, and I wouldn't be surprised to see some loose dirt over her grave right at this very moment.

૮ઝ • ઝ૭

UNCLE GEORGE AND THE FAMILY WHIPPING
by Archie P. McDonald
of Nacogdoches

Madison McDonald, my grandfather, a "squire" of Beauregard Parish, Louisiana, during the first part of the twentieth century, was the sire of a brood of eleven children. He was known as "Square Matt" to numerous business associates, but I never knew if the moniker testified to scrupulous honesty or was an ironic reference to shrewdness. At home he was a stern disciplinarian, as evidenced by this story about my Uncle George and the Family Whipping.

Business often called Square Matt out of town for several days at a time. My grandmother, Olivia Turner McDonald, had difficulty maintaining control over their boisterous children during these absences and dutifully delivered reports on their misbehavior when Square Matt returned. Square Matt would line them up, stair-stepped by age, and deliver chastisement to the miscreants all at once.

On one such occasion when offences were unusually numerous, my Uncle George, whose position in line was near the end, had a long time to dread the inevitable. He repeated over and over in his mind, "I hope he dies before he gets to me." About two lickings before George's own, Square Matt fainted dead away from exertion. George fell to knees, crying "Oh! Papa! I didn't mean it! I didn't mean it!"

Then, of course, when Papa awoke Uncle George had to explain himself to the other survivors of the family whipping. Uncle George never found this "family whipping" as humorous as did his brothers and sisters.

Madison ("Square Matt") McDonald, his wife Olivia and their eleven children, all of whom required regular whippings. The miscreant George is number five from the left

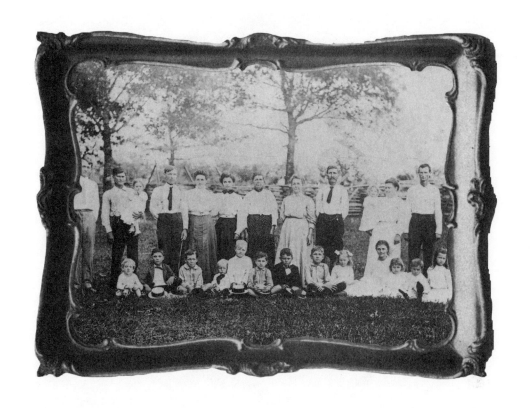

14.
Family Characters
Heroes, Black Sheep, and Eccentrics

I n all social and family circles, some folks stand out from the rest. Techni-
cally, they are the ex-centrics—without the same center, outside the circle.
This does not mean that they are not a part of the family. They might be, in
fact, the most important parts of the family. They might be the ones the
family most closely identifies with, the ones with the most memorable-ad-
mirable-interesting characteristics.

Take "interesting," for example: Grandad's half-brother Leslie showed
up at the ranch one day back in the 1930s in a green-and-yellow Model A
with the top down. By golly, but I thought that he was the keenest cutter I
had seen in the whole Panhandle of Texas, from Wheeler to Pampa Town.
But as a puzzle to my young mind, the next morning Leslie drove that Model
A back in among the sand hills along the Washita River—and he left it there!
Every time I went to the river I would go look at and sit in Leslie's Model A
convertible and wonder. I watched and puzzled, over my young years, as
the Dust Bowl sand slowly covered it up. It must still be there today, but I
imagine that you would have to dig deep to find it, or to find the whole
story behind its abandonment. I know I never got a straight story about it
from Grandad. But Leslie certainly became an interesting character in my
family's saga, with this story and others. In fact, I would have forgotten
Leslie by this time if I did not have that episode to hang my memory on.

COUSIN AD AND COUSIN NET
from an interview with Follis Bennett
by Patsy Johnson Hallman
of Nacogdoches

Now a little about Cousin Ad and Cousin Net, our oldest and strangest relatives. I remember both of them, because even though they were born during the Civil War, they lived until after World War II in 1945. They were two of our great-uncle Gideon Paschall's daughters. You remember Great-uncle Gideon was the eldest son of our great-great grandfather Jesse Paschall. Gideon was a founder and leader here in our town of Fulton, Kentucky. All his children were girls, and "Ad" and "Net" were the only ones who lived to an old age. They were very eccentric, trying always to live in the past, greatly exaggerating the prestige of the Paschall name.

When I was small I was scared to even be close to them; I thought that they were old and ugly. Their house (Uncle Gideon's once fine home in downtown Fulton) had deteriorated to the appearance of the one in the film *Psycho*. When my mother took me with her when she called on them, we always found them dressed in long black dresses. One would sit on one side of the livingroom, and the other would sit on the opposite side, usually sipping their drinks.

They spent most of their days watching the people of the town as they passed by their windows. They both stayed about half-drunk on whiskey. Even at age ten, I remember knowing that they drank 100-proof Colonel Lee Whiskey and diluted it with very little water. They would tell Mother that different members of the family returned from the spirit world to visit and talk with them. I imagine that was the 100-proof talking!

They would have Mr. N. G. Cook, president of City National Bank, to come by quite often for drinks. Then when he relaxed his guard, they questioned him about different people's bank accounts. If they learned that someone had more money than they had, they would be so mad at them that they would never speak to them again.

Grandad was a City Commissioner when the streets were first paved in Fulton, and because he voted against their wishes to keep the streets unpaved, they never spoke to him again either. Similarly, at one time the Methodist Church members here in Fulton wanted to buy their house and build a church on the site. That made them so mad they refused to talk with any member of the church again.

They would never wash a dish until they had used every dish in the kitchen. (Apparently they remembered the days of maids and slave help.)

Finally Cousin Ad died and the Presbyterian minister went to call on Cousin Net. She had taken to her bed, but she was a "Paschall" to the end.

As they talked, she said to the preacher, "Woe is me! I lost Father and Mother. Then all my older sisters died, and my young husband and two little children were killed. I had to come home to live with Ad, and now she has been taken from me. Oh, it's not to be borne!"

"Now, Miss Paschall," the preacher said, "I know the Lord will provide for you."

With that, Cousin Net rose up and said as only one of the Paschalls could say, "I have broken with the Lord!"

⊰ • ⊱

GUS HOOKS
OF THE BIG THICKET
by Callie Coe Wilson and Ellen Walker Rienstra
of Beaumont

There was a wild but widely circulated story that a Hooks—Gus Hooks, the eccentric son of Austin—had started the fire that burned the courthouse at Old Hardin and caused a new one to be built in Kountze. Gus was a capricious character whose strange antics were not all performed within the limits of the law—or even within the bounds of credulity. His most amazing performances involved his fleetness of foot. He seldom wore shoes and could run like a deer. At the courthouse fire, someone was sure he had seen Gus running away from the conflagration.

There are many stories about Gus's mercurial prowess. The best one concerns a footrace he ran and won against a man on a horse. It seems that his reputation for beating everyone who ran against him got around, and he was finally challenged by a man from Louisiana, a local champion, who rode over on his horse for the contest. After easily defeating his challenger, Gus, it is said, offered to run against his horse with him on it. Of course, he won that race too—by running backwards in front of the horse and successfully spooking both the rider and his steed.

"He would have won anyway," a member of his rooting section (and possibly of his family) said later. "That horse was handicapped to begin with—he was shod."

As for the story about the alleged burning of the courthouse at Old Hardin, Gus was cleared of the charges. The evidence was purely circumstantial. Men on horseback raced miles through the Piney Woods to Gus's house on the banks of Village Creek, hoping to apprehend him, but when they arrived, their horses hot and frothing at their bits, Gus was sound asleep in his own bed. The implications of such a story were apparently ignored by the Hookses. But then they were never ones to put much credence in stories that they didn't tell themselves.

Unconventional to the point of being perverse, Gus drank soft drinks out of a whiskey bottle, and whiskey out of a pop bottle—just to put people off, he claimed. A bootlegger of some renown, Gus had two houses, just around a bend in the road from each other, and a wife in each house.

Gus was a talented bee man. It was said that he could lead a swarm of bees ten miles through the Piney Woods, herding them like a sheep dog. He would lure the bees, folks said, by singing to them, a song he had learned from the bees themselves, just by listening to their humming. You might say that he spoke their language. Probably because of this proficiency, it was believed by some that he'd kept his money, mostly gold, in his bee-hives.

One of the stories involving Gus Hooks and one of his sons illustrates admirably that old adage about a wise parent knowing his own child. It seems the son had got himself into serious trouble and, after a day in court, was sentenced to the state penitentiary. Uncle Bryant Coe was district attorney at the time. After the trial, Gus approached him with admonition. "Bryant," he said, "you know there ain't no use sending that boy up there. He ain't gonna like it, and he ain't gonna stay."

Father knew best. The boy escaped so many times they quit coming after him, deciding, no doubt, to leave him where they knew they could always find him if they had to. That story was one of Uncle Bryant's favorites. Apparently it's a favorite among all the family storytellers; served up on frequent occasions, it has the unmistakable flavor of a family recipe.

ᴦᴑ • ᴓᴠ

GIDEON LINCECUM'S CHRISTMAS RITUAL
by Gideon Lincecum
edited by Jerry Lincecum
of Sherman

Gideon Lincecum (1793–1874), Jerry Lincecum's great-great-grandfather, was a botanical physician who spent six months exploring Texas in 1835 and returned in 1848 with his family of ten children to settle at Long Point in Washington County. This account of a family ritual he established in

Georgia and then carried out in Alabama, Mississippi, Texas, and Mexico comes from his autobiography, *Adventures of a Frontier Naturalist: The Life and times of Dr. Gideon Lincecum* (College Station, TAMU Press, 1994). At his request, the old black violin he used to play "Killiecrankie" was buried with him.

When I was seventeen years old and clerking in an Indian trading post in Eatonton, Georgia, my employer, Mr. Thompson, brought me a fine English violin as a Christmas present. When he knocked, early on Xmas morning, I answered the door without dressing, and there it was in his outstretched hands, handsome and shiny against the new fallen snow. When he handed the violin to me and wished me a happy Xmas Day, at first I was struck dumb. I could not utter a word. Soon I was gyrating around the yard outside in the snow, whooping like an Indian. The kindly merchant was right behind me, laughing and dancing with me. The only tune I knew how to play was a Mississippi version of an old ballad called "Killiecrankie," and I couldn't play very well. But I resolved to learn how and I did.

That violin became one of the treasures of my life and it led to the establishment of a personal and family ritual that occurred without fail for 63 years. Every Christmas morning, just before the sun came up, I would go out, in nightclothes and barefooted, to play three times the old Scottish bal-

Gideon Lincecum, who from 1810 to 1873 played "Killiecrankie" on his fiddle every Christmas morning just as the sun came up

lad that along with my grandmother Miriam Bowie, had come to America from Scotland. The ballad of "Killiecrankie" celebrated a Scottish defeat of English forces in 1689 and took its name from the mountain pass where the battle occurred.

As I lay on my deathbed in November, 1874, I made a game of calling up, one by one, memories of the sixty-three Christmases I had saluted the dawn by playing the Xmas tune on that old black violin. First I remembered triumphantly my most recent celebration of the Christmas ritual, only eleven months before. As I stepped out of the door barefooted on Christmas morning in 1873, I stubbed my toe on an old white petrified cactus that I had collected years before on the plains of Texas. As soon as the pain in my toes subsided, I once again enjoyed the life-giving freshness of the sweet morning; the bright old moon whirling her broad yellow face down behind the western edge of this little bad-fixed world; and at the moment the last thread of her silver light disappeared, the new day was peeping out from the fractured east where the sun's first rays were glimmering. Such was the bewildering power of my splendid surroundings that I could no longer keep from yelling out one of my big Indian whoops.

For an instant the sound of the whoop reverberated down the branch, and then the world rolled on as good as ever. Then I stood on my weary legs and completed the Christmas ritual for the last time.

᠀ • ᠀

MARINER WILCOX AND THE FABULOUS FIB
by Sybil F. Crawford
of Dallas

If necessity is the mother of invention, Mariner Wilcox, my grandfather's cousin, was the master inventor. He was born on August 6, 1847, on Wood Island, New Brunswick, a tiny speck of land jutting out of the chill North Atlantic waters off its larger island neighbor, Grand Manan. As his name suggests, he was from a long line of seafaring men. Island life not only ruled out a wide choice of outside entertainment, but fostered its fair share of superstition and storytelling, an art form still delighting islanders today. There were scores of fishermen and sea captains along the Atlantic coast and Bay of Fundy, but Mariner was, in his day and time, *the* master storyteller of them all.

After saying goodbye to his wife and children one gray morning in the early 1880s, Mariner and a helper set out for a day of fishing, hoping for a generous haul of herring. The wind came up soon thereafter and visibility suddenly dropped to zero. With the wind carrying the sound of the fog-horn in the opposite direction, it was impossible to hear it above the roar of the sea. Murr's Ledge (many a seaman's watery grave) and other dangers lurked not far away, but it was impossible to see them.

In spite of years of navigating experience and a thorough knowledge of winds and tides, it was well nigh impossible to return to harbor with nothing more for guidance than running time and compass bearings. Deciding to return home, the two men headed for Grand Manan, missed the buoy, and finally gave in to the realization that they no longer knew where they were. Seabirds circled ominously overhead, constant companions, and there were other forbidding signs as well; sudden squalls and wicked winds had the sea heaving angrily. Doing everything possible to keep the boat afloat, Mariner did not know at the time that this was to be the last journey he and his boat would make together.

The winds blew ever wilder and the two men bailed furiously. In the darkness, they called upon the Lord for wisdom and guidance in finding the mouth of a channel or locating a safe harbor, and He did not let them down. Having passed by Lubec and Eastport in the impenetrable fog, the boat went crashing up on the rocks at Cutler, Maine, smashed to a thousand pieces, but their lives were wondrously spared.

Mariner and his helper had not a cent of money between them, and everything in the boat was lost. Both were soaked to the skin and ravenously hungry. Oh, what would they do? More than a simple question, it was a plea for help.

Suddenly, out of the fog, a few sturdy residents of Maine's sparsely populated coastline appeared in their heavy oil slickers and boots and took Mariner and his helper to their home where a warm fire and steaming bowls of chowder awaited. As this was before the days of easy communication, there was no way to notify loved ones at home and seemingly nowhere to turn for further help.

Ingenious, ever witty, and never stuck for words, Mariner would at this time tell the most "fabulous fib" of his entire yarn-telling career. Reaching deep for a tale that would be both believable and make their return home possible, he told these gentle, trusting souls that he was there to hold a revival!!

The schoolhouse was opened that evening and for the next two weeks a revival meeting was held each and every evening. Mariner had a melodious, resounding voice, and the nightly meetings always opened with soul-stirring song. Then he preached, making the walls echo with his message of Heaven, Hell, fire and brimstone. Souls were saved, hearts rejoiced, lives were changed, and never did an altar-call go unanswered during his stay. His attentive listeners unfailingly delved deep into their meager purses each evening to further the Lord's work (so they supposed). After two weeks of rousing services, the offerings were sufficient to buy a small boat and a few supplies. The rescuers, still unaware that they had been so cleverly duped by this charmer, bid him a fond farewell, and Mariner headed homeward under the now-sunny skies.

At home on Grand Manan, Mariner's family, despairing of his life and in deep mourning, had held a solemn memorial service. Imagine their surprise and delight to look up with misty eyes and see him pulling up the rocky beach . . . jingling the few remaining coins from the offering in his pocket.

෨ • ෧

WILLIAM FLETCHER CROWELL
by Donna McFadden

In the Crowell family of Milam County, William Fletcher Crowell is the ancestor who receives the most attention at tale-telling time.

Will Crowell was the symbol of sturdiness. Part of his daily health plan included waking up at four o'clock a.m., eating a hearty breakfast, and walking to the oilfields five miles away, where he worked as a roustabout. He was a big man, standing 6'6" in his stocking feet and tipping the scales at 250 pounds. His outstanding features consisted of a thick handlebar moustache, bulging biceps, and a wart on the end of his nose. Will was a likeable person because he was always on hand to give muscular assistance whenever the job required it. The people of Cameron, Texas, were always obliged to him, and there was not doubt in their minds that Will was the strongest man within a hundred miles. Consequently, it was his powerful strength that hastened the end of William Crowell.

One summer, a pair of jealous brothers who worked with Will dared him to prove his strength once and for all by carrying a Model T car single-handedly from the oilfields to town, a distance of five miles. They stated that Will would be allowed as many resting periods as he desired, but he had to be entering the town limits at, or before, two o'clock p.m. The event would be scheduled at start at eleven o'clock a.m. the following Saturday if Will would consent. Needless to say, this proposition insulted Will; he not only took on the bet, but declared that he would cross the finish line in two hours instead of in three.

When the eventful day arrived, the town folk gathered on the outskirts of Cameron, eager to cheer for Will when he neared the finish line. At the other end of the stretch, Will began his five-mile trek in the heat of the August noonday sun just a little less confident than the people in town.

With a mile of dusty road behind him, Will set the car down for the first time, relieving the tension of his body. The deal proved to be more than Will had bargained for, but he picked up the car again, nevertheless, and started on his way. It was not long, however, before Will was compelled to stop for a second rest. This time Will knew he could not lift the tremendous load upon his shoulders again; but he also knew that the people of Cameron had faith in him, and he could not let them down. Fortunately, Will's brain was on the beam devising a plan, and before long, he had picked up the Model T and continued on his way. This time, the car was minus a few inconspicuous parts of considerable weight. Will made four other stops before he was through, and each time, he had made the car a little lighter by removing parts of the motor. He assured himself that his actions were not deceptive, by reasoning that the car was a tremendous load, and that this was a feat that no other human being had ever attempted.

Well, William Fletcher Crowell actually won the bet that Saturday, and the town folk still talk about his superhuman test of strength and stamina. It was unfortunate that Will was not able to boast about the phenomenon himself. As it turned out, poor Will died of heart strain at the feet of the cheering crowd, not knowing that his story would live on in his family and in the hearts of the people of Cameron.

Today, William Fletcher Crowell's grave is visible from the highway because the motorless car, which helped bring an early end to this boastful strongman, is still sitting next to his tombstone.

ꝏ • ꝏ

GRANNIE'S OLD PICKUP TRUCK
by Lora B. Garrison
of Utopia

Grannie's pickup truck is a genuine ranch vehicle, purchased new in 1956 by my Daddy who was at that time serving as Uvalde County judge.

Some folks at Utopia will remember the years Grannie Davis drove this same ol' blue pickup to church every Sunday, arriving perhaps two hours early so she could fold the bulletins and mow the lawn before other worshipers arrived.

The last few years Grannie drove "Ol' Blue" (as we once called the pickup), local people learned to recognize her from a distance and give her a wide berth. Grannie had plenty of room in that imaginary lane, and no one contested her at stop signs, which were not seen by those eyes that had grown dim.

Grannie was in Utopia one day when she heard someone say that the Sabinal River was rising. She remarked that she better hurry and cross before it got too high. Several people tried to convince her that she should stay in town, as the river was already too high to cross.

"No, I have to get home. My cow will need to be milked," Grannie said adamantly. So she headed out of town and across the Sabinal River. Jesse McFadin followed her to make sure she made it.

About halfway across, "Ol' Blue" washed off the slab and onto the riverbed below the crossing. As spectators on both sides of the river watched in amazement, "Ol' Blue" and Grannie continued on across the river, parting the raging waters like Moses at the Red Sea.

Finally "Ol' Blue" emerged on the other shore, cut back onto FM 1050 and headed for home. Nothing like a swollen river could ever stop "Ol' Blue" or Grannie.

Bob and Annie Lee Auld Davis on their wedding day in 1903

CUT OFF AT THE KNEES
by Robert Bethea

The Bethea family came from France to Louisiana some years before the turn of the century. After the first generation had settled, there were six sons born in as many years. This meant that under the customs of primogeniture the last-born sons were given very little inheritance. One of those sons came to Texas and obtained some land and managed a small herd of cattle. One afternoon, through circumstances that still remain a secret, he caught a man who had been stealing his cattle. This, of course, gave my distant ancestor the right to hang the man, which is exactly what he did. There was one difficulty, he was in an area of mesquite trees, none of which were high enough to hang anyone of any height. This didn't present a problem for long, through a bit of ingenuity, the origin of which I can only hope has been lost on some obscure branch of the family tree.

Mr. Bethea (or Berthier as it was spelled then) simply cut the thief's legs off at the knees, he was then suitable for hanging from even the lowest mesquite.

It was at this same time in history that Berthier became Bethea and all ties with France were severed. Whether or not it was because of this incident our name was changed, I'm not sure, but that's the way it was explained to me.

৵ • ৶

MY ANCESTOR WAS HANGED WHEN
HE WAS 14 YEARS OLD
by Mary Joe Clendenin
of Stephenville

When Charles Allen III, born in Charlotte, Virginia, in 1764, was just a young boy, his father Charles Allen II, was killed by the Tories. The Allen family had moved to what is now Laurens County, South Carolina, and were farming there when the death occurred. Mrs. Allen and her son, with the help of a few slaves, were trying to carry on with the farm while the heat of the Revolutionary War built around them in 1778.

It was cotton-picking time that summer. Because everyone else was busy with the cotton and they were in need of cornmeal, Charles was sent to the grist mill about two miles by a narrow lane through a dense wood. Mrs. Allen was reluctant to send the boy carrying a twenty-five pound bag of corn over his shoulder, but he assured his mother that he was man enough to take care of the job.

It was dark and scary deep in the wood when he had followed the crooked path through a few turns so that neither end of the lane was visible. When Charles heard horses thundering around a bend, he quickly hid his sack in the brush and climbed up a big tree that had limbs that stretched out over the lane. He flattened himself out on a limb, like butter on a roasting ear, completely hidden by the leaves.

Charles froze as the horses and riders, led by Tory General William "Bloody Bill" Cunningham, stopped right underneath the limb on which he lay. He scarcely dared to breath. The men talked over their plans to kill Patriot Officer William Hubbs, at his farm on the other side of the wood. Because they could not ride through the dense wood where no path had been cleared, they would have to go on to the junction near the mill and then around the wood.

As soon as the Tories rode on to complete their bloody task, Charles climbed down from his hiding place and set off through the wood to warn Mr. Hubbs. He fought his way through the brush, finding some animal trails to speed the way, praying with each breath that he would be in time. That was the same bunch of Tories that had killed his own father.

Finally, scratched, torn, panting and shouting to the Hubbs family, he broke into the clearing of the farm.

"Hide, Mr. Hubbs! Quick! Hide. The Tories are coming. Bloody Bill Cunningham is coming."

Mr. Hubbs knew they would search the house and the barn. Where could he hide? His son and wife were too scared to think. Hubbs quickly lay down in the barnyard and told the boys to cover him with hay. He told his wife to get her egg bucket and go to the hen house.

Soon they could hear the horses, but the haystack was pretty big by then. The boys tossed some hay over the fence to the two cows to make it look like they had just been feeding as the Tories rode into the yard.

First, the general questioned Mrs. Hubbs. "Woman, where is your husband?"

Mrs. Hubbs managed, in spite of her fear, to say, "He's back at camp with the men."

"I know he's home on leave. Tell me where he is," demanded Cunningham.

"He was home last week, but he went back."

Bloody Bill demanded answers from the son, too. But he gave the same answers his mother did. Seeing how scratched and torn Charles was, he turned his questions to him. "Did you warn them we were coming? Where is Hubbs?"

"I wouldn't tell you. You are the one that killed my dad!"

"You had better tell me or I'll string you to yon tree!"

"No!"

The general ordered his men to put a noose around Charles' neck and hang him to the big tree in the yard. They did so. They hanged Charles and immediately rode off.

The Hubbs family quickly ran to the tree. Mrs. Hubbs grabbed the end of the limb that was bending under the weight of the boy and swung with all of her weight. The Hubbs boy got his knife, but couldn't reach high enough. Mr. Hubbs plunged out of the hay and ran to cut Charles down. Charles was still alive and was soon revived.

Later in life, Charles Allen III became a well-known judge. He helped survey and establish Laurens County, South Carolina, and the town of Laurens. Judge Allen lived to be ninety-two years of age and died January 5, 1856. The Daughters of the American Revolution erected a marker at his grave in 1974. The story of his bravery and other deeds was published in the papers and celebrated at his funeral.

This is the line of descendents: Charles Allen III, Sophia Allen Lewers, Mary Lewers Love, Wirt Adams Love Womack, Mary Lucy Womack Fitzgerald, Mary Joe Fitzgerald Clendenin.

So, my great-great-great-grand father was hanged when he was 14 years old.

◡◠ • ◠◡

PATMAN TAKES IN WASHING
by Patsy Johnson Hallman
of Nacogdoches

Rebecca, Patman Paschall's wife, died just before the Civil War, and Patman moved from Eastland to Mineral Wells. The handsome, successful rancher didn't have any trouble finding another wife, but during the time when he was single he continued his cattle drives to the Kansas markets. Once during the War he was on a drive, and as he and his men came abreast of a farm, they saw a curious thing. A woman stood outside her house beside a wash pot crying as if her heart would break. Patman told the men to ride on while he stopped to offer assistance.

"Ma'am, what is the trouble?" he asked.

"My husband has gone to war; my last slaves have run away; and all the clothes we have are dirty. I'm trying to wash, but I don't know how it's done."

"I know how," replied the gallant Patman. "You just sit here in the shade and let me take over."

After a time the wash was drying on the line, and Patman was invited in for dinner.

The next day Patman caught up with the herd and rejoined his companions on the drive.

Women in the family who knew Patman did considerable talking about that episode.

∞ • ∞

MARTIN PARMER—THE RINGTAILED PANTHER
by Frances B. Vick
of Dallas

Little Mother, my mother's mother, used to tell stories that came down to her through her mother, about the trials and tribulations of the daughters of Martin Parmer at the hands of Uncle John (apparently Martin's son, as you will read later). John's meanness to Betsy (my ancestor), and her sisters Emily, Sarah Anne and Zina was legendary. On one occasion the girls wanted to go to a dance and John mixed two tubs of peas and beans in one large container and told the girls they would have to separate them out before they could go. Another time the girls had collected eggs to color for Easter eggs, which left John with fewer eggs for his breakfast. In a fury he stomped the saved eggs and told them they could make Easter eggs of them if they could get them back together. In later years we heard of the stories told about Martin Parmer, which we found far more exciting than those about Uncle John.

Before coming to Texas, and according to Martin's son, Thomas, Martin saved the neighboring McElwees' little red-headed daughter from the Osage Indians, who had kidnapped her, thinking she had powerful medicine and would keep their lodges warm. In the rescue, the stock of his gun was shot off, but Martin "caught the naked barrel in his hands with a giant's grip, his eyes blazing as a wounded tiger. . . . with one bound as a wild beast, and an unearthly scream, his gun-barrel high lifted in the air," proclaimed, "I'm the Ringtail Panther," killing several of the Osages and giving himself the sobriquet by which he would be known the rest of his life.

The Osages decided they had better go kill this Ring-tailed Panther, so Martin protected his forted-up family by planting ten five-pound canisters

Martin Parmer, the Ringtail Panther, Signer of the Texas Delaration of Independence, as painted by Charles Shaw of Dripping Springs

of powder along the hollow leading up to the fort. He ran a trail of powder through hollow canes from canister to canister and a second trail from the last canister to the spot where he intended to march out to meet the Osages. They believed him to be a great Medicine Man they called Big Thunder and he intended to play upon their superstitions to save his family and himself. When Chief Blundo of the Osages arrived with his warriors, Parmer waved them to a halt and lighted the powder, yelling "Big thunder comes!" The ensuing explosions scared the Indians so badly that "every savage that could run made for his wigwam; Blundo had seen enough."

According to legend, after hearing that a Sioux chief, Two-heart, received his name from ripping open a white man and eating his heart, Martin was so indignant that he force-fed Two-heart bear meat until he died. And he was famous for having called a preacher to come preach the funeral of his favorite bear dog, the preacher not knowing the funeral was for a dog until he had ridden fifty miles.

While he was in the assembly in St. Charles, Missouri, he introduced himself thus: "[I'm the] Ringtail Painter [panther] from Fishin' river, wild and wooly, hard to curry. When I'm mad I fight, and when I fight, I whip. I raise my children to fight. I feed 'em on painter's hearts fried in rattle-snake greese." A *History of Carroll County Missouri* says that when the members of the General Assembly engaged in a free-for-all, Governor McNair intervened and demanded peace in the name of the State of Missouri and Parmer knocked him down, "sending his Excellency gall west, and half a ride away."

While in the Missouri Assembly Martin came to know Moses and Stephen F. Austin where he no doubt heard about the land of milk and honey that was Texas. So Martin came to Texas in the spring or summer of 1824 with his wife Sarah, who was very ill and died at what is now Alto, Texas, and was buried by the old well adjacent to the Catholic mission. Martin intended to settle on the east side of the Neches River at the crossing of the Old San Antonio Road where another family was living, that of Peter Ellis Bean. Bean had been gone for two years and reportedly had been killed, so Martin noticing the presumed widow, Candace Bean, proceeded to marry her in the fall of 1826. However, Peter Ellis Bean was not dead at all and showed up, causing Martin to escape out the back window and ride away as Peter Ellis came in the front door.

Bean did not face Martin but began writing letters to discredit land titles and to get people expelled from their lands in the Ayish Bayou, where Martin had settled. Other persecutions of the colonists were most heavily centered on the Hayden Edwards' colonists in and around Nacogdoches. The unrest culminated in Martin, at the head of thirty-six men, riding into Nacogdoches on the morning of November 22, 1826, and calling the citizens together, proclaimed to them the Republic of Fredonia, which shortly collapsed from lack of support.

Parmer crossed the Sabine into the United States but apparently recrossed the Sabine in 1831 in the company of James Bowie, with the two of them making an appearance in San Antonio, where Bowie had a Mr. Black make him his first Bowie knife. But as popular as Bowie was with the Mexicans, he could not protect Martin from their fear of him, so Martin left.

Meanwhile, Martin had taken another wife, Mrs. Margaret Griffith Neal, who had a daughter by Martin and had died a year later. Martin found he could move back to Ayish Bayou so he took his boys and went back to the farm to get things straightened out. While Martin was there, John Lout, a neighbor and friend, died and Martin married his widow, Levisa Anderson Lout in 1833.

Martin received an invitation from the people in the "District of Teneha and the municipality of St. Augustine" requesting him to represent them at the Consultation in San Felipe in 1835, which he did. Then on the 2nd day of March, 1836, a convention of the people of Texas at Washington-on-the-Brazos, adopted a declaration of independence, signed by all, including Martin Parmer. On March 6, 1836, Martin wrote his wife, Levisa, and enclosed a copy of Travis's letter from the Alamo, asking her to have the letter read publicly in St. Augustine. He wrote her that "Unless we have a general turn out and every man lay his helping hand to, we are lost." He had learned that lesson during the Fredonian Rebellion.

That Parmer was a great "spinner of tales" is attested to by another delegate's statement that he "was the greatest wag in the Convention," and that on crossing the river on the way to the convention he told the ferryman such a good joke that the entire party was carried across without charge. Stephen Blount of San Augustine described him as "an interesting talker . . . frequently seen in the midst of an admiring group relating incidents of his adventures," most of them about his fights with the Indians.

At the conclusion of the convention, Sam Houston was organizing his army. He took a liking to Isom Parmer's (Martin's son) horse, Saracen, and bought it from Isom for $400. He then rode off with his army that he was gathering, ending up at San Jacinto. It was this horse that was shot out from under him at the battle on April 21. Isom was in the battle, but Sam Houston had told Martin that he was too old for battle and he wanted him to do something else. Houston appointed him "Impresario of Horses." After thinking about it, Martin declared he was the only duly-appointed horse thief in Texas.

Martin's wife Levisa died in 1839, leaving him with a young boy, John Martin Parmer, to raise. Their neighbor in Jasper County, where Martin had moved after his service to the Convention, was a Kelly family with a daughter named Zina. Zina apparently came to help Martin with his son and to be a housekeeper. She ended up marrying him although she was younger than most of Martin's children and therefore never accepted by them. Martin was sixty-two. Presumably the boy was the "Uncle John" who caused such misery to the Parmer girls.

In February 1850, Martin traveled to Walker County where his sons lived and where he intended to move and live in his old age. While there he was feted with a dinner given by his friend Sam Houston and other prominent citizens of Huntsville. Martin rode home to Jasper in very inclement weather, contracted pneumonia and died on March 2, 1850 at 72 years of age—on the fourteenth anniversary of the Declaration of Texas Independence that he had signed. He is buried in the State Cemetery in Austin.

᦮ • ᦭

THE BLACKBURNS
by Virginia Alexander
of Nacogdoches

In *The Family Saga*, Mody C. Boatright states, "I use the term mainly to denote a lore that tends to cluster around families, or often the patriarchs or matriarchs of families, which is preserved and modified by oral transmission, and which is believed to be true. Lore that is handed down as folklore is excluded. I am, then, not concerned with a type of tale, but with clusters of types, not with a motif, but with many motifs. These clusters never form a connected history. Such a coherent narrative requires research in libraries and archives."

The material in this paper was kept alive by oral transmission. It deals with members of three generations of the Blackburn family of Linn Flat in Nacogdoches County.

Mrs. Ella Lyles, whose maiden name was Blackburn, was the granddaughter of George Blackburn and the daughter of W. J. Blackburn, two of the main characters in these tales. She lives three miles south of Sacul and had lived there all of her married life. She was born February 14, 1870. She divorced her husband and reared their eight children without any help from him. Mrs. Lyles is the source of most of these family legends.

Members of the Blackburn family have resided in Nacogdoches County for many years. They first settled in Linn Flat located in the northwestern part of the county. When the last Blackburn moved out of the settlement, the people changed the name to Happy Valley. This is probably true because any "old timer" who has spent his life in Nacogdoches County can tell you about the notorious Blackburns, whose social values were not always in harmony with the accepted standards.

George Blackburn was the first of this family to settle in East Texas. He and his wife came here from either South Carolina or Georgia. George was half-Indian. He was a handsome man and exhibited a friendly magnetic personality. George owned farmland in Linn Flat. Bill Hudman, one of his Negro workers, was his favorite hired hand. Bill lived in a cabin behind

George's house. George and his wife had two sons, Little George and W. J. When their third child was born, it looked like a Negro baby. George's wife admitted to her husband that there was a possibility the child was Bill's. A few days later, George arrived home to find that his wife had taken her own life, and had killed the baby also by giving it Bluestone poison in tea. He then killed Bill. This was probably the first murder he committed. He stood trial, but he was acquitted. After that he was a changed man. He became involved especially in thefts.

Several years later, George and Doug Sanders, another of his Negro men, stole a drove of hogs. George was afraid Doug would tell, causing him to be sent to the penitentiary, so he decided to kill him. He rode his horse nearly to Doug's house, tied the horse to a tree, and walked the rest of the way to the house. He lay down behind a log and waited for Doug to come out. Doug and his wife had killed one of the stolen hogs and were "cooking it out" in an old black wash pot in the back yard. Doug finally came out of the house to stir it, and George shot him. The slug went through his neck and buckshot through his heart. George got his horse and started home. He had to cross a creek. He stopped in the middle of the bridge, removed his horse's shoes, and threw them in the river. Satisfied that he had erased his trail, he went on home. He was indicted, though, and had a trial. He was acquitted once again because of insufficient evidence.

Mr. Lloyd Cook, a retired farmer and a resident of Cushing, gave some of the information about Little George and W. J. He was just a child when these incidents occurred, but he remembers them vividly from stories his family handed down.

Little George was a chip off the old block. Their father had reared the boys with the idea that if they saw something they wanted and were men enough to take it, they were entitled to it.

Three horse traders with a herd of horses were traveling through their area. Little George tried to buy the horse one of them was riding, but the man didn't want to sell it. Little George then invited the men to spend the night at his father's house, which they did. Those three men were never seen again. The Blackburns told their neighbors the men had sold them the horses and gone on to gather another herd. A year or so later the brother of one of the horse traders came through inquiring about the traders. He became suspicious of the Blackburns, went to the law, and asked for an investigation. The property was searched for signs of the bodies, but no trace was ever found. Rumors went around that George and Little George had killed the traders, burned their bodies, and thrown the remains in an old well. The truth will probably never be known. The ironic thing is that Little George was later elected sheriff of Nacogdoches.

W. J., the youngest son of George, had gone away and fought in the Civil War. When he came back he was a colonel and from then on was known as Colonel Blackburn. When he returned, he got married, acquired a farm, and started his family. He was respected and had never been in as much trouble as Little George.

Alden Pitman, a friend of the family, was living with and working for Colonel. They were the best of friends. One night Colonel, his wife, and their children were coming home from a social. They were passing a house where a widow and her daughter lived. Screams were heard, and Colonel stopped to investigate. Alden was inside ranting, raving, and tearing things apart. Colonel saw that he was drunk and tried to stop him. Alden cursed, broke away, and pulled his pistol. One of the women grabbed for the pistol and caught her hand between the hammer and pin preventing the gun from firing. Colonel finally subdued Alden. Alden, in a drunken stupor, kept telling Colonel that he was going to kill him the next day for interfering in his business. Colonel took Alden to his house and put him to bed. He then took his family and went to his father's house to spend the night.

The next day, Colonel, Little George, and several other men went over to see if Alden had settled down. There was no trace of him in the house. Then they heard him calling from the backyard to Colonel. When Colonel opened the back door, he glimpsed Alden kneeling on the ground, aiming a gun at him. He jumped behind the door just as Alden fired. A slug went through a milk bucket that was hanging there, and the back door was sprayed with buckshot. Colonel opened the door, and the two men fired at each other simultaneously. Alden was killed instantly, but Colonel was not hurt. Alden, in loading the gun, had put the wadding down before the powder, and it didn't fire. The other men wanted to take Alden to the church to lay him out, but the Colonel insisted on laying him out in his house. An inquest was held, and Colonel was cleared.

Mrs. Lyles tells the following story about her father and brother.

Colonel and his eldest son, Frank, got into an argument. Frank threatened to cut his father's head off. Deciding to make an example of Frank for the benefit of the five younger children, Colonel disowned him and told him to get off the place. Frank went to Colorado and began trapping beaver and otter. This was illegal. A game warden who suspected Frank of trapping warned him to stop. Frank didn't, and the game warden caught him. Frank shot the game warden, tied a rock to the body, and threw it into a lake. He went to a lawyer and told him the details. About eleven months later, the body was found. The lawyer helped Frank get out of the state. He was never arrested for this murder.

Frank then settled in Breckenridge, Texas. He married a girl from there. Later his wife began running around with another man. Frank went to the man and told him he was going to kill him if he ever caught him with his wife, and this was fair warning. Frank went home early one afternoon and found the man with his wife. The man ran out the front door just as Frank shot. He was killed instantly. Frank then called the man's father and told him what he had done. The man's father came over and was going to kill Frank. Frank tried to talk him out of it, but failed. During the ensuing struggle, Frank killed that man too. He then went inside and called the police. He sat on the front porch and waited for the police to come after him. He stood trial and was acquitted.

Probably the most ironic aspect of all is the fact that each of these men died of natural causes. Another strange fact is the people who provided this information stated that almost everyone who knew these men liked them but were also afraid of them. There are many more stories about the Blackburns. Some of the other stories illustrated accommodating things they had done for people who lived in their neighborhoods, but the majority of the stories concerned incidents such as those told in this paper. At any rate, they lived adventurous lives.

ↄ • ৩

MEETING GRANDPA OWENS
by June Welch
of Dallas

My uncle told me about coming to Decatur from Davis, in the Indian Territory, to ask Grandpa Lucian Owens' permission to marry his daughter, Rebecca Jane, whom everybody called Jenny.

On the way down a couple of drunken louts had made life disagreeable for the other passengers. When the train stopped at Decatur, Uncle saw Grandpa Owens, wearing his marshal's badge, standing in the door of the station, meeting the train as he always did. The drunks got off, and one began talking to Owens. While Owens was distracted, the other picked up a rock large enough that it required both hands and hit the marshal on the side of the head.

Uncle said that Grandpa Owens shuddered, then shook his head to clear it. Then he whacked each assailant across the temple with his pistol. They dropped to the platform. Grandpa Owens picked up his hat and put it on his bloody head. With one oaf draped across his shoulder, fireman style, he dragged the other off in the direction of the jail.

And Uncle said, "That's the fellow I come to see about marrying his daughter!"

❧ • ❧

UNCLE MULE!
by John Graves
of Glen Rose

Sometimes the old earthy or ungenteel stories do come down in a family, usually through the male line. This is not any very great story but it's ours, which I guess is the main thing that can be said about most family anecdotes.

One of Papa's maternal aunts, long before he was born, had married a thoroughly disreputable, shotgun-assassin, mean-poor-white type known as "Mule" McGill. (That nickname is the actual one he bore, but the surname isn't.) Anyhow, her family and its connections were so disgruntled by the match that they stopped even talking about her, and my father as a child never heard her name and knew nothing of her existence.

One day when he was about twelve, a circus came to Cuero, and he and his best friend, a boy named Wofford Rathbone, rode their ponies over to watch the big tents being put up. While they were sitting there horseback and viewing the spectacle, a very dirty and disheveled man with a beard came slouching along and stopped to regard them. From Papa's description of him he must have looked a good bit like Huckleberry Finn's horrible sire. He was clearly about half drunk and was leaking tobacco juice at the corners of his mouth.

He said, "Hello there, Wofford."

"How're you, Mr. McGill," said my father's friend.

"Who's that you got there with you?"

"That's Johnny Graves."

"Johnny Graves!" the apparition said, peering up at Papa. "Why, boy, I'm yore damn *uncle*!"

Papa took a good look at him and hollered, "No, you ain't!" Then he turned his pony and ran it all the way home, where my grandfather told him at long last the story of Uncle Mule.

THE SHOOTOUT AT SUNSET
by June Welch
of Dallas

I want to tell you one of my family's stories about an old man who was not always old and tell you about a Sunday long ago when my folks took me to see him because he was my mother's grandfather. He sat on the front porch in a rocking chair, a huge man of great age with a white gunfighter's moustache, wearing black boots and a wide-brimmed black hat.

His name was Lucian Thompson Owens. He was born in Kentucky and brought to Wise County, Texas, at a tender age. He was a Confederate soldier at age fifteen. He married a girl with Cherokee blood named Tennessee Gift Barnes—the gift they got in Tennessee, I guess—and was a member of a Ranging Company that pursued, among others, the Comanche war party that massacred the Babbs and carried away their children. In later years he would draw a pension for service in the Indian wars from the State of Texas. On his application, which had been designed for use by veterans of wars

Sheriff Lucian Thompson Owens (1848–1933), who kept the peace in the County Seat of Wise

with battles that had names, in the space inquiring where he had fought, Owens wrote simply, "wherever the trail led."

Not long after Quanah Parker took his Quahadi Comanches onto the reservation at Fort Sill, still only a little more than a hundred years ago— around 1875—Owens became a peace officer in Wise County. He bought a new six–shooter, a .45-caliber Frontier Model Colt that was his proudest possession. A fair number of bad men sojourned in and around Decatur, perhaps accounting for that traditional call in a game of chance involving the casting of dice: "Eighter from Decatur" (and the refrain, "The county seat of Wise!"). Trail herds passed through, bound for Abilene, Kansas. Lots of effort was required to preserve the civilization recently set down in Wise County. Owens devoted himself and his pistol to that task. In the meantime the family was increasing and Tennessee was raising the children alone. His absences were frequent and extended as he trailed malefactors and escorted convicted felons horseback to the penitentiary at Huntsville.

Tennessee's daughters, in their old age, would speak of her beauty and of her grace and her goodness and how at night when she took her hair down she could sit on the ends of it. There were troubles. The house burned and a new one had to be built. A child died.

Then the responsible citizens of Sunset, a small town near Decatur, sought Owens' help. A gang led by two brothers was harassing their town, which was outside Owens' jurisdiction, just over the line in Montague County. But Owens buckled on the six-shooter and went up to Sunset to meet the gang. (I'll call them the Hunters; that was not their name.)

In that classic scene one afternoon the Hunter gang and Owens faced each other in the main street—probably the only street—in Sunset. Sunset has little more than that now. And they tried to ride him down. Owens shot one brother and dragged the other off his horse. Using the Hunter brother as a shield, he retreated, backing into a corner outside the depot. Keeping Hunter in front of him, he shouted through the window for the telegraph operator to wire Decatur for help. The gang was waiting him out.

Dan Waggoner, who had been his partner, was the man to whom Owens turned. Waggoner would found one of the great ranching and oil fortunes. Dan Waggoner ordered a flat car hooked onto a locomotive, recruited a couple of dozen well-armed, fun-loving souls, and they hurried to Sunset and successfully extricated Owens and his prisoner and broke the power of that particular band of ruffians.

This story did not end until a year later, when Mrs. Hunter, probably deranged by the death of one son and the incarceration of the other, came down to Owens' home carrying a pistol in her purse, intending to kill him. Owens managed to reason with her and that episode in West Texas gunfighting became local history.

15.
Miscellaneous

⤳

This Miscellaneous chapter is the "catch-all." We had some tales and entries left over that failed to fit comfortably in the fairly restrictive categories that we had established. As much as we would like to have a place for everything and everything in its place, some entries refused to be categorized, particularly in our limited table of contents.

◦ • ◦

NAMING THE TOWN OF ROCKNE
by Patrick Brannen Vick
of Austin

When the town of Rockne was first established it was called Lehman after the original Lehman pioneer. Later it became known as Hilbigville for another member of a pioneer family who had established a business in the community. The community received its present name of Rockne after representatives of the Humble Oil Company in 1930 showed an interest in developing an oilfield in the area and wanted to know the name of the town. Since it had never been named officially, no one could give them an exact answer. My wife, Nelda Ann Grohman Vick, tells the family's story of how her mother, Edith Goertz, was responsible for the naming of Rockne, Texas.

The parish priest, Father Strobel, made the motion at a parish meeting that the school children vote on either Joyce Kilmer, an American poet and journalist killed in France in World War I, or Knute Rockne, the famous Notre Dame football coach of the "Four Horsemen."

When the children's votes were tallied, the boys had voted for the football coach and the girls had voted for the poet, resulting in a tie. When the boys realized how the vote was split they started putting the pressure on Edith to change her vote. When she went home from school that night her father, who had found out about the vote, put more pressure on her because he was a big Notre Dame fan. The next day Edith Goertz changed her vote, giving the community its name, Rockne.

҂ · ҂

WHIZZERVILLE!
by Lou Rodenberger
of Baird

Nobody referred to his hometown as McMahan in my father Ben's day. It was Whizzerville where they went to buy staples and gossip. How McMahan earned its nickname has several versions, embellished each time family storytellers pass them along. Recorded as local history, after years of refining by local raconteurs, the following story reflects symbolically the easygoing spirit of this community balanced on the edge of the violent Texas frontier.

This, my father says, is how his hometown got its nickname. For the natives, two social events gathered the community—a protracted Primitive Baptist revival in the summer and a country dance anytime. Fiddlers—among them young Ben Halsell, my grandfather—showed off their skills regularly in homes where the host cleared out the furniture from the largest rooms and all generations stomped until dawn to "Leather Britches" and "Sally Good'un." On one summer evening, several women sat piecing quilt blocks and catching up on news in the kitchen apart from the hilarity on the dance floor. Unscreened doors and windows stood open. Suddenly, a young drunk on horseback leaped through the front door and out the back. Whooping, he streaked off down the road. The quilt piecers missed not a stitch. "My land," one said, "that boy's on a real whizzer." This wide spot in the road, officially designated McMahan at the post office, would be called Whizzerville by natives ever after.

҂ · ҂

E-HEART—E ♥
by Frances B. Vick
of Dallas

Where did my great-great-grandfather, Lewis Dial, get the old family cattle brand, E-Heart? My aunt, Bess Brannen, thinks it came about this way; at least this is the story she used to tell. When Lewis came across the Sabine, on the run because of the Rawhide Fight, he headed down to Castroville, where there were friends who would hide him. While he was down in that area he ran across the old Mission Espiritu Santo brand—E S—spirit of the saint. She thinks Lewis was inspired by it and came up with E-Heart—E ♥—espiritu del corazon. I have a set of the old branding irons. And my brothers were among the last to ride a horse with the E-Heart brand, a descendant of the old Lewis Dial stock.

∾ • ∾

FAMILY FOLKLORE: NAMES
by Jerry Bryan Lincecum
of Sherman

According to family tradition, the origin of the unusual spelling of the name "Lincecum" came about as follows. During the early 1700s, an English common soldier named Linseycomb went to France on a military expedition and was left behind as an unexchanged prisoner. Remaining in France, he married a Frenchwoman, and they had only one son, whom they named Paschal. On him they bestowed all the learning that their means would allow, and he grew up with some knowledge of the literature of France. Not fancying the English orthography of his surname, he gave it a decidedly French spelling: "Lincecum."

In due time Paschal took a wife, and their union was blessed with the birth of a son, whom they named Gideon. Because Paschal and his wife sided with the Republican Party, which at that time was rising up against the French government, they refused to take the oath of allegiance that was required of Protestants, and which amounted to renouncing their faith.

With their young son, Paschal and his wife gathered up their personal effects and sailed to America. They settled in Maryland, where three daughters were born to them, but no more sons.

This Gideon Lincecum was the namesake and grandfather of my own great-great-great-grandfather, Gideon Lincecum (1793-1874). There is one small problem with this story, however, in that there are today a number of families named "Linthicum" which trace their origin back to Maryland in the eighteenth century, and even a town in Maryland named Linthicum Springs. The simplest explanation for this anomaly is that another branch of the English Linseycomb family settled in Maryland, and their patriarch spoke with a lisp, which resulted in his name being recorded incorrectly.

The Lincecum family can also illustrate some changing patterns in assigning Christian names to children. The second Gideon Lincecum was named for his grandfather, but his naming was unusual because he was not given a middle name. He himself chose to break tradition by giving his sons first names beginning with "L" that came not from ancestors or family friends but from Greek literature and history: Lycurgus, Lysander, Leonidas, Leander, Lachaon, Luculllus, and Lucifer. There were actually two Lysanders, Lysander M., who died young and Lysander Rezin, born later. Gideon and his father Hezekiah did not enjoy good relations, so it was not until the last-born son came along that one was given the middle name of Hezekiah (Lucifer Hezekiah did not survive infancy.). The daughters were given more conventional names: Martha Ann Elizabeth, Mary E. Catherine, Leonora, Cassandra, and Sara Matilda.

My father, known throughout his life as "Jack" Lincecum, was officially christened "John Aubyn," the first name coming from a maternal uncle and the second from a paternal uncle. He never liked his formal name, and when names were chosen for his two boys he insisted that they have first names they would be known by rather than formal names: thus my first name is not "Gerald" but "Jerry" and my brother's official name is "Joe Jack." I now have three granddaughters, and the names their parents chose for them have no roots or precedents in family history. Their parents simply chose names they considered appropriate and distinctive: Hannah Faith, Zoe Kate, and Erin Tess. I suspect that is more often the norm these days than any other criterion.

୫ • ୬

A CURE FOR FREE
by Eleanor Monroe
of Sherman

My father, who managed a Farmer's Co-op in the early 1900s, told this story about one of his farmer friends.

Mr. Whoopenhorst believed that asafetida (a bad-smelling gum resin) worn in a little bag around the neck would repel disease. One day, during a flu epidemic, he went into a drugstore and asked for five cents' worth of asafetida. When the druggist handed it to him, he said, "Charge it."

The druggist looked at him for a minute and then said, "Just take it. I'm not going to write down asafetida and Whoopenhorst for a nickel!"

VIGILANTE RAID
by Jean G. Schnitz
of Boerne

When the C. A. Lee family arrived in Comanche County, Texas, in 1878, they settled in a part of Texas that did not take kindly to Yankees. Having served in the Union Army, C. A. Lee was considered to be a Yankee. Though he became a music teacher and song leader in the local church and community, he continuously experienced problems because of his affiliation during the Civil War.

The Lee family had never owned slaves, but they brought with them to Texas a Negro family that had worked for them in Missouri for many years. My grandmother described in frightening detail the raids on the Lee homestead during which masked "hoodlums and ruffians" rode horses around the Lee home at night, shooting guns into the air and shouting threats against the Negroes and the family. This happened on several occasions.

One day in the early 1880s when C. A. Lee was in town (Desdemona—then known as Hogtown), someone warned him that he should send his Negro employees away because a raid on the Lee property was planned for that very evening. The Ku Klux Klan (which was active in the area during the post-Civil War years) did not want Negroes to come into the county, so they planned to run them out one way or another. C. A. Lee rushed home. He quickly provided the Negro family with horses and a wagon, food, and money and told them to seek shelter and employment elsewhere because he feared they were no longer safe in Comanche County.

That night, there was a raid on the Lee homestead and someone knocked on the door to demand that C. A. Lee produce his Negro employees. He was able to truthfully tell them that the Negroes were no longer on the premises. The fact that the raiders came again several times after that led the Lee family to believe that their fleeing employees had escaped safely.

Though no one in the Lee family was ever injured in the raids, Lee feared for the safety of his family. C. A. Lee moved his family to Seymour in Baylor County during the late 1880s. Eventually, the family moved to Paducah where there was a more tolerant attitude toward "Yankees."

FROM HOGTOWN TO SEYMOUR
by Jean G. Schnitz
of Boerne

That Ku Klux Klan story made me think of another related story that was one of Aunt Esther's favorite stories to tell. My Grandmother told me both stories many times. This one is about the move from Hogtown to Seymour.

When the C. A. Lee family moved from Hogtown in Comanche County to west of Seymour in Baylor County around 1889 or 1890, it took several trips to move the family and their household goods, and to drive the cattle to their new location. When Dora Belle Lee (my grandmother) was fifteen years old, she and her sister, Cora Lee, went along as cooks for her father and the cowboys who were driving the cattle on one of the trips.

My grandmother told me about the dusty ride in the wagons, the hard work cooking for the men and cleaning the dishes after mealtime. She remembered the fun that they had also, including the singing around the campfire in the evening. There was plenty of fresh beef, venison, and fish. The trip took several days.

One afternoon, the men were tending the cattle while the two girls were preparing food for supper. A storm was coming up. Lightning flashed and thunder roared as the cloud approached. They heard a distant shout they could not understand. Then they recognized their father's voice shouting, "Get in the wagon!" The girls quickly climbed into one of the wagons. The reason for the warning became apparent as the stampeding herd came by like an avalanche, with horns hitting the wagon and nearly overturning it. The terrified girls stayed in the wagon until the herd was past. They had to stay at that camp for several days while the men herded the cattle back together.

৵ • ৶

GRINDING THE CORNMEAL
by Barbara Pybas
of Gainesville

Ben Pybas brought wonderfully smooth grinding stones when the Pybas clan came, lock, stock and barrel, from Tennessee to Texas. He built a gin on the upslope above Warrens Bend located on the Red River in Cooke County, Texas, in 1884. Soon there were lots of sharecroppers farming the one-team and two-team acreages, turning out good cotton crops and making a living for their families.

The grinding stones required power and Pybas put in a small mill at the gin, using the wood-powered steam engine first, later fired with crude oil from the Empire Oil Company pipe line which was laid across the river less than a quarter mile from the gin.

Ben would fire up the steam engine and hook up the mill every week or so after ginning season, and tell the neighbors when it would be in operation. They would shell fifty to a hundred pounds of corn stored in their cribs and bring their own sacks to be ground. The stones made fine corn meal because it contained the whole kernel, the heart, also. Since the meal might become rancid and weevily if it was not used regularly, it was best to have freshly ground meal as often as possible. In the winter time the meal would keep for some time, but in the summer, the heat would make the oil in the ground corn get rancid more quickly.

Grinding days were also a time to talk to a neighbor or two, passing the time it took to mill the corn. Perhaps they planned to cook fish from the river, roll it in corn meal and fry it and make hushpuppies to go with it.

ৰঙ • ঔৰ

GRANDMOTHER PERKINS: HEALER
by Kenneth W. Davis
of Lubbock

When she came to Texas with her family from Gravelling Springs, Alabama, in the early 1880s, my grandmother Perkins brought with her traditional folk remedies for a variety of ailments. She made cough syrup from the hoar hound weed, bourbon whiskey, and sugar that alleviated all symptoms of then common "winter coughs." For insect stings she used a mixture of baking soda and vinegar. For the grandchildren's summertime sunburned arms and legs, she applied sweet cream from her cotton seed-fed cows. From some vile smelling weed she fashioned with whiskey, sugar, and vinegar, a sure remedy for the "summer complaint" (vomiting and diarrhea). For sinus drainage, then sometimes call catarrh, she had a remedy whose ingredients included bark from the gum elastic tree as well as some from the mesquite bushes. This remedy also included the juice from the third parboiling of leaves from gourd vines. She also added a generous portion of brown sugar to 'cut the bitter,' as she said

The remedy for which she was best known was one for the complaint now called strep throat. In the mid-1930s a virtual epidemic of this disease spread throughout central Texas causing numerous deaths particularly of small children of many white as well as black sharecroppers. For this dreaded

sickness my grandmother made a swab of boric acid and some other ingredient whose identity is not known, as is the case in many traditional tales
about the prowess of folk healers. But whatever was in the remedy, it was
effective. My grandparents at that time had six sharecropper families who
worked the section of blackland my grandfather bought after he immigrated
to Texas from Mississippi. Of the two or so dozen sharecropper children,
not one of them died from the throat condition. My grandmother swabbed
each child's throat with the potion. Word of her success at treating the po-
tentially deadly malady reached the doctors at Temple's famed Scott and
White Hospital. One bitterly cold January afternoon, two big Buicks full of
doctors drove to the Perkins home near Bartlett to confer with my grandmother about her cure. She gave them all the information they wanted. I do
not know what the proportions were for her various folk remedies nor in
the case of the throat swab do I know what was the ingredient that comple-
mented the boric acid. I do know that the remedies she used with me and
the other grandchildren were sure-fire.

CONTRIBUTORS

F. E. Abernethy is the Secretary-Editor of the Texas Folklore Society and Regents Professor Emeritus of English at Stephen F. Austin State University.

Hazel Shelton Abernethy is a retired teacher of history at Stephen F. Austin State University, a writer, speaker, and actress, and a participating grandmother of six.

Mary M. Aikman was a Kilgore student at SFA in this editor's folklore class in 1970. Her paper was the result of an assignment to collect and write family legends. We hope that this writer reads her paper and contacts the editor, who occupies the same office as he did in 1970.

Jim H. Ainsworth is a business entrepreneur who founded several diverse small businesses including a CPA firm, Financial Planning Firm, a Broker-Dealer, and a western wear store. He is also the author of five books. His latest, *Biscuits Across the Brazos*, is a narrative of a 325-mile journey by covered wagon and horseback that Jim and his cousin took to test their mettle against that of their ancestors. They traveled the same route that their ancestors had taken eighty years earlier. The author still lives in Northeast Texas near the area where his ancestors first camped on their original journey. He enjoys writing and team roping.

Virginia Alexander was a student at SFA in this editor's folklore class in 1970. Her paper was the result of an assignment to collect and write family legends. We hope that this writer reads her paper and contacts the editor, who occupies the same office as he did in 1970.

Jeanne Blackstone Almany, a Spanish teacher at Central Heights High School, graduated summa cum laude from SFASU in 1968, and received her master's in secondary education in 1975. She has taught for twenty-six years. She is married to Sammy Almany, a semi-retired band director, and they have two daughters and one granddaughter.

Elaine Brown Ascher was born and raised on Long Island, New York. She attended the University of Michigan and graduated from New York Medical College. After practicing on Long Island for twenty-five years, she and her family moved to Denison, Texas, where she is currently practicing. She published a volume of her memoirs, *Window On My World.* She was married to the late Laurence I. Ascher and has two sons and five grandchildren.

Martha Baxley of Denison is a retired schoolteacher with two daughters and three grandchildren. Her avocations are dancing, public speaking, painting, traveling, and studying her family's genealogy.

Robert Bethea was a student at SFA in this editor's folklore class in 1970. His paper was the result of an assignment to collect and write family legends. We hope that this writer reads his paper and contacts the editor, who occupies the same office as he did in 1970.

Carole Hensley Bergfeld, daughter-in-law of Mrs. Caroline Nash Bergfeld, is a sixth-grade Language Arts teacher at Hubbard Middle School. She has been teaching for thirteen years and has also supervised student teachers for the University of Texas-Tyler for eleven years. She is married to Bob Bergfeld and they have two boys: Robert, twenty-eight, and Chris, twenty-four.

Alice Dial Boney spent many hours sitting on the floor listening to the tales told by her great-grandmother, **Mary Ann Long Ferguson**. Her mother, **Odessa Hicks Dial**, recorded many of these in *Musings of My Grandmother as She Neared the Century Mark*. Her handwritten manuscript is one of Alice's most prized possessions. Alice worked for Magnolia Petroleum and taught school in addition to rearing a son and daughter and now enjoying four grandchildren.

Silva Boze Brown was a native of Fannin County, Texas, who chose teaching as a profession in 1926 and spent more than forty years as a teacher in Childress County and Hunt County, Texas. A graduate of East Texas State Teachers College, Silva was a star basketball player and was inducted into the East Texas State Athletic Hall of Fame in 1995. Always a yarn spinner, she chose to write about her life when she was ninety years old and published her stories in *Silva by Silva, 1905–1996*. At age ninety-six, she was still writing stories at the time of death, March 10, 2002.

Sandra Brownlow of Timpson is the President of the Timpson Area Genealogical and Heritage Society of Shelby County and can tell a good story.

Carole Bruce was a student at SFA in this editor's folklore class in 1970. Her paper was the result of an assignment to collect and write family legends. We hope that this writer reads her paper and contacts the editor, who occupies the same office as he did in 1970.

Jane Barnhart Burrows was a student at SFA in this editor's folklore class in 1970. Her paper was the result of an assignment to collect and write family legends. We hope that this writer reads her paper and contacts the editor, who occupies the same office as he did in 1970.

Mary Margaret Dougherty Campbell was born in Alice, Texas, and raised in Live Oak and Jim Wells Counties in deep South Texas, where her family ranched. Her ancestors' playing vital roles in settling and developing the area has provided a rich oral history tradition in her family. Mary earned both a BA and MA in English from Texas Tech University and an MS in educational administration from Texas A&M University-Corpus Christi. Currently, she is the chair of the English Department at George West High School, where she teaches English and Speech.

Thomas P. Carolan is a retired trial attorney from the United States Department of Justice. He was born in Iowa and grew up in Washington, D. C. He attended Georgetown Prep, College and Law School. He currently resides in Sherman, Texas.

Nancy Carr was a student at SFA in this editor's folklore class in 1970. Her paper was the result of an assignment to collect and write family legends. We hope that this writer reads her paper and contacts the editor, who occupies the same office as he did in 1970.

Alice Cashen was a legendary teacher of English at South Park High School in Beaumont. She was born and raised in the Batson oilfield in the heart of the Big Thicket of Southeast Texas, and she knew all of its stories by heart.

Martha Cavness was a student at SFA in this editor's folklore class in 1970. Her paper was the result of an assignment to collect and write family legends. We hope that this writer reads her paper and contacts the editor, who occupies the same office as he did in 1970. Martha's husband's family, the Cavnesses, proved out their 160 acres and became leading citizens of Harmon County when Greer County became part of Oklahoma.

Tom Chesnut was born in Childress, Texas, and grew up listening to the stories of life in West Texas. After graduation from high school, Tom attended the University of Texas, from which he graduated with a degree in geology. He is involved in the highway and heavy construction business and has spent his working life in El Paso, Dallas, and Austin.

Gwen Choate is a native of Nacogdoches County, Texas, and a graduate of Stephen F. Austin State University. She is a former magazine editor and has had four novels published (by Doubleday and New American Library/Signet Books). She is presently a free-lance writer living in Nacogdoches, Texas.

Mary Joe Clendenin was drafted into teaching in WWII, when a local rural teacher had ambitions to be "Rosie the Riveter." After fourteen years, which included marriage and three children and five years of teaching, she completed her B. S. at Abilene Christian University. She obtained two other degrees—an M. S. in Natural Science from New Mexico Highlands University and an Ed. S. in Guidance and Counseling from New Mexico State University. She is currently a Professor Emeritus at Lubbock Christian University, author of ten books, and writes a weekly column for *The Stephenville Empire Tribune*.

Gloria Counts was a Ware family genealogist from North Little Rock, Arkansas.

Margaret A. Cox of Austin grew up in Eden, Texas, fourth generation of 1886 Concho County pioneers. She worked thirty-five years with the University of Texas library, but maintained her close ties to Eden. Margaret served on the founding board of the Eden Historical Preservation Association, which opened the Don Freeman Memorial Museum of Concho County in February 2003. Margaret currently sells vintage fabric folk art and collectibles in Austin, Georgetown, and Eden.

Sybil F. Crawford retired as documentation coordinator for an international commercial lender in 1990. She attended what is now the University of Arkansas-Little Rock and has written extensively on local history, fine arts, and gravestone studies subjects. Her research paper, "Dionicio Rodriguez: The *Faux Bois* Sculptor," was the 2001 winner of the F. Hampton Roy History Award.

Jennifer Curtis is a transplanted New Englander, freelance writer, and storyteller who has always enjoyed writing, history, storytelling, and family. She has a B. A. in History from the University of Houston-Clear Lake, an M.Ed in Storytelling from East Tennessee State University, and has developed a specialty in English. She teaches writing courses and English at San Jacinto College South. Her six children and many grandchildren also share a love of family, history, and stories.

Lillian Ellisene Rumage Davis was raised on a ranch near Jacksboro, Texas. She earned a B. S. in home economics from Texas Tech, an M. Ed. from North Texas State University with chemistry as her teaching field, and certification to teach special education from Texas Woman's University. Ellisene is a published writer and a student of creative writing. She presently lives in the mountain community of Angel Fire, New Mexico.

Kenneth W. Davis, a past president of the Texas Folklore Society, is professor emeritus of English, Texas Tech University. He continues to read papers now and then and to publish essays about folklore and Southwestern literature. His most recent article is in *Southwestern American Literature*. Titled "Kelton's Clio," it comments on Elmer Kelton's fiction as well as his beliefs about the proper uses of historical writing.

Tom Davison, a native of Nacogdoches, wrote his family saga story when he was a twenty-year-old journalism student at the University of Texas in Austin. He graduated with a degree in journalism in 1941, worked for a short time at the *Galveston News* and served three years in the Army Air Force, working part time as a field correspondent for *Yank* magazine, the army weekly, in the European Theater. Tom was also a golf columnist and football writer for the *Houston Post* for fifteen years. He now lives in Austin.

Robert J. (Jack) Duncan is one of Ross Estes's grandsons. Jack is a former TFS president. He a writer-researcher-editor for Retractable Technologies, Inc., an adjunct English professor at Collin County Community College, and a widely-published freelance writer. He has written both for scholarly and popular periodicals, including *Reader's Digest*. He lives in McKinney with his wife Elizabeth, his McKinney High School sweetheart.

Ross Estes was born in 1889 near Tioga, Texas, and lived virtually his whole life in that area until his death in 1982. Around 1920, he farmed sixty-five acres while so crippled that he couldn't walk. For more than fifty years he played Santa Claus nearly every Christmas. He owned a horse or team of horses for seventy years. Other of his stories can be found in *Paisanos* (PTFS XLI), and in his book, *I Remember Things: An Informal History of Tioga, Texas*.

Robert Flynn Professor Emeritus at Trinity University and a native of Chillicothe, Texas, is the author of twelve books: seven novels, a dramatic adaptation of Faulkner's *As I Lay Dying*, a two-part documentary—"A Cowboy Legacy," shown on ABC-TV—a nonfiction narrative, *A Personal War in Vietnam*, an oral history—*When I was Just Your Age*, two story collections —*Seasonal Rain* and *Living With the Hyenas*, and a collection of essays, *Growing Up A Sullen Baptist*. Flynn is a member of the Texas Institute of Letters, from which he received the Distinguished Achievement Award in 1998, The Writers Guild of America, The Marine Corps Combat Correspondents, and P. E. N.

Lora B. Garrison has been twice president of the Texas Folklore Society and a long-time storyteller at the Texas Folklife Festival. She has an educational background in Anthropology and Creative Writing. She also collects oral history, is a newspaper columnist and a storyteller. During her early life she was a fashion and millinery designer to first ladies and senator's wives and other dignitaries in Washington, D. C.

John Graves was born in Fort Worth, Texas in 1920. He graduated from Rice University and was a Marine during WWII. After the war he received a Master's Degree in English from Columbia University and has done some college teaching along the way. His main ambition was to write, however, and during the early and mid-1950s he lived all over the map on this continent and in Europe. After coming home in about 1956, he taught at TCU, got married and started a family, and published his first book, *Goodbye to a*

River. Later came *Hard Scrabble* and *From a Limestone Ledge.* More recently he has published *A John Graves Reader* (1996), *John Graves and the Making of Goodbye to a River* (2000), and, with photographer Wyman Meinzer, *Texas Rivers* (2002). He has also published a good many articles, book introductions, and short stories, some of which have been made into small books, and has been the recipient of a few honors, among them Guggenheim and Rockefeller fellowships.

Lottie Lipscomb Guttry grew up in Kilgore, Texas, attended Sweet Briar College and received a Bachelor of Music from the University of Texas at Austin, an M A from Stephen F. Austin State University, and an Ed.D. from Texas A&M University at Commerce. She has taught at Kilgore College, the University of Texas at Tyler, and has owned and directed a Sylvan Learning Center in Longview. Her publications include a musical, *Boom,* based on the history of the East Texas oilfield; a play for children, *The Enchanted Swan;* a critical article published in the *Walt Whitman Review;* a devotional published in *The Upper Room* and numerous feature articles for *The Longview News and Journal.* She lives on Lake Cherokee, Longview, Texas, with her husband, John, a retired dentist. She volunteers at First United Methodist Church, plays golf, writes, and travels. She has three grown children and seven grandchildren.

Patsy Johnson Hallman is the daughter of Don and Edna Johnson, Miller Grove, Texas (Hopkins County). She received degrees from Texas A & M, Commerce, Stephen F. Austin State University, and Texas Woman's University. Dr. Hallman's teaching experience spans K-16, but for the past ten years she has been in administration at SFASU, where she currently serves as Dean of the College of Education. Her research interests are in best educational practice, with several books and numerous articles to her credit. A favorite hobby is family folklore. She is married to Dr. Leon Hallman and is the mother of Dave Lyndon Spurrier and Bethany Spurrier.

Myrtle Oldham Ham was born in 1886 in Navarro County, Texas. She moved with her family to Alexander, Texas, and later settled near there on Alarm Creek. In 1905 Myrtle married Robert Edwin Ham and they were the parents of eight boys and two girls. She and Ed lived all their lives on farms in the Alarm Creek area. Myrtle was a natural born storyteller and her descendants thank her for a rich heritage.

Carol Hanson is the daughter of August and Mary Helen (Worthy) Stanglin and a native of Dallas, Texas. She was a librarian at the Dallas Public library in the Texas/Dallas History Division, the Genealogy Section, and the Government Information Center. She also worked as a Children's Librarian at the public library in Cedar Hill, where she and her husband, Pete, and their son, Erik, live. Currently she is a Reference Librarian in the Grand Prairie Library System. Her grandmother, Nettie (Baldwin) Worthy, was the storyteller in the family, and she inspired Carol to collect family stories.

Lucille Harris, a retired teacher, was born at home in 1939 in rural Denton County, Texas, the first child of Jimmie and Oneita Patterson. She graduated from Lewisville High School in 1957 and married T. J. Harris (deceased 1998) in 1958. She graduated from T.W.U. in 1971 with a B.S. in education. She taught special education in Grapevine and Anna. She has two children, five grandchildren, and two great-grandchildren with another on the way! Lucille has been active in *Telling Our Stories* at Austin College and has received awards. One of her stories was published in *Texas Millennium Book: The Way Things Used To Be.*

Waun Harrison was a student at SFA in this editor's folklore class. His paper was the result of an assignment to collect and write family legends. We hope that this writer reads his paper and contacts the editor, who occupies the same office as he did in 1970.

J. Willis Hastings was born in Chester, South Carolina, in 1924. He attended public schools there and graduated from Chester High School in 1940. He worked for two years in a local textile plant before he enlisted in the U. S. Army Air Corps in 1942 and became a bombardier with the Fifteenth Air Force, where he flew combat missions until his plane was shot down. He spent almost nine months as a POW in Germany. He held the rank of 1st Lieutenant and was awarded the Air Medal with Oak Leaf Clusters, five Battle Stars in the European Theater, and a Purple Heart. He returned home and was discharged in October 1945. He enrolled in Clemson University and after graduating with a B.S. degree he pursued a career in the textile industry with Burlington Industries, Inc. at Sherman, Texas. He was married to Ruth Wallin and they had three children: Helen, Mark and Paul and one grandchild, Preston Willis Hastings.

Margaret L. Hewett from Moss Hill in the Big Thicket of East Texas is a natural born storyteller and a repository of the rich history and folklore of the southeast Texas area.

Georgeanne Hitzfeld is a native Texan and a graduate of Trinity University in San Antonio with a B.A. in Sociology. She has published in various poetry anthologies and is a listener and storyteller of the many voices of her family.

Joanna Hurley works with her husband, former University of North Texas Chancellor Al Hurley, on behalf of the University. She has a BA in French from St. John's University, and a master's degree from Colorado College. Currently, she is President-Elect of the Texas Board of the National Museum of Women in the Arts in Washington, D. C., has been on the board of Texas Women's Alliance, and is a member of the Denton Benefit League, the Greater Denton Arts Council, Denton Tennis Association, and the Allocations Committee for United Way of Denton. Her personal interests include visiting her eight grandchildren, playing tennis, and surfing the web.

Janet Jeffery is the great-great-granddaughter of Elizabeth Russell Baker. Janet graduated with a B. S. in Art from the University of Texas at Austin in 1967, and more recently earned an M. A. in English in 1997. After a career in technical writing, performance consulting, and curriculum design, she retired from Dell Computer Corporation in April 2000. In the last half of the 1990s, she designed a number of online courses for Dell employees to access on the corporate intranet. These days, she uses the Internet for more personal reasons; it has allowed her to locate a number of distant cousins on the Russell-Baker side and gather even more family stories that describe the realities of the Texas frontier.

Timothy Lee Jones was a student in this editor's folklore class in 1970. His paper was the result of an assignment to collect and write family legends. We hope that this writer reads his paper and contacts the editor, who occupies the same office as he did in 1970.

Elmer Kelton of San Angelo, Texas, is Texas' foremost western fiction writer and for forty-two years was also an agricultural journalist. Among his better known books are *The Time It Never Rained* and *The Good Old Boys*, which won for him two of his seven Spur Awards from Western Writers of America. He is a Distinguished Alumnus of the University of Texas at Austin.

Austin T. King was born on a farm in Camp County, Texas. He was educated in Pittsburg, Texas, and took a B.A. at the University of Texas in 1948. Austin taught school and worked in real estate and insurance. The focus of his life has been prospecting and looking for lost mines, and he has traveled in the western States and Mexico in pursuit of that passion. Austin now lives in semi-retirement on his La Babicora ranchita back in Camp County. He has four grown children and a grandson, his blessings.

James Ward Lee, a former president of the Texas Folklore Society and a former Radarman Second Class, USN, is Emeritus Professor of English at the University of North Texas. He now lives in Fort Worth and is Acquisitions Editor at TCU Press. Lee's latest book is *Literary Fort Worth* (edited with Judy Alter).

Faye Leeper was an instructor of English at Robert E. Lee High School and Midland Community College for twenty-five years. She received a B.S. from Southwest Texas and an M.A. from Texas Tech. Her interest in folklore has taken her to graduate schools on seven campuses, including two in the British Isles. She has been active in many academic organizations over the years, and has served in almost all of their offices, including president of the Texas Folklore Society. Writing is still her favorite pastime in retirement. She is now serving as Librarian of the Poetry Society of Texas and Executive Board Member to Lyric Stage in Irving, Texas. Faye has been a TFS member longer than anyone else in the Society.

Dorothy Kennedy Lewis of Ore City was an outstanding folklore student of mine at Stephen F. Austin State College sometime in the 1970s. She was a fine writer with a wealth of stories to tell, and if she is still around I wish she would report in.

Jerry Bryan Lincecum, a sixth-generation Texan and a past president of the Texas Folklore Society, is the Shoap Professor of English at Austin College, having taught there since 1967. He has served as the lead editor for three volumes drawn from the letters and papers of his ancestor, Dr. Gideon Lincecum (1793–1874). He and his wife, Dr. Peggy Redshaw, Professor of

Biology, are well known in the Sherman area for creating in 1990 the "Telling Our Stories" program in autobiography and family history and sustaining it to the present time.

Al Lowman of Stringtown, Texas, is a long-time member and past president of the Texas Folklore Society. His contributions have appeared in several of the Society's annuals over the last two decades. He is also past president of the Book Club of Texas and the Texas State Historical Association, not to mention his status as a notorious bibliophile. Having spent twenty-one years on the staff of the Institute of Texan Cultures in downtown San Antonio, he now devotes dwindling time and remaining energy to a prominent role as a sedentary lifestyle activist on his home turf in Stringtown.

Cynthia Lowry was a student at SFA in this editor's folklore class in 1970. Her paper was the result of an assignment to collect and write family legends. We hope that this writer reads her paper and contacts the editor, who occupies the same office as he did in 1970.

Jo Wilkinson Lyday was born August 1, 1931, in Keatchie, Louisiana. She graduated from Alamo Heights High School in San Antonio, Texas, in 1948 and married John Thomas Lyday, Jr., in Beaumont, Texas, in 1949. After attending Baylor University and Southeastern State in Durant, Oklahoma, she earned a B. A. and M. A. from Lamar State College and a Ph. D. from the University of Houston. Her career included six years of teaching English in Pasadena, Texas, public schools and twenty-one years at San Jacinto College South to tutor in the Writer's Center. The Lydays have one daughter and one granddaughter. Before 2002 is out, their great-grandson will be born. It will be up to him to keep the saga alive.

Marilyn Colegrove Manning is a practicing psychotherapist in her treehouse in Houston. She has two smart and handsome adult sons, a fine friend in her former husband, and alas, no grandchildren. Her parents lived hearty, productive lives, and contributed greatly to their spot in Texas, and passed in 1999 (Mom) and 2000 (Dad).

Louise Martin was born May 14, 1919, in the Bland Lake Community near San Augustine, Texas. The family moved from Bland Lake to Houston, Texas, when Louise was about six years old. Her father worked for Southwestern

Bell Telephone Company and her mother taught school in Houston. She married Thomas Ernest Martin on April 8, 1939, and they are the parents of two sons. In 1973, Louise and her husband retired to their farm in Garrison, Texas. They raise cattle and are active members of the Lions Club, Eastern Star, and FFA activities involving their son Marvin Martin and granddaughter Ashley Martin. Tom has celebrated fifty years as a member of the Masonic Lodge. Louise and Tom are members and attend the First Baptist Church in Garrison, Texas.

Sloan Matthews of San Antonio was born and raised a cowboy in Coleman County. In the early 1950s he wrote down stories of his life as a bronc buster and working cow hand. In 1954 Mr. Matthews sent a copy of his reminiscences to Mody Boatright, who put his stories in the State Archives. His daughter-in-law, Mrs. Tom Matthews of Houston, had typed up Mr. Matthews' stories, and Mody had kept a copy of the manuscript in a "consider for publication" file. Mr. Matthews told a lot of good stories. I used one of them.

Laurette Davis McCommas was born in Dearborn, Michigan, in 1934 under the shadow of Henry Ford. Many of her stories stem from that area. She moved to Texas in 1980. She has written a book, *Secrets from the Trunk*, which is now in its second printing. Other stories of hers have been printed in the *Herald Democrat*, a newspaper for Sherman and Denison, Texas.

John Artie McCall is a Doctor of Optometry in Crockett, Texas, who is in practice with his son, Dr. John McCall, Jr. John Artie's ancestors were long-time settlers in Anderson County, and he grew up in Grapeland and Palestine, where he and the editor attended school together. He is a hunter and fisherman with a camphouse on the Trinity River, and he is a genealogist who has recorded stories of his family in his book, *I'll Never Forget*.

Archie P. McDonald, a child of the Depression, grew up in Beaumont, Texas, where he was graduated from French High School and Lamar Tech, moved on to the Rice Institute, and finished off at LS&U. In Beaumont he also married above his station, and the poor bride has made the best of a bad bargain (for her) for near half a century. Archie has taught at Stephen F. Austin State University in Nacogdoches, since Stephen was a student there. He has written some books, made some speeches, but none of it ever amounted to much. Archie does not plan to retire; instead, he will just quit working one day and not tell anyone so they will keep the paychecks coming (this may have happened already).

Karen McDonald was a student at SFA in this editor's folklore class in 1970. Her paper was the result of an assignment to collect and write family legends. We hope that this writer reads her paper and contacts the editor, who occupies the same office as he did in 1970.

Donna McFadden was a student at Lamar State College in this editor's folklore class in 1964. Her paper was the result of an assignment to collect and write family legends. We hope that this writer reads her paper and contacts the editor.

JoEllen Ham Miller, the granddaughter of Myrtle Ham and the carrier of her family's treasure of tales, was also raised in the Alarm Creek area of Erath County, and married and raised her own four children there. JoEllen is the one who found the stories Grandma Ham had stored in the old quilt box with her other prized possessions, and she is the one we have to thank for passing them on to the readers of this book of family legends.

Eleanor Monroe was born in Pawnee Rock, Kansas, but grew up in Liberty, Missouri, where her father's family had resided for four generations. She attended the University of Missouri's School of Journalism. She and her husband, Dr. Stanley Monroe, moved to Sherman, Texas, in 1948. They have five children, twelve grandchildren and six great-grandchildren. She was a founding member of "Telling Our Stories," a writing group under the direction of Dr. Jerry Lincecum at Austin College, Sherman, Texas.

Patrick Mullen was born in Beaumont and educated at Lamar State College, the University of North Texas, and the University of Texas. He teaches folklore and American Literature at Ohio State University and is the author of *I Heard the Old Fishermen Say: Folklore of the Texas Gulf Coast, Lake Erie Fishermen: Work, Identity, and Tradition,* and *Listening to Old Voices: Folklore, Life Stories, and the Elderly.* He has lived in Ohio for thirty-two years but still considers himself a Texan and can be found periodically collecting shells on the beaches of Bolivar Peninsula or catching fish in East Galveston Bay.

Palmer Henry Olsen of Clifton, Bosque County, is a second-generation Texan, his father and mother both coming from Norway to Clifton in the early 1880s. Palmer grew up in Clifton and got a civil engineering degree from Texas A&M, where he was an outstanding athlete. He served in World War I and World War II. In WWII Palmer received a personal citation for service to Norway from Crown Price Olav. He later served as a military governor in occupied Germany. He was married to Esther Swenson, his childhood sweetheart, and they had two daughters.

Paul Patterson was born east of Seminole, Texas, on Brennan Ranch in 1909. He cowboyed four full years and seven summers. Broke a few broncs. Learnt bronc-riding "from the ground up." Other words "Laid groundwork" for bronc-riding. Sometimes laid there several minutes at a time—gasping for breath. He taught school for forty years in Marfa, Sanderson, Crane, and Sierra Blanca.

Elizabeth Stanley Pope was born in 1892 in rural north central Texas. A hardy individual, she was picking cotton while still in grammar school. Married three times, she said she'd been a widow all her life. Miss Lizzie lived on her own well into her nineties, sharing family stories on visits to her small house in Bluff Dale, Texas. She enjoyed *Wheel of Fortune* during the last years of her life, and hacked off the head of a rattler with one stroke at the age of 94. She died in Dallas, Texas, in 1987, fighting until the end.

Grace Fisher Porch was born in 1904 in Tishomingo, Oklahoma, soon after her parents moved from their claim in what had been Old Greer County, Texas. Grace Fisher married Richard Porch, and they had three children. Grace worked for twenty-six years for Seismograph Service Company.

"Wildwood" Dean Price of Bonham began designing and building furniture from varieties of dogwood in 1986. He had learned of the excellent properties of dogwood for building furniture from his dad who used it for net hoops. Price received the Texas Forestry Award for Architectural Excellence in wood design in the Special Projects category in 1998. Then he received an invitation to read a paper at the Midland Texas Folklore Society meeting. He has recently signed to write a column, "Backyard Discoveries," for an online regional newspaper that was inspired by his recent Red River Expedition and will appear on a weekly basis beginning August 1,

2002. "Wildwood's" education came from operating successful businesses and from "a salutary diet of reading."

Barbara Pybas lives in Cooke County, Texas, on a ranch bordering the Red River. She immigrated to Texas from western Oklahoma in 1949 by marrying a Marine veteran and coming fresh from Oklahoma A&M University. Barbara became enamored with Texas history, first checking out a seventh grade textbook upon her arrival. Since that time, she has read, studied, and written many stories and historical articles, sometimes using much of the Pybas family lore from stories of the ancestors. She is one of the Cooke County representatives of the Texas Historical Commission. She attends Sivells Bend United Methodist Church, established in 1869. Barbara and her husband, Jordan E. Pybas, are still in the ranching business in the Sivells Bend community of Cooke County. They are parents of six children who attended the country school, but are all professionals in other fields, living away from Cooke County.

Edward R. Raasch was born October 14, 1914, retired twice: one time at sixty-five and one time at eighty. He managed radio stations, anchored noon news, emceed musical programs, and was a disk jockey during the late 1940s. He wound up in the lumber business from the 1950s through the 1990s. He lost his partner, friend, and wonderful artist, Grace, in February 2000. He has a daughter and a son and three grandchildren. He attended the Lincecum-Redshaw "Telling Our Stories" classes in Sherman, Texas. He has served on the Board of Adjustment and as President of the Kiwanis and the Coastal Bend Lumber Association, as well as the director of the Lumber Association in Corpus Christi, Texas.

Ellen Walker Rienstra is a sixth generation resident of Beaumont, Texas, who holds Bachelor's and Master's degrees in English Literature from Lamar University. With her sister, Judith Walker Linsley, Ellen co-authored *Beaumont: A Chronicle of Promise*, as well as numerous steamy historical novels and historical articles, including several in the *New Handbook of Texas*. With Callie Coe Wilson, she co-authored *A Pride of Kin*. Linsley's and her new collaborative effort, *Giant Under the Hill: A History of the Spindletop Oil Discovery at Beaumont, Texas in 1901*, was co-written with Lamar History professor Jo Ann Stiles. Also forthcoming is a January 2003 publication by Linsley and Rienstra entitled *Historic Beaumont*. Rienstra is a violinist, currently holding positions in the Symphony of Southeast Texas and the Lake Charles Symphony and the Rapides Symphony in Louisiana. She performs numerous free-lance orchestra, quartet, and solo engagements in Southeast Texas and Southwest Louisiana.

Joyce Gibson Roach holds BFA and MA degrees from TCU and taught there as a member of the adjunct English faculty from 1984 to 1997, specializing in Western Novel and Life and Literature of the Southwest. She is a three-time Spur Award winner from Western Writers of America for *The Cowgirls*; short non-fiction "A High-Toned Woman," from *Hoein' the Short Rows*; short fiction, "Just As I Am," from *Women of the West*; and a finalist for short fiction "In Broad Daylight" from *Texas Short Stories*. She is a fellow of the Texas State Historical Association, Clements Center at SMU, and a member of the Texas Institute of Letters.

Lou Rodenberger, now a professor emerita of English at McMurry University, has published essays on the experiences of her parents as rural schoolteachers, as well as on Texas women writers and southwestern life and literature. She is a Fellow of Texas State Historical Association, member of Texas Institute of Letters, and past president of the Texas Folklore Society and West Texas Historical Association. Her most recent publication is the introduction to *31 by Lawrence Clayton*, a collection of essays which she also edited. She is co-author with Sylvia Grider of *Texas Women Writers: A Tradition of Their Own* and *21 Short Stories by Texas Women: Then and Now*, forthcoming from A&M University Press. Other works include *Her Work: Stories by Texas Women* and a monograph-length critical study of West Texas writer, Jane Gilmore Rushing. A second longer biographical/critical study of Rushing for the University of North Texas Press' Texas Writer's Series is forthcoming.

Marlene Rushing was born in Russellville, Arkansas, but has lived in Texas all of her life. She has been married to Paul D. Rushing for forty-five years. She has one son, J. Rhett Rushing and two grandsons, Zane Tyler and Wyatt Luke Rushing. Marlene recently retired after thirty-eight years of teaching Theatre Arts and being a guidance counselor in the public school system. She has a B.A. from Baylor University, an M. Ed. from the University of Houston, an M. A. from Lamar University, and is A. B. D. from Texas A & M University. She holds certification in teaching, counseling, and school administration.

J. Rhett Rushing is a native teacher and Texan who, after fifteen years of chasing his education around the country, has finally come home to roost. Happy to no longer be shoveling snow or chipping through ice to fish, he divides his professional energies between consulting and folklore fieldwork. Currently A. B. D. in Folklore at Indiana University, Rhett lives in San Antonio and is writing his dissertation about the wealth of popular religious expression in South Texas. He is teaching Texas folklore at Southwest Texas State and anticipates his Ph.D. this winter from Indiana University. In the meantime, he is also teaching a writing course based on Texas folk narrative at Texas University in the fall of 2002.

Herb Sanders is a native of Dallas, Texas. He was educated in the Dallas Independent School District and at Southern Methodist University. He served in the U. S. Navy and was employed by Southwestern Bell Company. After thirty-two years with SBC, holding a number of managerial and engineering positions, he retired in April of 1981. After retirement he and Pat, his bride of fifty-two years, moved to their summer place on Lake Texoma. Sanders spent ten years with Grayson County Community College and was Director of the Pottsboro Area Library for five years. Now he is really retired and he and Pat do what they darn well please. They have two sons and three grandsons.

Ruth Garrison Scurlock was a professional writer-journalist, poet, historian, and beloved teacher of English at Lamar State College.

Jean Granberry Schnitz was born in Spur, Texas. She graduated from Raymondville High School in 1948 and from Texas A & I College in Kingsville in 1952. She married Lew Schnitz in 1953, and they have three sons and one grandson. A retired legal secretary, she lives near Boerne. As of 2002, Jean has presented six papers to the Texas Folklore Society since 1990. She served as a Councilor on the Board of the Texas Folklore Society 1999–2002, and was elected as a Director in 2002.

Mildred Boren Sentell was born in Post, Texas, and grew up in Post and Crane. She has three grown children: two daughters and one son, and retired from the English Department at Angelo State University in 1993 when she married Joe Sentell of Snyder. Joe died in January of 2002 and Mildred still lives in Snyder.

John F. Short, at one time of Center, Texas, wrote an outstanding research paper on the Regulator-Moderator War for a graduate class in folklore at Stephen F. Austin State College in 1966. The John Short articles in *The Family Saga* were taken from his paper. If John is in reading distance of this editor, please give him a call.

Dianna Shull was a student at SFA in this editor's folklore class in 1970. Her paper was the result of an assignment to collect and write family legends. We hope that this writer reads her paper and contacts the editor, who occupies the same office as he did in 1970.

Gail Simon was a student in this editor's folklore class in 1970. Her paper was the result of an assignment to collect and write family legends. We hope that this writer reads her paper and contacts the editor, who occupies the same office as he did in 1970.

Thad Sitton, historian, is a native of Lufkin, Texas, and currently lives in Austin, Texas. His special area of interest is rural Texas in the twentieth century, and he has published books about East Texas "backwoodsmen," cotton farmers, sawmill towns, rural sheriffs, country schools, and other things. Sitton is currently working on a study of Texas freedmen's settlements.

Elaine Scherer Snider is a native of Beaumont, Texas, where she graduated from Lamar University in 1966 with a bachelor's degree in English and French. She married Gilbert Snider and moved to Fort Worth to begin her teaching career and to work on her master's degree in English, which she received in 1974 from Stephen F. Austin State University. At both universities, she was fortunate enough to have Dr. Abernethy as an instructor in several courses. She has one son and lives in Conroe, Texas, where she serves as Department Chair of the English Department at Conroe High School.

Ernest B. Speck of Alpine is a native of Llano County. He left the worn-out, sandy-land cotton patches of his youth to become an English teacher at Sul Ross State College. Ernest married Mody Boatright's daughter and edited *Mody Boatright, Folklorist* in 1973. Ernest was a dedicated member of the Texas Folklore Society, and he served it faithfully in words and deeds for over forty years.

Artiemesia Lucille Brison Spencer of Pittsburg, Texas, corresponded regularly with this editor during the 1970s, when I first began working with family legends. Artie traveled the length and breadth of Camp County collecting history and folklore, which she used in her weekly newspaper column, "The Story of Camp County." She intended to put together a book by that title. I hope she made it. She was a dear.

Sheila J. Spiess graduated from Our Lady of the Lake University in 1958. She and her husband chose to live and raise their family in San Antonio, her hometown, and Helotes, Texas. They continue to live in Helotes where their children and grandchildren are now "raising" them.

Mary Means Sullivan is a graduate of Stephen F. Austin State University with a B. A. in English and Secretarial Science and M. A. in English. After teaching at Alto and Nacogdoches High Schools, she moved to Brownsville, Texas, and began teaching in the Office Occupations Department at Texas Southmost College. She was selected as the Outstanding Collegiate Business Teacher by the Texas Business Education Association in 1997 and received the University of Texas Chancellor's Award for Outstanding Teaching in 1998. She is married to James Rodney Sullivan of Nacogdoches, Texas, Associate Professor of Biology at UT-Brownsville.

Estella Wright Szegedin was a genealogist for the Wright family in Fort Smith, Arkansas. Her stories of her family's past included the story of Rev. Josiah Bolton's preaching in Arkansas before he moved with his family to Old Greer County, Texas.

James Vause was born in Apalachicola, Florida, on June 10, 1928, and lived in the surrounding rural areas near there until his family moved to Panama City, Florida, where he finished high school. After spending three years in the Marine Corps, he received a Master's Degree in Geology from Florida State University in 1957. While working with Humble Oil & Refining Company, he was transferred to Houston in 1968, and Houston has been home since then. He married Elizabeth Berry, a Texas lady, in 1986, and plans to stay in Texas. Jim has three sons from a previous marriage and Elizabeth has a son and a daughter from a previous marriage and two grandsons.

Frances Brannen Vick is the retired director and co-founder of the University of North Texas Press and founder and president of E-Heart Press, Inc. She holds B. A. and M. A. degrees in English from the University of Texas at Austin and Stephen F. Austin State University, respectively, and a Doctor of Humane Letters (honoris causa) from the University of North Texas. She is a member of the board of the Texas Council for the Humanities, secretary of the Texas Institute of Letters; the Book Award Chair in The Philosophical Society of Texas; Life Member in the Texas State Historical Association, the East Texas Historical Association. She is married to Ross Vick, and they have three children, six grandchildren and three great-grandchildren.

Patrick Brannen Vick, a sixth generation Texan and active in the Texas Folklore Society, is Vice President of Data Entry at Ross Vick and Associates, a manufacturer representative firm in Dallas. He holds a B. A. degree in history from St. Edwards University in Austin and is a member of the Longhorn Foundation, the Littlefield Society, and a lifetime member of the University Club at The University of Texas. With his brother and sister, he is part of a performing group, E-Heart Land & Cattle Company, and is married to Nelda Grohman, a Hill-Country German from Rockne, Texas.

June Welch was a graduate of Texas Christian University, U. T. Arlington, Texas Tech, and George Washington University. He practiced law for fifteen years before becoming Chairman of the Department of History and later Academic Dean at the University of Dallas. June was a facile and a prolific writer, publishing over a dozen books on Texas history and folklore.

Sue Wenner was born and raised in Dallas, but always held a deep affection for the piney woods around Nacogdoches and Appleby, where her father's family had taken root. She met her husband, Drew, in college at Stephen F. Austin State University. They have two daughters, Andrea and Melinda. She currently teaches English at Connally ISD in central Texas.

John O. West, Texas Folklore Society member for thirty plus years, has served the Society as Councilor, Vice-president, and President. He has contributed to the American Folklore Society and the Texas Folklore Society for over forty years as editor of the AFS Newsletter and as the author of *Mexican-American Folklore*. He was installed in 2002 as a Fellow of the Texas Folklore Society.

Lucy Fischer West was born in Catskill, NY, but raised in El Paso, Texas. She has done freelance editing primarily in the field of Southwestern history, worked with non-profit agencies, and is currently teaching provisional students at the University of Texas at El Paso. Her presentation entitled "Folklore by Osmosis: Three Decades with John O." was included in the Writer's AudioShop "The Best of Texas Folklore Volume 2" and two memoir pieces have appeared in the creative writing journal *BorderSenses*.

Florena Williams was born in Whitewright, Texas. After attending public schools there, she attended and graduated from Texas Woman's University in Denton. She also did graduate work at East Texas State University in Commerce. She taught speech and English for ten years in Sour Lake, Texas, and twenty-seven years in Sherman. She was told family history stories by her father, who was the youngest of the nine children of a Methodist minister who was a Circuit Rider. The oldest of the children was twenty-nine years older than the youngest, and no doubt the baby of the family was entertained by his older brothers and sisters with their adventures as well as family lore passed down from the time before the family came to Texas from North Carolina in a covered wagon before the Civil War. She attended the "Telling Our Stories" workshops sponsored by Austin College in Sherman and several of her stories were printed in collections of this group.

Callie Coe Wilson, born April 8, 1917, in Pitkin, Louisiana, is the only member of her family to be born outside of Texas for several generations. She was educated in Beaumont public schools, Lamar Junior College, and Stanford University, and pursued a career as manager of Szafir's and Taylor's bookstores in Beaumont before her marriage to Waldo Wilson. She wrote a newspaper column, the "Calico Column," featured for several years in the *Beaumont Enterprise*, and "April Wedding," a short story published in *Redbook* in the 1940s. With her cousin, Ellen Walker Rienstra, she co-authored *A Pride of Kin*. Mrs. Wilson has two children, Waldo "Pasq" Wilson, Jr., and Nancy Wilson Scanlan; two grandchildren, Laura Scanlan Cho and Wilson McAllen Scanlan; and one great-granddaughter, Callie Marguerite Cho, who is her namesake.

Gwendolyn Wingate of Hamshire was a student in one of this editor's first folklore classes in Lamar State College. Gwendolyn was the area's social and religious historian.

Lee Winniford graduated from high school and left the little town of Cumby in northeast Texas where she was born and grew up. She was still a teenager when she received her B. A. in English, magna cum laude, from East Texas State Teacher's College and began teaching in the Texas public schools. In 1957–58, she spent a year at Louisiana State University and obtained her M.A., soon after which she taught for two years at Lamar State University and then married. As part of mid-life rejuvenation, she earned a Ph.D. in English and folklore from the University of Houston in 1994. Her dissertation became a book, *Following Old Fencelines: Tales from Rural Texas*. She currently resides in Houston, teaching on the adjunct faculty of the University of Houston and doing volunteer work at a women's detox center. She has completed a novel, *Blood in the Yolk,* and a collection of women's recovery narratives, *Surviving their Lives: The Women of Telephone Road*. She has three children, two daughters and a son, and five grandchildren.

Henry Wolff, Jr. has been a Texas journalist for more than four decades, most of his adult life. He has worked for the *San Angelo Standard-Times*, the *Abilene Reporter-News*, and the *Victoria Advocate*. In South Texas, he is a popular speaker and storyteller at history, folklore, and civic gatherings. He joined the *Advocate*, the second oldest existing newspaper in Texas, in 1963 and has been a fulltime columnist since 1979, having written more than five thousand of his "Henry's Journal" columns since.

Sarah M. Winstead Zoda was born in Smith County, Mississippi, but got to Texas as quickly as she could, the following year. She grew up in Richland and has been a homemaker, a beautician, and a realtor. She and the late Harry L. Zoda were married more than fifty years. She has one daughter and a grandchild.

Index

Note: Page numbers in **bold** indicate entire chapters dedicated to particular subjects. Page numbers in *italics* indicate photographs and illustrations.